NONRESIDENTIAL
PARENTING

OTHER RECENT VOLUMES IN THE
SAGE FOCUS EDITIONS

NONRESIDENTIAL PARENTING
New Vistas in Family Living

Charlene E. Depner
James H. Bray
editors

SAGE PUBLICATIONS
International Educational and Professional Publisher
Newbury Park London New Delhi

Copyright © 1993 by Sage Publications, Inc.

For information address:

SAGE Publications, Inc.
2455 Teller Road
Newbury Park, California 91320

SAGE Publications Ltd.
6 Bonhill Street
London EC2A 4PU
United Kingdom

SAGE Publications India Pvt. Ltd.
M-32 Market
Greater Kailash I
New Delhi 110 048 India

Printed in the United States of America

Library of Congress Cataloging-in-Publication Data

Main entry under title:

Nonresidential parenting : new vistas in family living / edited by
   Charlene E. Depner, James H. Bray.
       p. cm.—(Sage focus editions : vol. 155)
   Includes bibliographical references and index.
   ISBN 0-8039-5050-0 (cloth).—ISBN 0-8039-5051-9 (pbk.)
    1. Parenting, Part-time. 2. Divorced parents. 3. Children of
divorced parents. 4. Custody of children. I. Depner, Charlene E.
II. Bray, James H.
HQ755.8.N64 1993
306.85—dc20
                                         92-37537

93 94 95 96 10 9 8 7 6 5 4 3 2 1

Sage Production Editor: Judith L. Hunter

Contents

Acknowledgments

This collection was undertaken out of the conviction that there was a need to expand the scope of inquiry about the role of contemporary nonresidential parents. We would like to thank a number of people who have made our vision a reality. The collegial spirit of the contributors fostered a lively and challenging exchange of ideas. We all feel indebted to scholars, across a wide range of disciplines, whose work is contributing to a more richly diverse image of families. Roxy Cuddy edited and reviewed all the manuscripts. We are grateful for her insistence on technical and conceptual clarity. The advice and support of our editor, C. Deborah Laughton of Sage Publications, were invaluable in the conceptualization and production of the volume. We also acknowledge the contributions of the Department of Family Medicine at Baylor College of Medicine in supporting the preparation of this book.

We are indebted to our own families, who provided inspiration and support. Dr. Bray expresses his appreciation for the support and patience of his wife, Juneau N. Shepherd, and their children, Lindsey, Jessica, and Matthew, during the process of preparing this book. Their tolerance for weekend absences to work on this book is greatly appreciated. He dedicates this book to his parents, Jamie and Joveda Bray, who have always been present in his life with their love and support. Dr. Depner expresses special thanks to her husband, Mitchell Chyette, for his critical insights, affection, and good humor. She dedicates her work to her loved ones—especially Elaine and Cy Chyette, Cher Depner, and Jan Bean—a family that daily demonstrates the strengths of kinship while defying simplistic structural classification

PART I

Nonresidential Parents:
Who Are They?

1

Perspectives on Nonresidential Parenting

JAMES H. BRAY
CHARLENE E. DEPNER

Although it has become fashionable to nostalgically evoke a bygone era of family stability, the historical course of the American family is one of transformation and diversity. Family configurations have ascended and diminished in prevalence, reflecting the social forces of the times (Skolnik, 1991). In the past two decades, a sharp upswing in the divorce rate and exponential growth in the number of children born outside of marriage have produced a populous cohort of parents who live apart from their children (Glick, 1988b; National Center for Health Statistics, 1990, 1991b). This dramatic reshaping of family structure has prompted a fundamental reassessment of the role of the nonresidential parent in family life and has challenged family policymakers and other professionals to address the diverse emotional and financial needs of children who do not reside with both parents (Depner & Bray, 1990).

In this book, the authors attempt to reframe monolithic approaches to nonresidential parenting. Our multidimensional perspective is influenced by the need to recognize the demographic and cultural variations

AUTHORS' NOTE: This chapter is partially based on Depner, C. E., & Bray, J. H. (1990). Modes of participation for nonresidential parents: The challenge for research, policy, education and practice. *Family Relations, 39*, 378-381. Copyright 1990 by the National Council on Family Relations, 3989 Central Ave. NE, Suite 550, Minneapolis, MN 55421. Used with permission. Dr. Bray's contribution was partially supported by NIH grant RO1 HD22642 from the National Institute of Child Health and Human Development.

in families and to be visionary about the factors that will facilitate the functioning of children and families who are forging new family patterns. The family is viewed as a dynamic entity that can be expected to transform structurally and behaviorally over time. This book responds to a compelling need to integrate knowledge from research, practice, and policy sources and to devise innovative ways of thinking about family change and its implications for our society.

Conceptual Distinctions and Terminology

The focus of this volume is on the *de facto* living arrangements of children. Legal custody labels do not always match the day-to-day responsibilities assumed by parents. Children may reside with a parent who does not have legal custody and, conversely, parents who have legal custody do not always assume full-time child care responsibilities (Clark, Whitney, & Beck, 1988; Fischer & Cardea, 1984; Mnookin, Maccoby, Albiston, & Depner, 1990). In order to keep this distinction clear, the term *custody* is reserved for *de jure* status, and terms such as *domestic arrangements, caretaker,* and *residential parent* are used when referring to *de facto* residential arrangements.

Throughout this volume, terms such as *primary caretaker* and *residential parent* are used to refer to the parent with whom the child lives. The chapters move beyond the realm of the primary caretaker to consider the patterns of involvement of both parents in the life of the child and treat such parenting functions as caregiving, social interaction, and decision making as continua, not dichotomies.

Most nonresidential parents are fathers; however, some observations generalize to nonresidential mothers as well. Authors use gender-neutral terminology when referring to all nonresidential parents and gender-specific nomenclature when a point applies only to fathers or to mothers. For example, the term *nonresidential parent* is used generically for mothers and fathers, and *nonresidential father* is used when a gender-based differentiation is implied.

Demographic Origins of Nonresidential Parenting

The upsurge in the number of nonresidential parents can be attributed to simultaneous changes in patterns of childbearing and marital stability. Because nonresidential parenting occurs for varied reasons and in diverse contexts, nonresidential parents and their children defy simplistic characterization and policy formulation.

One source of nonresidential parenting is marital dissolution, which is rapidly becoming the norm rather than the exception. The overall rate of divorce has declined since 1979 from a high of 5.3 per 1,000 population to a low of 4.7 per 1,000 population during the 3-year period of 1988 to 1990 (National Center for Health Statistics, 1991a). Despite this leveling of the divorce rate, it is estimated that about half of all marriages will end in divorce (National Center for Health Statistics, 1991a; Norton & Moorman, 1987). In addition, dissolution is forecast for two-thirds of recent marriages (Castro Martin & Bumpass, 1989). With an estimated 60% of divorces granted to parents of minor children, millions of children are reared in single-parent homes as a result of divorce (Glick, 1988a; Norton & Glick, 1986).

Available information indicates that there are different patterns of separation and divorce for African-Americans and Caucasians (London, 1991). For example, Caucasian women are more likely to divorce their husbands than are African-American women, 86.7% versus 61.8%. However, African-American women are more likely to separate and not divorce their husbands than Caucasian women, 32.9% versus 8%. As a result of this cultural variation, African-American women and children are more likely to be living in single-parent homes and experiencing a series of cohabiting partners.

Dramatic transformations in childbearing patterns have also generated millions of nonresidential parents (National Center for Health Statistics, 1990, 1991b). In 1988 and 1989 more than one million babies were born to unmarried mothers. This is the culmination of a general upward spiral in births outside marriage—a 64% increase since 1980 (National Center for Health Statistics, 1991b). In 1988, 26% of all babies were born to unmarried mothers, compared to 18% in 1980.

Births outside of marriage vary substantially within different subgroups of the population. Caucasian mothers had 11% of their babies outside of marriage in 1980 and 18% in 1988. In comparison, African-American mothers had 55% of their babies outside of marriage in 1980 and 64% in 1988. Longitudinal comparative data are not available for Hispanic mothers. However, in 1989, 36% of births to Hispanic women were outside marriage (National Center for Health Statistics, 1991b). Although most babies born outside marriage have teenage mothers, there is also an increase in nonmarital births to mothers over age 25; about one-quarter in 1980, compared to about one-third in 1988.

Implications for Family Relationships

Both marital dissolution and nonmarital births have been linked to poor financial consequences for children (Teachman & Paasch, this volume; Zill & Rodgers, 1988). In addition, there are variable, often circumscribed, social and legal entitlements of nonresidential parents. Expectations are even less clear when the nonresidential parent has not married the residential parent, or when paternity of the nonresidential father is not legally established.

Although regional estimates vary, in 85% to 90% of post-dissolution families children live with their mothers and have some type of access to their nonresidential fathers (Glick, 1988a). An even higher percentage of children born outside marriage reside with their mothers. Thus, nonresidential parents are usually biological fathers who vary with respect to the nature of their level of family connections and legal entitlements.

Many children born outside marriage have no legal ties to their fathers (Peterson & Nord, 1990). Child support and visitation arrangements are more variable and less likely to be legally formalized when parents have not married (Seltzer, 1991). For divorced or separated families, there have been powerful shifts in prescriptions for nonresidential parenting. At the onset of the "divorce revolution" (Weitzman, 1985), legal and mental health professionals advised that the discretion of the residential parent should regulate the child's relationship with the nonresidential parent (Goldstein, Freud, & Solnit, 1973). This position gave way to both enthusiastic aspirations for shared parenting after divorce and pervasive reformation of child custody legislation (Folberg, 1991).

A longstanding concern of mental health professionals and family policy specialists is the potential for complete disengagement of the nonresidential parent (Depner, 1987). Early research painted a bleak picture of the nonresidential parent's ongoing involvement. In 1981 Furstenberg, Nord, Petersen, and Zill (1983) collected retrospective data about families, most of whom had separated in the early 1970s, concerning contact between children, ages 11 to 16, and their nonresidential parents. They found that more than 50% of the children had not seen their fathers within the preceding year. In addition, only 17%

reported visiting their fathers on a weekly basis. Furstenberg and colleagues detected decrements in visitation as early as 2 years following the marital separation.

This alarming level of disengagement has not been replicated in subsequent studies of nationally representative and regional samples (Braver, Wolchik, Sandler, Fogas, & Zventina, 1991; Bray & Berger, 1990; Depner, Maccoby, & Mnookin, 1988; Maccoby, Depner, & Mnookin, 1988; Seltzer, 1991), perhaps due to changes in social norms and legislation governing parenting opportunities for nonresidential parents. In addition, longitudinal data suggest more complex patterns of association, with disengagement of some parents and reinstatement of others (Bray & Berger, this volume; Maccoby & Mnookin, 1992).

Seltzer's (1991) work offers a nationwide comparison of patterns of involvement among differently situated nonresidential fathers. Using the nationally representative sample from the *National Survey of Families and Households* (NSFH) (Sweet, Bumpass, & Call, 1988), Seltzer found that only 18% of previously married fathers had not visited with their children during the past year and about 25% had contact at least once a week. In contrast, 40% of fathers who were not previously married to the mothers had no contact with their children in the past year, although 20% of unmarried fathers saw their children at least once a week. Economic involvement was also related to marital history, with 64% of married fathers paying child support and only 29% of unmarried fathers paying child support. Fathers who pay some type of child support are more likely to have visits with their children than fathers who pay no child support. Seltzer's cross-sectional data showed that fathers who had been separated from their children for longer periods had less social and financial involvement with them.

The NSFH data and those from regional samples suggest that nonresidential parents continue their involvement with their children at a higher rate than previously documented. Nonetheless, the dynamics of involvement deserve further inquiry. Substantial proportions of nonresidential parents do not develop or maintain close emotional and financial ties to their children. What factors presage and influence a sustained relationship between parent and child? The challenge for research and social policy is to identify such factors and promulgate changes that promote the beneficial aspects of children's relationships with their nonresidential parents.

Each chapter in this book approaches this challenge from a slightly different vantage point, considering the positions of different family members and the powerful forces of culture, social context, economics, legal policy, and family life cycle on family dynamics. What are the different models of participation? What is proving feasible? What are the implications for the welfare of various family members? What interventions and service delivery approaches facilitate family functioning and adaptation? This book begins to answer some of these questions and in the process raises other important ones. Each chapter evaluates the state of knowledge in a particular area and provides suggestions for further research, clinical interventions, and changes in social policy.

Cross-Cutting Themes in a Multidimensional Perspective

Nonresidential parenting exists in the context of diverse family forms. Nonresidential parents are themselves different in respects that are consequential for their family relationships. Over the life course, a child's family may assume myriad structural variations. Rather than cataloging the many permutations, this volume attempts to think about strategies for research, practice, and policy that acknowledge and are responsive to the fact of diversity.

Often, chapter authors find that research has not kept pace with the stunning proliferation of patterns of nonresidential parenting. There are many gaps in the knowledge base. Fundamentally, although we know that alternative scenarios eventuate in nonresidential parenting, there is a paucity of theoretical and empirical work about different situations of nonresidential parents. We cannot say with certainty what the nonresidential parent's gender, ethnicity, or marital history portend for parent-child relationships over time. It is too early to know to what extent models developed on predominantly white, middle-class divorcing families generalize to the wider spectrum of nonresidential parents in our society.

Several chapters address important gaps in theory by extending and adapting existing formulations to address issues in nonresidential parenting. Social exchange theory, family systems theories, individual development theories, and legal theories of dominance and gender are used as organizing frameworks for the disparate literature on participation of nonresidential parents. In keeping with wider systems thinking, the authors also seek a broader contextual understanding of nonresidential parenting. Social institutions and community relationships also are consequential for family outcomes. Each chapter raises questions about the ways in which social relationships and organizations can facilitate family functioning.

The significance of multivariate models is also underscored. Family outcomes are multiply determined. Identifying central variables and disentangling causal relationships is a major challenge for research on nonresidential parenting—one that is crucial in the formation of policies that will have the greatest benefits for families. Implications for further research and social policy are discussed. Several chapters also grapple with the complexities of concurrent temporal dynamics. Processes are superimposed—the course of the child's development, parental adaptation, and family transitions.

Overview

Part I, "Nonresidential Parents: Who Are They?" reviews what we know about the different patterns of residential parenting that exist in our culture. Rebecca del Carmen and Gabrielle Virgo provide a multicultural perspective on nonresidential parenting. Despite the significance of cultural heritage and the increasing ethnic diversity in our society, Del Carmen and Virgo find that many ethnic and cultural differences have been overlooked by study designs that are limited in scope. Although particular ethnic differences in family forms have been documented by demographers, the cultural significance of these variations deserves particular attention. Their chapter reviews culturally relevant themes among African-American, Asian-American, and Hispanic families. They find substantial variation in nonresidential parenting across different ethnic groups. The role of the extended family and the strength of kinship bonds emerge as key contextual variables. Salient ethnic distinctions are also found in links between legal and emotional bonds with children.

The next chapter examines parental role reversal. Charlene Depner traces the history of social and legal ideology about the respective roles of mothers and fathers and concludes that, although role reversal households grapple with many of the normative issues in single-parent living, the wider context of law and social attitudes creates unique challenges for role reversal families. Moreover, ideological underpinnings of custody legislation are being challenged by revisionist theory. Underscoring the variability of residential and visitation arrangements over time, Depner emphasizes the importance of longitudinal models for understanding the meaning and impact of the nonresidential parent role.

Part II, "Using Social Science Research in Policy and Practice," turns to complex interactions of family pluralism and social policy. The financial implications of parenting apart are central issues for nontraditional families. Jay Teachman and Kathleen Paasch use nationally representative data to illustrate the severe financial jeopardy of residential mothers and their children. Adequate support of children who do not reside with both parents is a policy imperative that has generated heated debate. There is no consensus about strategies, or even objectives, of a comprehensive family economic policy. This chapter assesses the feasibility of social interventions in light of the scope of the problem and economic circumstances within population subgroups.

Contributions to theory-building are found in the chapter by Sanford Braver, Sharlene Wolchik, Irwin Sandler, and Virgil Sheets. They extend social exchange theory to organize and integrate the disparate literature on patterns of involvement of nonresidential parents. Previous researchers have applied social exchange hypotheses to the study of adult relationship formation, maintenance, and dissolution, but this chapter extends the formulation to nonresidential parent-child relationships. The chapter reviews empirical evidence that supports the social exchange perspective.

Obstacles to ongoing relationships between nonresidential parents and their children are considered in the chapter by Janet Johnston. Children's reluctance or refusal to visit is a perplexing dilemma for mental health professionals and the legal system, but it has rarely been the subject of systematic inquiry. Drawing from research and clinical experience, Johnston considers the roots of visitation resistance in different, multiple, and often interlocking psychological, developmental, and family systemic processes. The overall thesis of this chapter is that children's resistance or refusal to visit a nonresidential parent is generally multidetermined, and each case needs differential assessment and intervention.

Joan Kelly's chapter accentuates the importance of creating a forum in which mothers and fathers can work together to set the stage for their ongoing parental relationship. What resources exist for developing parenting agreements between mothers and fathers who live apart? When disagreements exist about the appropriate role of the nonresidential parent? What dispute resolution forums should be considered? Kelly weighs the relative advantages of mediation as a forum where parents can establish operating principles for their respective parental roles.

The chapter by James Bray and Sandra Berger presents a developmental family systems model of divorce and remarriage concerning the nonresidential parent. Data from the *Developmental Issues in StepFamilies Research Project* is presented on the effects of the nonresidential parent-child relationship on children's behavioral adjustment. Their data suggest that after the early months of remarriage the nonresidential parent-child relationship has few effects on children's adjustment. These authors take a long-term view of divorce and remarriage and argue that it is important to understand the longitudinal process of multiple family transitions in studying nonresidential parenting.

Each chapter considers implications for further research and social policy. In the final chapter, we comment on these recommendations and offer new directions for multidimensional approaches in research, policy and practice.

References

Braver, S. H., Wolchik, S. A., Sandler, I. N., Fogas, B. S., & Zventina, D. (1991). Frequency of visitation by divorced fathers: Differences in reports by fathers and mothers. *American Journal of Orthopsychiatry, 61*, 448-543.

Bray, J. H., & Berger, S. H. (1990). Noncustodial father and paternal grandparent relationships in stepfamilies. *Family Relations, 39*, 414-419.

Castro Martin, T., & Bumpass, L. (1989). Recent trends and differentials in marital disruption. *Demography, 26*, 37-51.

Clark, S. C., Whitney, R. A., & Beck, J. C. (1988). Discrepancies between custodial awards and custodial practices: De jure and de facto custody. *Journal of Divorce, 11*(3/4), 219-229.

Depner, C. E. (1987, August). *Child residence in the post-divorce family.* Paper presented at the annual meeting of the American Psychological Association, New York City.

Depner, C. E., & Bray, J. H. (1990). Modes of participation for nonresidential parents: The challenge for research, policy, education and practice. *Family Relations, 39*, 378-381.

Depner, C. E., Maccoby, E. E., & Mnookin, R. H. (1988, August). *Assessing father participation in the post-divorce family.* Paper presented at the Annual Meeting of the American Psychological Association, Atlanta, GA.

Fischer, J. L., & Cardea, J. M. (1984). Mother-child relationships of mothers living apart from their children. *Family Relations, 32*, 351-357.

Folberg, J. (1991). Custody overview. In J. Folberg (Ed.), *Joint custody and shared parenting* (2nd ed., pp. 3-10). New York: Guilford Press.

Furstenberg, F. F., Jr., Nord, C. W., Peterson, J. L., & Zill, N. (1983). The life course of children of divorce: Marital disruption and parental contact. *American Sociological Review, 48*, 656-668.

Glick, P. C. (1988a). The role of divorce in the changing family structure: Trends and variations. In S. A. Wolchik & P. Karoly (Eds.), *Children of divorce: Empirical perspectives on adjustment* (pp. 3-34). New York: Gardner Press.

Glick, P. C. (1988b). Fifty years of family demography: A record of social change. *Journal of Marriage and the Family, 50*, 861-873.

Goldstein, J., Freud, A., & Solnit, A. J. (1973). *Beyond the best interest of the child.* New York: Free Press.

London, K. A. (1991). Cohabitation, marriage, marital dissolution, and remarriage: United States, 1988. *Advance data from vital and health statistics; No. 194.* Hyattsville, MD: National Center for Health Statistics.

Maccoby, E. E., Depner, C. E., & Mnookin, R. H. (1988). Child custody following divorce. In E. M. Hetherington & J. D. Arasteh (Eds.), *Impact of divorce, single-parenting and step-parenting on children* (pp. 91-114). Hillsdale, NJ: Lawrence Erlbaum.

Maccoby, E., & Mnookin, R. H. (1992). *Dividing the child: The social and legal dilemmas of custody.* Cambridge, MA: Harvard University Press.

Mnookin, R. H., Maccoby, E., Albiston, C. R., & Depner, C. E. (1990). Private ordering revisited: What custodial arrangements are parents negotiating? In S. D. Sugarman & H. Hill Kay (Eds.), *Divorce reform at the crossroads* (pp. 37-74). New Haven, CT: Yale University Press.

National Center for Health Statistics (1990). Advance report of final natality statistics, 1988. *Monthly vital statistics report* (Vol. 39, No. 4, Supp.). Hyattsville, MD: Public Health Service.

National Center for Health Statistics (1991a). Annual summary of births, marriages, divorces, and deaths: United States, 1990. *Monthly vital statistics report* (Vol. 39, No. 13). Hyattsville, MD: Public Health Service.

National Center for Health Statistics (1991b). Advance report of final natality statistics, 1989. *Monthly vital statistics report* (Vol. 40, No. 8, Supp.). Hyattsville, MD: Public Health Service.

Norton, A. J., & Glick, P. C. (1986). One-parent families: A social and economic profile. *Family Relations, 35*, 9-17.

Norton, A. J., & Moorman, J. E. (1987). Marriage and divorce patterns of U.S. women. *Journal of Marriage and the Family, 49*, 3-14.

Peterson, J. L., & Nord, C. W. (1990). The regular receipt of child support: A multi-step process. *Journal of Marriage and the Family, 52*, 539-551.

Seltzer, J. A. (1991). Relationships between fathers and children who live apart: The father's role after separation. *Journal of Marriage and the Family, 53*, 79-101.

Skolnik, A. (1991). *Embattled paradise: The American family in an age of uncertainty.* New York: Basic Books.

Sweet, J. A., Bumpass, L. L., & Call, V. (1988). *The design and content of the National Survey of Families and Households* (NSFH Working Paper No. 1). Center for Demography and Ecology, University of Wisconsin-Madison.

Weitzman, L. J. (1985). *The divorce revolution: The unexpected social and economic consequences for women and children in America.* New York: Free Press.

Zill, N., & Rogers, C. C. (1988). Recent trends in the well-being of children in the United States and their implications for public policy. In J. L. Palmer & I. V. Sawhill (Eds.), *The changing American family and public policy* (pp. 31-115). Washington, DC: The Urban Institute Press.

2

Marital Disruption and Nonresidential Parenting

A Multicultural Perspective

REBECCA DEL CARMEN
GABRIELLE N. VIRGO

Understanding parenting in the context of marital disruption is enriched from a perspective informed by the cross-cultural and comparative literature. From a multicultural viewpoint, marriage and marital disruption take various forms and meanings according to a person's sociocultural situation. Lancaster (1989) notes that the cross-cultural record of human adaptation provides us with a wide spectrum of marital patterns, ranging from polygyny, monogamy, serial monogamy, and polyandry to single parenthood. Others have acknowledged a variety of family groupings, including the nuclear family, the joint or extended family, or the *famille-souche* or stem family (Arensberg & Kimball, 1965). There is substantial variation in family adaptations across different ethnic groups.

Variations of marital patterns and family formations throughout all segments of American society are increasingly acknowledged. However, there still exists a chasm in the social sciences between family patterns that are fully recognized and the variety of individual adaptations evolving out of current social, economic, and political realities influencing family life. This is true particularly for ethnic minorities.[1] For example, researchers highlight the increasingly large numbers of

13

female-headed households while alluding to the possibility that true levels of father involvement are not known. Some suggest that there may be a greater influx of fathers or father figures in these homes or even improved "quality" time between nonresidential fathers and their children (Mott, 1990).

In this chapter, we assess marital and family patterns, including marital disruption, post-divorce parenting, and nonresidential parenting from a multicultural perspective. A multicultural perspective provides a rich source of broader, more complex models for understanding the participation of nontraditional or nonresidential parenting. Family patterns and life cycle phases vary by ethnicity (McGoldrick, 1982). Further, they are influenced by the factors unique to each group, such as particular sociohistorical events, migration, patterns of acculturation, and discrimination. Yet, the literature in the area of divorce and post-divorce adjustment has focused primarily on nonminority individuals. There is a lack of empirical data in this area on families from different ethnic groups, particularly studies that focus upon healthy minority families and successful marital patterns in minority communities. Even less research exists regarding divorce and its impact in these communities. Often, when minority families are studied, individual differences within the group such as socioeconomic factors are not adequately controlled. As a result, cultural diversity is not adequately reflected in the literature on marriage, divorce, and post-divorce parenting.

The aims of this chapter are to: (a) provide a context for a multicultural viewpoint in understanding of family patterns, divorce, and nonresidential parenting by highlighting factors that can provide a culturally sensitive framework; (b) review the research on cultural values, family structure, marital disruption and nonresidential parenting among African-Americans, Asian-Americans, and Hispanics; and (c) highlight the neglected areas in the literature and propose directions for future research.

The Need for a Multicultural Perspective

A multicultural perspective is required to adequately examine adaptation to divorce in both minority and nonminority families. In this section we review the literature, highlighting the salient factors that can form the basis of this perspective, including demographic patterns and family structure.

Family Demographic Patterns

The Two-Parent Household. The American, middle-class, nuclear family has been characterized as two-parent, immediate or biological, mobile, and short-lived (Arensberg & Kimball, 1965). In the context of the variety of family forms that anthropological, historical, and cross-cultural studies reveal, this pattern of family life is relatively unique. Even if we trace this form of family life back to its historical roots in seventeenth-century England and Europe, the characteristics of the two-parent nuclear family form a striking contrast to those family groupings that were "production units," including a variety of adults, children, kin, and workers living and working under the same roof (Rosenthal & Keshet, 1981). Arensberg and Kimball note that the special features of the American nuclear family pose certain problems, including isolation of family members; dependence upon the competence, cooperation, and adjustment of the spouses for the well-being and socialization of the children; and growing segregation of the elderly. Similarly, Rosenthal and Keshet note that: "We can easily see how the increased demands on the parents, on the small isolated nuclear family, both intensified and confused the parental relationship" (p. 21).

In fact, the number of children being raised in two-parent, nuclear family units has been declining dramatically (Bumpass, 1990). The proportion of households across all ethnic groups involving two-parent households with children under 18 years of age has dropped from 40% in 1970 to only 26% in 1990 (U.S. Bureau of the Census, 1990a). In the past 30 years, certain trends have been documented across ethnic groups in the United States. These trends include lower marriage rates and older median age at first marriage, higher divorce rates, lower birth rates, earlier and increased sexual activity among adolescents, and a higher proportion of births to unmarried mothers (National Research Council, 1989). These changes may be more or less pronounced for certain subgroups of American society, such as for the African- or Asian-Americans, resulting in increasingly different marital and family experiences for individual members of these groups.

The Single-Parent Family. The number of single-parent households has increased dramatically from 3.8 million family groups in 1970 to 9.7 million in 1990 (Bureau of the Census, 1990a). Families maintained by women (with no husband present) accounted for 44% of households for blacks, 13% for whites, 12% for Asians, and 23% for Hispanics.

Families maintained by men (with no wife present) accounted for 6% of family households for blacks, 4% for whites, 6% for Asians, and 7% for Hispanics.

Virtually all single-parent situations are the result of (a) birth outside of marriage, (b) adoption, (c) marital separation, (d) divorce, or (e) widowhood (U.S. Bureau of the Census, 1990a). The primary causes for the single-parent status may vary by ethnic group and may reflect the unique sociocultural characteristics and economic challenges faced within each group.

As shown in Table 2.1, divorce is the major source of single-parent household status among white families. In contrast, out-of-marriage parenthood is driving single parenthood for black families, and separation (without divorce) is the major cause for this household pattern among Hispanic families. For emigrating Asian families, the cause of single-parent status may be linked to the process of immigration.

From an evolutionary and cross-cultural perspective, Lancaster (1989) notes that the primary determinant of human family formation and parent investment approaches is "the needs of women for access to resources to rear children. In some contexts, women may find that the best and most predictable access to resources is through a male mate; in others, through their own kindred; and in still others, through their independent efforts" (p. 67). She suggests that under a wide variety of conditions, male mating patterns are secondary or dependent on female strategies, and that males adjust their behavior to the ways in which "females must distribute themselves in space in order to rear their offspring successfully." Thus, patterns of nonresidential (predominantly father) parental involvement in child rearing following divorce may reflect the culturally determined needs of the residential parent (mother). For ethnic minority families, examination of the role of the extended family in determining the nonresidential parental role is key.

Fine and Schwebel (1988) note that in some ethnic minority groups such as African-Americans, single parenthood may last longer than in nonminority families. Further, Takai (1981) found that black single women use kinship support to replace lost income of their husbands more successfully than do white women. In contrast, there may be a stronger motivation to remarry among white families. As a result, blended or stepfamily situations may be more prevalent among nonminority families. For example, Lee, Zimiles, and Ladewski (1991) reported that Hispanics are less likely to live in stepfamilies. The lower prevalence of stepfamilies may provide a different context for nonres-

Table 2.1   Etiology for Children Under 18 Years of Age Who Live
With One Parent, by Percentage

Race	Divorced	Married Parent Absent	Widowed	Parents Never Married
Black	20	23	5	52
White	49	24	8	19
Hispanic	27	34	7	33

SOURCE: From U.S. Bureau of the Census (1990b)

idential parenting in the minority families. When conflicts arise for the
nonresidential parent in minority families, they may be more likely to
involve biological relatives than stepparents.

The links between socioeconomic factors and family living arrangements are not well understood. Some suggest that economic hardship
deters marriage among couples (Bishop, 1977; Furstenberg, 1976;
McLoyd, 1990). Wilson (1987) proposed that increasing unemployment may make marriage less attractive to both men and women.
McLoyd reported that compared to parents whose economic circumstances are more favorable, parents who are financially distressed
experience more depression and marital conflict; further, these effects
are more pronounced and enduring among disadvantaged black men
compared to disadvantaged white men. Low-paying insecure jobs resulting from discriminatory practices toward some ethnic groups may
discourage men from marriage or may promote an unwillingness on the
part of women to risk possible loss of kin support for an uncertain future
with the child's father (Ladner, 1971; National Research Council, 1989;
Stack, 1974). Clearly, socioeconomic and demographic factors are
critically important in determining family structural patterns and post-
divorce adjustment of ethnic minority groups.

Socioeconomic status also may play a critical role in determining the
level of parental involvement of the nonresidential father. Although
there is uncertainty regarding established guidelines for the role and
behavior of nonresidential parents (Seltzer, 1991), one widely acknowledged obligation is the provision of financial support. In ethnic minority
families, particularly black families, the role of the extended family in
providing emotional and child-rearing support is salient. The black

nonresidential father may respond to economic disadvantage with a more hands-on approach in concert with the extended family, or he may withdraw from the family network if he feels less dependence from his former spouse and children (Isaacs & Leon, 1988). This decision may largely be determined by the support of the extended family and the various perceptions of role of the nonresidential father in that extended family context.

Differential Family Structures

A major issue for divorced families is the role of the nonresidential parent, and where he or she fits into the larger family structure. Given no clear legal guidelines defining the place of the nonresidential parent, societal and subcultural norms often determine the role. In ethnic minority families, there are several facets of family concept and organization that may influence the role of the nonresidential parent and the level of involvement with the children.

Family and Kin Support. In contrast to the isolated nuclear family, ethnic minority families generally have been characterized by the traditional extended family structure, which includes many siblings, relatives, and grandparents living in the same home or in proximity. Although among Asian-Americans the residential extended family pattern is quite rare as there is a gradual shift to the nuclear structure, the Asian-American family appears to have retained some aspects of the extended family pattern (del Carmen, 1990). For example, extended family ties are maintained with grandparents living in the home or in proximity (Wong, 1985). The first- and second-generation Asian-American family is less likely than the Asian family in Asia, but more likely than the non-Asian-American family, to include a grandparent or relative living in the home (del Carmen, 1990; Liu & Fernandez, 1987).

For black Americans, the family structure appears to have evolved patterns of "kinship" networks and social support systems that are not necessarily drawn along biological lines (Hines & Boyd-Franklin, 1982). Others have noted the active role of black grandparents in the socialization of children (Cherlin & Furstenberg, 1986; Pearson, Hunter, Ensminger, & Kellam, 1990). Even among middle- and upper-middle-income African-American families, the extended family concept remains strong, although actual dependence upon extended family may be relatively minimized due to greater financial independence and mobility. In times of marital stress or marital disruption, these patterns may come to the surface.

Kellam and colleagues (1977) assessed varying family structures in economically disadvantaged families and reported that mother or father presence in the home was a protective factor to child adaptability and psychological well-being, but that the grandparent in the home also was strongly protective for a child of either sex. However, they did not investigate the nature and extent of involvement of the nonresidential parent in the mother-grandmother-child triad. Examining how the non-residential father is integrated into this extended family situation is critical to understanding the role of the nonresidential parent in the well-being of the successfully adapted child.

In a 1978 study by McAdoo, 178 middle- and upper-class black families in the greater Washington, D.C., area were studied to determine whether extended family variables were supportive of family members' stability and upward mobility. The majority of these families were two-parent, some were single-parent, and all had school-age children. McAdoo found that the parents, other family, and non-biological relatives of the couples were extensively involved in an "extended kinship network" that facilitated their mobility. In a previous study (1980) McAdoo reported that the success of the black middle-class mothers and their school-age children was tied to their participation in the "kin-help exchange network," which often involved "fictive" kin who functioned as aunts and uncles. She concluded that the black family has maintained a system of kin-help family extension that is a viable historical and ancestral part of the culture of African-Americans, operative at all income levels.

Differential Effects. The literature suggests that there may be differential effects of extended family and kin support across different ethnic groups in times of transition such as divorce. If so, these differences would clearly impact upon patterns of nonresidential parenting.

Several studies suggest that the involvement of extended family may not always be positive for nonminority families. Hawkins and Eggebeen (1991) reported that white children in a three-generation living arrangement with grandfathers present were more likely to experience problems in psychosocial functioning. Similarly, Bray and Berger (1990) reported a negative relationship (including increased behavior problems and poorer self-esteem) of grandparent involvement in a white, middle-class sample in stepfamilies. Spanier and Hanson (1981) assessed the role of extended kin in the adjustment to marital separation in a nonminority sample of individuals who were separated 26 months or less. They predicted that interaction with and support of kin would lead to better adjustment following separation. Their findings did not support this prediction.

Hawkins and Eggebeen suggest that the norm of the two-parent, nuclear family and its independence is strong and pervasive among nonminorities, and that violations of this norm for any length of time "create potential difficulties for all three generations" (p. 968). Similarly, Clemens and Axelson (1985) suggested that Caucasian mothers who return to live with their parents following divorce may revert to the role of dependent child, which may have negative consequences for grandchildren. Thus, some studies that have investigated the extended family structure among nonminority families suggest that neither the adult children nor their parents find this family structure the preferable one (Cherlin & Furstenberg, 1986; Hawkins & Eggebeen, 1991).

Sibling Relations. Sibling relationships also are relevant to the adjustment of children after divorce and to their relationship with nonresidential parents, particularly for certain minority families, which often include a large number of adults and a larger number of children than Caucasian families (Garcia-Coll, 1990). In a study of successful rural African-American adolescents, Lee (1985) reports that the average number of children per home was five. Hispanics also tend to have higher fertility and higher birthrates than the non-Hispanic population (Ventura, 1987). Among Mexican-Americans, the ties of siblings are very strong, and birth order or age hierarchies are important in family life throughout childhood and often into adulthood (Falicov, 1982).

The effect of these age hierarchies in understanding post-divorce adjustment and nonresidential parenting has not been assessed in the literature on minorities or nonminorities. It can be theorized that the sibling subsystem may foster or hinder post-divorce adaptation for children. In the ethnic minority family, the sibling support network may already be in place before the advent of a separation or divorce. Sibling ties within the immediate family may provide additional protective mechanisms for children of divorce. However, there may be a differential effect depending on birth order. Upon divorce, older children may serve as surrogate caretakers or disciplinarians for younger children. This new and increased responsibility may foster or hinder the older child's functioning in other areas of development, such as academic performance or peer relations (Amato, 1987). Also, depending on birth order, this dynamic may have a differential influence on the child's relationship to the nonresidential parent. For example, the older child may be at risk for more conflict in his or her relationship with the nonresidential parent, given any additional burdens and responsibilities in caring for younger siblings. The effects of the sibling subsystem and birth order of the child on post-divorce adjustment and nonresidential parenting are fruitful areas for culturally relevant research in this area.

Ethnic Differences in Family Functioning and Divorce

The value of examining differences in coping with divorce is that it allows us to appreciate the wide range of cultural variation and to remain open to the broad possibilities in our search for effective modes of adaptation to divorce, regardless of ethnicity. There is substantial variation across ethnic groups regarding divorce and nonresidential parenting. The difficulty in studying perceptions and adaptations based on ethnicity is that within each of the innumerable ethnic groups, one can find as many differences based upon social, economic, and religious lines as can be found within the majority population. In this section, we attempt to examine post-divorce adaptation in three ethnic minority groups. We chose the largest three groups for reasons of brevity and available research. While examining each ethnic group, we attempt to delineate individual and group differences in family functioning as well as adaptation to marital disruption and divorce. This section examines the research on African-American, Asian-American, and Hispanic family life and marital disruption.

African-American Families

Although the ancestral roots of the majority of black families in the United States can be traced to the African continent, the migratory route that their ancestors followed differs as greatly as does the cultures of countless ancestral African homelands. The cultural backgrounds of black families whose roots trace back several generations in the countries of Brazil, Jamaica, the Cape Verde Islands, the United States, and Cuba are each distinct and vastly different (Bryce-Laporte, 1972; Nobles, 1974). Further, the economic and social status of black families has as broad a range as any group. Clearly, the behavioral practices of a six-figure income, northeastern African-American family whose roots trace back to the Colonial days cannot be classified together with the practices of a rural southern family of farmers. This sort of generalization can be misleading and detrimental in our attempt to accurately delineate ethnic differences.

However, there may be broad generalizations that can be applied to black families as a whole, given the political and social reality of being "black" in the United States (Hines & Boyd-Franklin, 1982). Given the obstacles posed for black Americans, regardless of place of origin, throughout this country's history, there may be a commonality in ways of understanding and adjusting to disruptive situations including divorce.

The resilience of the black family has been emphasized in the literature on African-Americans. A striking finding to emerge from modern historical accounts of the black family is that stable, two-parent families were maintained during slavery and survived the vicissitudes of poverty, migration, and urbanization (Billingsley, 1968, National Research Council, 1989). Until the 1960s, statistical accounts of intact black families including both husband and wife were as high as 75% (National Research Council, 1989). The dramatic changes, including a shift to more single-parent households, have come only in more recent decades.

Given the economic and social realities faced by many black families, black parents have by necessity been individually prepared to function as both mother and father in the best interest of their family's survival (Hill, 1972; Martin & Martin, 1978; Rosser, 1979). This particular adaptability is one of the themes of Hill's *The Strengths of Black Families* (1972), in which he attributes the survival of black families to their strong kinship bonds, flexibility of family roles, and high value placed upon religion, education, and the work ethic. Several authors place the origins of this flexibility of family, particularly the parental roles, in the West African ancestry of African-American and Afro-Caribbean people (Diop, 1987; Hill, 1972).

Hines and Boyd-Franklin (1982) noted that role flexibility is a strength that can be mobilized in times of crisis, such as separation or divorce. For a variety of social, historical, and economic reasons, black women often worked outside the home. If their spouses faced unemployment, the women were sole wage earners in the household and relied heavily upon the extended family unit to assist in child rearing. Philips and Alcebo (1986) noted that black women have often assumed nontraditional roles within the family, and that this pattern may buffer them from the more "traditional" effects of divorce upon women. Brown, Perry, and Harburg (1972) explored the ethnic differences in women's psychological response to divorce. They reported that during the divorce process, white women reported significantly lower self-esteem, less well-being, and less personal growth than black women.

Others have noted that the effect of divorce appears to be more negative for whites than for blacks (Amato & Keith, 1991; Fine & Schwebel,1988; Katz & Piotrokowski, 1983) in terms of healthy psychological outlook. However, it may be that patterns of coping are not necessarily better, but simply different for blacks than for whites. For example, the extended family may envelop the broken family to assist everyone, particularly children, through the transition. Another possibility is that the black woman may express her distress differently. For example, the stress of divorce may simply be internalized by black women to a greater degree than by white women, given the pressures on African-Americans in this country to maintain a certain degree of stoicism in order to survive (Bryce-LaPorte, 1972; Hill, 1972). Hines and Boyd-Franklin (1982) note that a woman may feel empathy for her husband's frustrations in coping with discrimination and have difficulty holding him fully responsible for his situation, or may feel reluctant to publicly express her dissatisfaction. The cross-pressures between ethnicity and gender in response to divorce are a relatively unexplored area.

Another relevant factor may be the presence or absence of stepfamily or blended family situations in adjustment to divorce. For whites, the subgroup norm to remarry may create different types of pressures (for example, competition among stepchildren and biological children for resources) for white families than for blacks, who may rely more on kin for support upon divorce. Thus, the challenges in the post-divorce adjustment may be different in the two groups. The role of the grandparent or other extended family member may become more salient in the post-divorce period in certain ethnic groups, leading to different post-divorce behaviors for nonresidential parents across ethnicity. For example, conflicts arising over parenting for the nonresidential parent from certain minority groups may involve the grandparents rather than the stepparents. Also, given greater extended family support and less financial pressure to remarry, there may be higher cohabitation or "living together" arrangements for blacks than for whites.

The role of the father is central to understanding nonresidential parenting patterns among African-Americans. With respect to the position of the father in the family, Hines and Boyd-Franklin (1982) suggest that the issue of "peripheralness has been vastly overstated in the literature" (p. 87). Following divorce, the degree of involvement of a nonresidential parent with the children is determined by a number of factors, including the precipitating reason for divorce and the ongoing relationship between the parents. This is certainly no different for the black divorced family.

In 1986 Isaacs and Leon conducted a study examining the frequency of visitation of both black and white nonresidential fathers, as well as certain circumstances surrounding the divorce situation, for each of 96 families in the Philadelphia area. Their fundamental hypothesis was that differences in visitation, if found, might be accountable on the basis of differences in family structure between white and black families, rather than on the degree of desired involvement of the father. They based their hypothesis on the acknowledged strong kinship bonds and the adaptability of family roles, identified by Hill in the 1970s as two of the major strengths of black families in this country. They also hypothesized that father involvement was not as necessary in divorced black families as in white families due to the willingness of black women to assume full head-of-household responsibility, thus minimizing dependence upon the nonresidential parent.

Isaacs and Leon found several interesting things. Ethnicity had a significant effect upon each of the predictors of father visitation, while having no direct effect on the frequency of visitation for the nonresidential parent. Specifically, being black increased self-reliance in divorced women and increased the likelihood of extended family support. Black women were more likely to move in with their parents after separation and were more likely than white women to have decided to separate in the first place. The general finding was that black fathers were no less likely than white fathers to have consistent relationships with their nonresidential children but were, in a sense, rendered less necessary by the family adjustment following divorce, given the way black women coped with divorce.

There is not strong support in the literature for the assumption that black nonresidential fathers are less interested or involved with their children than white nonresidential fathers, particularly in middle-class families with resources. In a study of professional middle-class blacks who grew up in single-parent families, Morris (1977) reported that the subjects felt that their fathers were very important in their lives, regardless of residential status.

Other investigators have failed to find ethnic differences in economic involvement of nonresidential fathers, which may be a reflection of consistently low involvement across groups. However, ethnic differences in levels of participation in child rearing have been noted. For example, in another study on nonresidential parenting among African-Americans, Seltzer (1991) found that black fathers not living with their children had significantly higher probabilities of visiting and participating in child rearing decisions than nonblacks, although they did not differ from white fathers in terms of their levels of economic participation and support.

Few studies have directly examined nonresidential parenting patterns among African-American families. However, the literature suggests that black children, as well as their residential parents, are supported by and involved with both extended kin and nonresidential parents following divorce (Fine & Schwebel, 1990; Isaacs & Leon, 1988; Morris, 1977; Seltzer, 1991).

Asian-American Families

Patterns of marriage, divorce, and post-divorce functioning among Asian-Americans is a relatively unexplored area of research. There are only a few relevant articles and papers. These describe traditional values of Asian families (Shon & Ja, 1982), delineate current marital and divorce trends of Asians living in Asia (Bjorksten, 1984; Ho, 1987), or include Asians as subjects in empirical studies of adjustment to divorce (Mechanic & Hansell, 1989). Also available are current census statistics on Asian-American families (U.S. Bureau of the Census, 1990a, 1990b) as well as more extensive reports published on ethnic minority families, based on 1980 census information (Hernandez, 1986). There is a scarcity of empirical work on post-divorce and nonresidential adjustment patterns of Asian-Americans. This section will review the available literature and highlight issues relevant to an understanding of marriage and divorce patterns for Asian-Americans. These issues include background information and cultural values, family functioning of Asians in Asia and in the United States, and patterns of divorce and post-divorce adjustment among Asian-Americans.

Currently, Asians make up approximately 2.9% of the total U.S. population, although this figure varies greatly by state. Like other ethnic minorities, the subgroups that fall under the Asian/Pacific-American rubric are very diverse in terms of nationality, socioeconomic status, and level of acculturation (Fugita, 1990). Some scholars in the area estimate that there are more than 20 different cultural or nationality groups included in this category (Yoshioka, Tashima, Chew, & Murase, 1981). The three largest Asian-American groups are, in order, Chinese, Filipino, and Japanese.

Despite such diversity, one common and unifying theme to emerge from the literature on values among Asian-Americans is the importance of the family. Several characteristics have been observed that appear to reflect this cultural value. In comparison to other ethnic groups in the United States, Asian-Americans have the lowest proportion of households headed by a woman, the lowest rate of divorce, and the lowest rate of fertility (Momeni, 1984). The proportion of Asian families of divorced or widowed parents in the United States is lower than that of nonminority Caucasian Americans, but still higher than Asians living in Asia (del Carmen, 1990; Momeni, 1984).

In the past, the traditional Asian family has been characterized by a large and extended family structure, which included many siblings and their spouses who lived with their parents and other relatives spanning two or three generations. There has been a shift from the extended family structure to the nuclear family in Asia. Recent surveys suggest that 27% of Japanese and 40% of Chinese families have retained some aspect of the traditional, extended structure in the form of a "stem-family" with at least one grandparent living in the same home (Sorifu, 1985; Tseng, Kuotai, Hsu, Jinghua, Lian, & Kameoka, 1988).

In 1980 about 85% of Asian-American children lived with two parents, more than white (83%), Hispanic (71%), Native American (63%), or black (46%) (Hernandez, 1986). Those Asian children living with one parent included: Chinese, 8.5% living within mother-only homes and 4.7% living in father-only homes; Filipino children, 11.8% in mother-only homes and 4.6% in father-only homes; Japanese children, 11.9% in mother-only homes and 4.0% in father-only homes; and Korean children, 10.8% in mother-only homes and 3.2% in father-only homes (Hernandez, 1986; U.S. Bureau of the Census, 1980). In contrast, 13.5% of white children lived in mother-only homes and 1.6% lived in father-only homes.

This pattern differs from single-parent family situations for Asians living in Asia, with respect to the sex difference between mother-only and father-only homes as well as the overall prevalence. For example, a survey conducted on Chinese living in Hong Kong (Kang, 1985) revealed that 2.6% of 3,554 children were living in single-parent families. Of these, the proportion of children in mother-only homes (1.4%) was approximately equal to the proportion of children living in father-only homes (1.2%).

Ho (1987) suggests that sex difference in single-parent homes in Asia reflects several interesting differences in family and social background between the two cultures. First, it is very probable that in the extended family or stem-family arrangement, there would be older female relatives in the father-resident homes. Second, Chinese women traditionally did not have equal rights to family property and child custody in divorce, remarriage, or death. Finally, more fathers may be granted custody in Asia, reflecting the economic differential between Asian women and men.

Two additional family patterns have been observed among Asian-Americans that may relate to nonresidential parenting. Researchers have described the "incomplete family," in which family members are temporarily separated over a number of months or years in the process of migration from Asia to the United States (Liu, 1987; Wong, 1985). This arrangement might increase the prevalence of nonresidential parenting among Asian-Americans in that many parents may not reside with their children at various times during the process of migration. Few studies have examined how the migrating Asian families successfully cope with this arrangement, although this situation may provide a model for examining the impact of nonresidential status of a parent on the parent-child relationship.

Another family pattern observed by researchers is the nonresidential or "modified-extended," family in which the residential pattern is nuclear in its structure, but extended family ties are maintained with grandparents and other relatives living in proximity (Wong, 1985). While there have been several studies examining the kinship system and its impact in times of transition, such as divorce and remarriage, among white and black Americans (Hawkins & Eggebeen, 1991; McAdoo, 1977), few researchers have empirically examined the impact of such support among Asian-Americans. Serafica (1990) suggests that the loss of familiar social support among the Asian-American immigrants may weaken the ability of the parents to deal with cultural conflict and, as a result, threaten the stability of the family.

Similarly, losses of support may occur when Asian-Americans relocate from areas in the country where Asians are highly concentrated, such as the West, to other parts of the country where there may be less community support. It may well be that the social support of the Asian-American community in some parts of the country provides a buffer from some of the stressors that ordinarily contribute to increased marital disruption and divorce. The relationship between community support and patterns of marriage and divorce is an unexplored area.

There is a dearth of empirical information on divorce and visitation patterns among Asian-Americans. However, there have been some reports and cross-national comparisons based on surveys of Asians living in Asia. These studies may be suggestive of how cultural values play a role in post-divorce adjustment patterns, including nonresidential parenting.

In a study conducted by Kang (1985), 38 children from nonresidential-father families were matched with 38 children from intact families on the basis of the child's sex, age, grade, birth rank, and the educational/occupational status of the mothers. Among the 38 children from nonresidential-father families, 21% had weekly contact with their nonresidential father, 24% had monthly contact, 10% had yearly contact, and 45% had no contact at all. Also, the children's identification with and relationship to the nonresidential father were weaker in comparison to the residential father-child relationship seen in intact families.

Shon and Ja (1982) contrast the Asian family structure with the American structure. While the American family has an emphasis on the single nuclear family with a "time-limited" life span, the Asian family extends both "backward and forward" and the individual "is seen as the product of all the generations of his or her family from the beginning of time" (p. 211). From this perspective, an individual's actions are a reflection of not only the individual and his family, but also preceding and future generations. This deeply ingrained cultural value may influence the prevalence of divorce and post-divorce patterns of nonresidential parenting once marital disruption has occurred. Specifically, the salience of the value regarding continuity of family may preserve the role of parents in the lives of Asian-American children, regardless of residential status.

On the other hand, the pressures of cultural conflict, social change, and race relations (Sue & Chin, 1983) may interact with internal pressures within the family to create additional stress on the migrating Asian-American family. Serafica (1990) notes that if encounters with prejudice and discrimination have already engendered in Asian-American parents a feeling of inability to control outcomes in the workplace or the community, "it can be devastating to have husband-wife and parental roles within the family challenged as well" (p. 227). This may lead to a more conservative approach among members in order to maintain a minimum level of stability within the family. How these cross-pressures interact and influence nonresidential parenting among Asian-Americans is an unexplored area.

Hispanic Families

Like the research on Asian-Americans, there is minimal empirical work that examines divorce among the distinct ethnic subgroups within the Hispanic population. Even less investigated are issues of custody and nonresidential parenting arrangements among divorced Hispanic parents that reflect the diversity of nationality, socioeconomic status, and acculturation level.

Generally speaking, diversity within the Hispanic population is seen in several areas. First, there are many historical and ethnic differences among the heritage of Mexican, Puerto Rican, and the many other Hispanic families; a common theme, however, is the influence of Spain and Spanish culture. Second, the socioeconomic diversity that exists within the Hispanic community precludes generalization because Latino families can be found at every level of class description of the United States. As with the Asian-Americans, issues of immigration and acculturation play a significant role in the adaptation of the family unit to the stress and disruption of divorce. Families who have recently entered this country may adhere more closely to their cultural legacy than those who have been in the United States for several generations. Family patterns are often determined by the balance between the culture of origin and the practices found in the new culture.

Hispanic family relations are characterized by respect and honor as well as strong patriarchal sex roles. These include a belief that the men work outside the home and are to be ultimately respected by their wives and children to maximize the man's sense of machismo (Alverez, 1977; Fernandez-Mendez, 1970). Catholicism as well as the concept of "familism" (Alvirez & Bean, 1976) are other fundamental values pervasive in Hispanic culture. "Familism" is defined as the extension of kinship ties to family and community members outside the nuclear family. The extended family network exists as a support system to ensure the well-being of the children.

While these values mark Hispanic culture in general, each subgroup has a unique way of reconciling many of its more traditional beliefs. Thus, the practical expression of these family values is very dependent upon ethnic subgroup, socioeconomic level, and religious and acculturation factors (Falicov, 1982). For example, in some ethnic and socioeconomic subgroups, the sex roles are much more flexible, despite a strong patriarchal tradition. In such groups, women may be strongly encouraged to develop themselves intellectually and professionally.

There are broad degrees of variation across the different subgroups within the Hispanic population with respect to divorce (Frisbie, 1986). Generally speaking, divorce in the Hispanic family has been frowned upon by the extended family and community, due, in part, to the influence of Catholicism. This is also true of Filipino families. However, recent statistics show that separation and divorce rates have increased over the past 20 years for Hispanic families living in the United States as well as in their homelands (U.S. Bureau of the Census, 1979). Cultural conflict between traditional values and mainland American values may lead to conflict, including divorce (Garcia-Preto, 1982). Patriarchal sex role definitions were often challenged and reversed in households where Puerto Rican women frequently were the only adults in their households able to obtain employment. Census reports have demonstrated an increasing divorce rate and prevalence of female-headed households for Puerto Rican women from 1960 to 1980 (Garcia-Preto, 1982; Rodriguez, 1980; U.S. Bureau of the Census, 1988). Some have suggested that this is due, in part, to the clash between the traditional and the new values as well as the Puerto Rican wife's diminished dependence upon her spouse (Comas-Diaz, 1988). However, Frisbie (1986) found that greater educational attainment for Puerto Rican women increased marital stability, while it had the opposite effect for Mexican and Cuban-American families.

Factors including acculturation, ethnicity, and ongoing bilateral migration may also influence divorce and parenting patterns, although these factors are not well investigated. Muschkin and Myers (1989) noted that more recent Puerto Rican immigrants are overrepresented by families that are disrupted, particularly in comparison to the native island population (Vega, 1990). In this situation, the role of the noncustodial parent may be even further diminished due to significant physical and cultural distancing.

Mexican-American families, more so than their Puerto Rican and Cuban counterparts, tend to remain as married, two-parent families throughout the lifespan. Census data (Frisbie, 1986) demonstrate that Chicanos have a lower proportion of divorced persons than other Hispanic ethnic minorities. Hispanic women, like African-American women, may adapt to divorce successfully because they have had extensive experience balancing both domestic and employment roles in this country. Wagner (1988) found that Catholic Mexican-American women with blue-collar fathers experienced more critical, nonsupportive parental responses to their divorced status than did their white counterparts. The response of members of the Hispanic community to divorce often depends on such factors as familial and religious background, socioeconomic status, and degree of acculturation. For many Hispanic families, the withdrawal of extended family support could be perceived as punishment for behavior that is viewed as counter to the traditional family concept. Taylor, Hurley, and Riley (1986) noted that since less-acculturated single-parent Hispanic women relied more heavily upon their family support system for help, their adaptation to single parenthood following divorce may be easier than their more acculturated counterparts. However, given Wagner's findings, these less-acculturated women in the Chicano community may be the least likely to have a supportive kin network willing to assist them following separation and divorce. The study of the extended kinship network in its relation to nonresidential parenting among Hispanic families is a fruitful area of research.

Conclusions and Directions for Future Research

A multicultural perspective is badly needed in the area of post-divorce adjustment and nonresidential parenting. Progress in elucidating the current patterns of family life is hindered by a paucity of literature on marriage, divorce, and post-divorce adjustment among ethnic minority families. This review suggests that nonresidential parenting may take different forms depending upon culture. Yet there is a dearth of empirical information on divorce and residential patterns among African-American, Asian-American, and Hispanic families that could inform culturally sensitive policies.

Implications for Policy

Family dissolution is a difficult reality of American society. Although divorce is universal, migrating to the United States increases the risk of marital dissolution for couples of many ethnic groups. Clearly planned policies that respect cultural diversity are critical to the public mental health interest. Several unique characteristics of ethnic minority families in the context of divorce, which have been discussed in this chapter, have important implications when considering policy directives for ethnic minority families. The role of the extended family and the strength of the kinship bonds emerge as important themes that could underlie effective social policies. The literature suggests that the extended family provides tremendous social support among the different ethnic groups. Also, non-residential parents within certain ethnic groups, for example African-American and Asian-American, may be less involved with the courts regarding divorce and custody decisions, but they may be more involved with their children than nonminority nonresidential fathers. In the clinical literature, there is some evidence (Ko, 1986) that professionals can successfully utilize family members and authority figures in minority families to mediate disputes among conflicted couples. To form the most effective public policies that respect the increasing cultural diversity found in American society, we need to examine the different mechanisms regarding conflict resolution found among ethnic minority families.

Future Research

The literature we reviewed suggests several important areas for future research. These involve the following: (a) examination of the extended family in relation to the nonresidential parent and its differential effect across ethnic groups; (b) assessment of the effects of the sibling subsystem within the family on post-divorce adjustment and nonresidential parenting; and (c) comparative studies regarding mechanisms for resolving and mediating disputes within families. Culturally sensitive studies in this area are needed to reflect not only the cultural variations found between ethnic groups in coping with increasing divorce rates but also the subcultural variations, including socioeconomic level, acculturation factors, and nationality differences. Socioeconomic and demographic factors are critically important in determining family structural patterns and post-divorce adjustment of ethnic minority groups. Yet these relationships are not well understood. Studies assessing how the process of migration impacts upon marital and divorce patterns also could be conducted. Finally, the relatively low prevalence of stepfamilies among ethnic minorities as it impacts upon nonresidential parenting is another area that could be explored in future work. A culturally sensitive perspective heightens our awareness of how nonresidential parenting can be linked to a broader context as it evolves.

Note

1. Data from the 1990 U.S. Census (U.S. Bureau of the Census, 1990c) reveals that 12.1% of the U.S. population is African-American, with a 13.2% increase from the 1980

census; 9% is of Hispanic descent, marking a 53% increase; and 2.9% is of Asian-Pacific Island origin, marking a 107.8% increase in number. Census predictions for the year 2000 note a steady increase in ethnic minority group percentages in the United States.

References

Alvarez, A. (1977). The development of the Puerto Rican child. Unpublished manuscript, University of Massachusetts, Amherst.

Alvirez, D., & Bean, F. D. (1976). The Mexican American family. In C. Mindel & R. Habenstein (Eds.), *Ethnic families in America*. New York: Elsevier.

Amato, P. R. (1987). Family processes in one-parent, stepparent, and intact families: The child's point of view. *Journal of Marriage and the Family, 49*, 327-337.

Amato, P. R., & Keith, B. (1991). Parental divorce and adult well-being: A meta-analysis. *Journal of Marriage and the Family, 53*, 43-58.

Arensberg, C. M., & Kimball, S. T. (1965). *Culture and community*. New York: Harcourt Brace and World.

Billingsley, A. (1968). *Black families in white America*. Englewood Cliffs, NJ: Prentice-Hall.

Bishop, J. (1977). *Jobs, cash transfers, and marital instability: A review of the evidence*. Madison: University of Wisconsin Institute for Research on Poverty.

Bjorksten, D. J. (1984). Current marital trends and outcome of marriage counseling in Japan: 1982. *Journal of Sex and Marital Therapy, 10*(2), 123-136.

Bray, J. H., & Berger, S. H. (1990). Noncustodial father and paternal grandparent relationships in stepfamilies. *Family Relations, 39*, 414-419.

Brown, P., Perry, L., & Harburg, E. (1972). Sex role attitudes and psychological outcomes for black and white women experiencing marital dissolution. *Journal of Marriage and the Family, 39*, 549-562.

Bryce-LaPorte, R. S. (1972). Black immigrants: The experience of invisibility and inequality. *Journal of Black Studies, 3*, 29-56.

Bumpass, L. L. (1990). What's happening to the family? Interactions between demographic and institutional change. *Demography, 27*(4), 483-498.

Cherlin, A., & Furstenberg, F. F. (1986). *The new American grandparent: A place in the family, a life apart*. New York: Basic Books.

Clemens, A. W., & Axelson, L. J. (1985). The not-so-empty nest: the return of the fledgling adult. *Family Relations, 34*, 259-264.

Comas-Diaz, L. (1988). Mainland Puerto Rican women: A sociocultural approach. *Journal of Community Psychology, 16*, 21-31.

Del Carmen, R. (1990). Assessment of Asian-Americans for family therapy. In F. C. Serafica, A. I. Schwebel, R. K. Russell, P. D. Isaac, & L. B. Myers (Eds.), *Mental health of ethnic minorities* (pp. 139-166). New York: Praeger.

Diop, C. A. (1987). *Precolonial black Africa*. Westport, CT: Lawrence Hill.

Falicov, C. J. (1982). Mexican families. In M. McGoldrick, J. K. Pearce, & J. Giordano (Eds.), *Ethnicity and family therapy* (pp. 134-163). New York: Guilford Press.

Fernandez-Mendez, E. (1970). *La identidad y cultura*. San Juan: Instituto dé Cultura Puertorrequena.

Fine, M. A., & Schwebel, A. I. (1988). An emergent explanation of differing racial reactions to single parenthood. *Journal of Divorce, 11*(2), 1-15.

Fine, M. A., & Schwebel, A. I. (1990). In W. A. Rhodes & W. K. Brown (Eds.), *Why some children succeed despite the odds* (pp. 23-40). New York: Praeger.

Frisbie, W. P. (1986). Variation in patterns of marital instability among Hispanics. *Journal of Marriage and the Family, 48*, 99-106.

Fugita, S. S. (1990). Asian/Pacific-American Mental Health: Some needed research in epidemiology and service utilization. In F. C. Serafica, A. I. Schwebel, R. K. Russell, P. D. Isaac, & L. B. Myers (Eds.), *Mental health of ethnic minorities* (pp. 66-83). New York: Praeger.

Furstenberg, F. (1976). *Unplanned parenthood: The social consequences of teenage childbearing*. New York: Free Press.

Garcia-Coll, C. T. (1990). Developmental outcome of minority infants: A process-oriented look into our beginnings. *Child Development, 61*, 270-289.

Garcia-Preto, N. (1982). Puerto Rican families. In M. McGoldrick, J. K. Pearce, & J. Giordano (Eds.), *Ethnicity and family therapy* (pp. 164-186). New York: Guilford Press.

Hawkins, A. J., & Eggebeen, D. J. (1991). Are fathers fungible? Patterns of coresident adult men in maritally disrupted families and young children's well-being. *Journal of Marriage and the Family, 53*, 958-972.

Hernandez, D. J. (1986, May). *Demographic and socioeconomic circumstances of minority families and children*. Paper presented at a conference on Minority Families and Children, sponsored by the National Institute of Child Health and Human Development, Bethesda, MD.

Hill, R. B. (1972). *The strengths of black families*. New York: Emerson Hall.

Hines, P. M., & Boyd-Franklin, N. (1982). Black families. In M. McGoldrick, J. K. Pearce, & J. Giordano (Eds.), *Ethnicity and family therapy* (pp. 84-122). New York: Guilford Press.

Ho, D.Y.F. (1987). Fatherhood in Chinese culture. In M. E. Lamb (Ed.), *The father's role: Cross-cultural perspectives* (pp. 227-245). Hillsdale, NJ: Lawrence Erlbaum.

Isaacs, M. B., & Leon, G. H. (1988). Race, marital dissolution and visitation: An examination of adaptive family strategies. *Journal of Divorce, 11*(2), 17-31.

Kang, T. K. (1985). *Mother-child relations in single-parent families*. Unpublished master's thesis, University of Hong Kong, Hong Kong.

Katz, M. H., & Piotrkowski, C. S. (1983). Correlates of family role strain among employed black women. *Family Relations, 32*, 331-339.

Kellam, S. G., Ensminger, M. E., & Turner, R. J. (1977) Family structure and the mental health of children. *Archives of General Psychiatry, 34*, 1012-1022.

Ko, H. Y. (1986). Minuchin's structural therapy for Vietnamese Chinese families. *Contemporary Family Therapy, 8*, 20-32.

Ladner, J. (1971). *Tomorrow's tomorrow: The black woman*. New York: Doubleday.

Lancaster, J. (1989). Evolutionary and cross-cultural perspectives on single parenthood. In R. Bell and N. Bell (Eds.), *Sociobiology and the social sciences* (pp. 63-72). Lubbock: Texas Tech University Press.

Lee, C. C. (1985). Successful rural black adolescents: A psychological profile. *Adolescence, 20*, 129-142.

Lee, V. E., Zimiles, H., & Ladewski, B. (1991, April). *Family structure and its effect on behavioral and emotional problems in young adolescents*. Paper presented at the biennial meeting of the Society for Research on Child Development, Seattle.

Liu, W. T. (1987). *The Pacific/Asian American Mental Health Research Center*. Chicago: University of Illinois at Chicago.

Liu, W. T., & Fernandez, M. (1987). Family reunification. In W. T. Liu (Ed.), *The Pacific Asian American mental health research center.* Chicago: University of Illinois.

McAdoo, H. P. (1980). Black mother and the extended family support network. In La Frances Rodgers-Rose (Ed.), *The black woman* (pp. 125-144). Beverly Hills, CA: Sage.

McAdoo, H. (1978). Factors related to stability in upwardly mobile black families. *Journal of Marriage and the Family, 40,* 761-776.

McAdoo, H. (1985). *Black children: social, educational, and parental environments.* Beverly Hills, CA: Sage.

McGoldrick, M. (1982). Ethnicity and family therapy: An overview. In M. McGoldrick, J. K. Pearce, & J. Giordano (Eds.), *Ethnicity and family therapy* (pp. 3-30). New York: Guilford Press.

McLoyd, V. C. (1990). The impact of economic hardship on black families and children: Psychological distress, parenting, and socioemotional development. *Child Development, 61,* 311-346.

Martin. E. P., & Martin, J. M. (1978). *The black extended family*. Chicago: University of Chicago Press.

Mechanic, D., & Hansell, S. (1989). Divorce, family conflict and adolescents' well-being. *Journal of Health and Social Behavior, 30,* 105-116.

Momeni, J. A. (1984). *Demography of racial and ethnic minorities in the United States.* Westport, CT: Greenwood Press.

Morris, R. B. (1977). *Strengths of the black community: An investigation of the black community and broken homes.* Unpublished doctoral dissertation, Columbia University Teachers' College, New York.

Mott, F. L. (1990). When is a father really gone? Paternal-child contact in father-absent homes. *Demography, 27,* 499-517.

Muschkin, C., & Myers, G. C. (1989). Migration and household family structure: Puerto Ricans in the United States. *International Migration Review, 23,* 495-501.

National Research Council (1989). Washington, D.C.: National Academy Press.

Nobles, W. (1974). Africanity: Its role in black families. *The Black Scholar, 5,* 10-17.

Pearson, J. L., Hunter, J. L., Ensminger, M. E., & Kellam, S. G. (1990). Black grandmothers in multigenerational households: Diversity in family structure and parenting involvement in the Woodlawn community. *Child Development, 61,* 434-442.

Philips, R. M., & Alcebo, A. M. (1986). The effects of divorce on black children and adolescents. *The American Journal of Social Psychiatry, 6,* 69-73.

Rodriguez, C. E., Sanchez-Korrol, V., & Alers, J. O. (1980). *The Puerto Rican struggle: Essays on survival*. New York: Puerto Rican Migration Research Consortium.

Rosenthal, K. M., & Keshet, H. F. (1981). *Fathers without partners: A study of fathers and the family after marital separation.* New Jersey: Roman and Allanheld.

Rosser, P. L. (1979). *Research on the black child and family at Howard University: 1867-1978.* Washington, DC: Howard University Institute for Child Development and Family Life.

Seltzer, J. A. (1991). Relationships between fathers and children who live apart: The father's role after separation. *Journal of Marriage and the Family, 53,* 79-101.

Serafica, F. C. (1990). Counseling Asian-American parents: A cultural-developmental approach. In F. C. Serafica, A. I. Schwebel, R. K. Russell, P. D. Isaac, and L. B. Myers (Eds.), *Mental health of ethnic minorities* (pp. 222-244). New York: Praeger.

Shon, S. P., & Ja, D. Y. (1982). Asian families. In M. McGoldrick, J. K. Pearce, & J. Giordano (Eds.), *Ethnicity and family therapy*. New York: Guilford Press.

Sorifu. (1985). *White paper on youth*. Tokyo: Prime Minister's Office.

Spanier, G. B., & Hanson, S. (1981). The role of extended kin in the adjustment to marital separation. *Journal of Divorce, 5*, 33-48.

Stack, C. B. (1974). *All our kin: Strategies for survival in a black community*. New York: Harper & Row.

Sue, S., & Chin, R. (1983). The mental health of Chinese-American children: Stressors and resources. In G. J. Powell, J. Yamamoto, A. Romero, & A. Morales (Eds.), *The psychosocial development of minority group children* (pp. 385-397). New York: Brunner/Mazel.

Takai, R. T. (1981). Marital separation in first marriages and remarriages of women: An examination of divergent patterns. *Dissertation Abstracts International, 42*, 2, 875A.

Taylor, V. L., Hurley, E. C., & Riley, M. T. (1986). The influence of acculturation upon the adjustment of preschool Mexican-American children of single-parent families. *Family Therapy, 13*(3), 249-256.

Tseng, W. S., Kuotai, J. H., Hsu, J., Jinghua, C., Lian, Y. & Kameoka, V. (1988). Family planning and child mental health in China: The Nanjing survey. *American Journal of Psychiatry, 145*(11), 1396-1403.

U.S. Bureau of the Census (1980). *Persons of Spanish origin in the United States: March, 1979* (Series P-20, No. 354). Washington, DC: Government Printing Office.

U.S. Bureau of the Census (1988). *Population characteristics* (Series P-20, No. 438). Washington, DC: Government Printing Office.

U.S. Bureau of the Census (1990a). *Current population reports. Household and family characteristics: March 1990 and 1989.* (Series P-20, No. 447). Washington, DC: Government Printing Office.

U.S. Bureau of the Census (1990b). *Current population reports. Marital status and living arrangements: March 1990.* (Series P-20, No. 450). Washington, DC: Government Printing Office.

U.S. Bureau of the Census (1990c). *Projections of the population of the U.S. by age and race from 1988 to 2080* (Series P-25, No. 1018). Washington, DC: Government Printing Office.

Vega, W.A. (1990). Hispanic families in the 1980s: A decade of research. *Journal of Marriage and the Family, 52*, 1015-1024.

Ventura, S. J. (1987). Births of Hispanic parentage, 1983 and 1984. *Monthly Vital Statistics Report, 36*, 1-19.

Wagner, R. M. (1988). Changes in the friend network during the first year of single parenthood for Mexican American and Anglo women. *Journal of Divorce, 11*, 89-109.

Wilson, W. J. (1987). *The truly disadvantaged: The inner city, the underclass, and public policy*. Chicago: University of Chicago Press.

Wong, B. (1985). Family, kinship, and ethnic identity of the Chinese in New York, with comparative remarks on the Chinese in Lima, Peru, and Manila, Philippines. *Journal of Comparative Family Studies, 16*(2), 231-252.

Yoshioka, R. B., Tashima, N., Chew, M. & Murase, K. (1981). *Mental health services for Pacific/Asian Americans*. San Francisco: Pacific Asian Mental Health Research Project.

3

Parental Role Reversal

Mothers as Nonresidential Parents

CHARLENE E. DEPNER

Despite unprecedented changes in family demographics and a national revolution in child custody provisions, it is still the case that the vast majority of nonresidential parents are fathers. This chapter examines "parental role reversal"—the relatively uncommon situation in which traditional gender-based family roles are switched. The father takes on primary parenting while the mother assumes the role of nonresidential parent. To what extent is this domestic arrangement simply the mirror image of the mother-resident family? What are the distinctive dynamics and concerns?

Trends in Law and Ideology

American custody law betokens a longstanding cultural ambivalence. Throughout the history of our nation, child custody standards have shifted, ratifying trends in social attitudes about the respective parental entitlements of mothers and fathers (Clingempeel & Reppucci, 1982). The fledgling social science literature on parental role reversal is best understood within this broader cultural context.

American courts in the nineteenth century adopted, with some exception (Mnookin, 1975), an English common law tradition that accorded the father exclusive property rights to children and their services, a valuable commodity in an agrarian society (Foster & Freed, 1978). Within this tradition, financial support and custody were inextricably linked. Fathers who were denied custody of their children were not held responsible for their financial support (Bishop, 1881).

By the end of the nineteenth century, social forces had apportioned children's financial support and physical care along gender lines. The Industrial Revolution physically separated work and family functioning, moving fathers into the workplace as women maintained primary parenting functions in the home (Stack, 1976). Emerging interest in child welfare and growing acceptance of psychoanalytic and child development theories accentuated the unique significance of maternal care. Maternal preference standards emerged with acceptance of the notion that a mother "alone has the patience and sympathy required to mold and soothe the infant mind in its adjustment to its environment" (*Jenkins v. Jenkins*, 1921, quoted in Little, 1982).

For most of this century, under the principle that mothers offered superior care to children of "tender years," it was an unquestioned assumption that mothers were more capable than fathers to rear minor children (Mnookin, 1975; Warshak & Santrok, 1983). A father who wanted custody had to prove that the mother was an exception to this general rule, in some way unfit to raise the children (Benedek & Benedek, 1974).

In the 1970s, maternal preference was challenged in defiance of gendered role prescriptions. It was argued that gender-based standards reified the traditional homemaker/breadwinner dichotomy, restricting women to child-rearing responsibilities and discriminating against fathers who wanted to assume them. At the same time, social science offered poignant documentation that the assignment of exclusive parental rights to mothers was linked to widespread paternal disengagement and rampant noncompliance with child support orders (Furstenberg, Nord, Peterson, & Zill, 1983; Wallerstein & Kelly, 1980). Fueled by optimistic visions of egalitarian social change, "gender-neutral" standards swept the country in the 1980s.

Legislative changes in custody and child support enforcement in the 1980s sent forceful social messages that, regardless of the status of the parental relationship, both fathers and mothers were expected to maintain responsibility for children. By 1991, 40 states had enacted some form of joint custody or shared parenting legislation (Folberg, 1991). The current legal climate offers parents wide discretion in the assignment of parental rights and responsibilities. In some relatively rare situations, parents divide responsibilities equally. Among the rest, one parent adopts a primary parenting role and there is considerable variability across families in the nature and extent of the other parent's involvement. Families who adopt role reversal arrangements today, when the law encourages shared parenting, may be very different from those who did so in an era when the law emphasized the assignment of exclusive rights to one parent. In the contemporary legal context, families with either sole maternal or sole paternal legal custody are selecting the extremes of a continuum of possible arrangements for dividing parental responsibilities (Albiston, Maccoby, & Mnookin, 1990).

The same powerful social forces that swing the pendulum of law and custom have also created a schism in role reversal scholarship. This chapter draws from two parallel and complementary traditions, one following the experience of fathers and the other the perspective of mothers. As custody revisionists challenged maternal preference, a fledgling scholarship in the 1970s established that it was possible for fathers to competently care for children all or part of the time. Investigations into the origins of father custody arrangements, taken from the vantage point of fathers and reflecting custody standards of the time, sometimes characterized mothers as unstable or unfit in some respect. Another prominent theme was the mother's quest to establish professional credentials deferred during her stint as primary caretaker.

By the 1980s feminist scholars spearheaded investigations of the consequences of custody reform for mothers. This literature accentuated concerns that mothers were being dislodged from the primary parenting role as the result of coercive processes and/or a double standard for the evaluation of parental adequacy (Chesler, 1986). It was argued that such injustices were transmitted to children because valid considerations of best interests were obviated.

Within each scholastic tradition, the theoretical framework and data collection emphasized one parent, often to the exclusion of the other. Stereotypes of unfit mothers and coercive fathers sometimes substituted for actual information. The resulting picture is incomplete, lacking integration of the perspectives of all family members.

The two dominant streams of research rely heavily on convenience samples composed of professional referrals, members of special interest groups, or respondents to advertisements. Such samples are likely to overrepresent parents who are sensitized, if not politicized, to a particular stance on the issues. Is it the case that mothers and fathers view role reversal very differently? Or are the complementary views found in the two literatures an artifact of the type of parents drawn to represent each point of view?

The remainder of this chapter attempts to integrate material from a variety of sources to produce a more balanced picture of role reversal families. Conforming to the general approach of this volume, this chapter reserves terms such as *custody* for *de jure* status and labels such as *domestic arrangements, caretaker* and *residential parent* for *de facto* residential arrangements.

Prevalence of Role Reversal Families

Role reversal families are not common (see Teachman & Paasch, this volume). The 1990 U.S. census revealed an upswing in paternal residence since 1980, from 2.1% to 4.9% of all households with children. The increment may be attributable to children living with their fathers part of the time in shared parenting arrangements (Miller & Schreiner, 1992).

Cross-sectional measurement cannot enumerate either the mothers who may, at some point, assume nonresidential status or the volatile nature of that role. Role reversal situations are highly fluid over time (Furstenberg & Spanier, 1984). Some are expressly temporary (Mendes, 1976). Others come about after a maternal residence arrangement has faltered (Bray, 1991; Giles-Sims & Urwin, 1989; Greene, 1978; Greif, 1985, 1987). Still other role reversal situations revert to shared or maternal residence. Maccoby and Mnookin (1992) report that more than half of the children who resided with their fathers at the time a divorce was initiated had changed residence within 3 years.

Conceptualizing Role Reversal

Is there a discernible profile of the role reversal family? Only a tentative analysis is possible, since most of the research is based on samples that were not designed to yield population estimates. Nonetheless, a cautious review that pools material from the two dominant lines of inquiry reveals distinctive features, such as unique forms of nonresidential parent participation, greater heterogeneity and transience. A comprehensive review does not offer strong support for common stereotypes of role reversal families—that they customarily involve male children, fathers with long-standing tenure as caretakers, or inadequate mothers.

Variability and Heterogeneity

The episodic nature of role reversal was documented in the previous section. Role reversal families are heterogeneous. A wide range of legal and residential configurations involve fathers who reside with at least some of their children. Many studies pool families in which caretaker fathers were never married, widowed, separated, divorced, remarried, and those who assumed custodial responsibilities during the mother's extended but temporary absence (Lewis, 1978). Often some children remain with the mother when another child moves in with the father.

Child Characteristics

There is no strong support that role reversal is more common when the family includes male children. The findings are equivocal, with some cross-sectional studies showing that sons are more likely than daughters to live with their fathers (Greif, 1985; Spanier & Glick, 1981) and others reporting no sex differences (Chang & Dienard, 1982; George & Wilding, 1972). At the onset of marital dissolution, paternal residence is only slightly more common for boys, most likely for boys approaching adolescence (Maccoby, Depner, & Mnookin, 1988); but boys are no more likely than girls to move in with their fathers later on (Maccoby & Mnookin, 1992).

In general, more older children live with fathers than younger ones (Greif, 1985; Maccoby et al., 1988). Fathers are more likely to assume a primary caretaking role in families with multiple children (Maccoby et al., 1988) or when mothers have children from previous relationships (Depner, Maccoby, & Mnookin, 1987).

Maternal Competence

Primary caretakers usually report that they feel they are doing a good job and maintain that they are the more capable, nurturant, or stable parent (Chang & Dienard, 1982; Depner et al., 1987; Greif, 1985; Mendes, 1976). Like residential mothers, caretaker fathers have qualms about the nonresidential parent's caretaking ability (Maccoby & Mnookin, 1992). Most role reversal studies include a small subset of families in which the fathers claim that the nonresidential mothers lack the ability or motivation to act as the primary caretaker and/or are incapacitated by emotional or substance abuse problems (Gersick, 1979; Greene, 1978; Greif, 1985; Maccoby & Mnookin, 1992; Mendes, 1976; Orthner, Brown, & Ferguson, 1976; Keshet & Rosenthal, 1978; Turner, 1984; Watson, 1981). This stream of research relies primarily on paternal reports, not independent data on maternal competence.

The feminist rebuttal to this image of the nonresidential mother challenges both standards and evidence. Chesler (1986) insists that a "double standard of parenting" exists in our culture, whereby mothers are evaluated by more stringent criteria than fathers. Thus, she argues that the same circumstances that might "disqualify" mothers as primary caretakers would not weigh as heavily against their husbands.

At this writing, the debate has not been resolved empirically. There are no sound prevalence data to measure the frequency with which maternal competence is challenged or rebutted. Multisource data to evaluate claims and counterclaims is also needed.

Parental Roles

The distribution of parental responsibilities in role reversal families does not mirror that found in maternal residence arrangements. In all two-parent households, including those in which parents ultimately reverse roles, it is most common for fathers to place primary emphasis on the development of career assets while mothers, regardless of their employment status, remain the primary caretakers of children (Hochschild, 1989; Maccoby & Mnookin, 1992; Weitzman, 1985). A generation ago, gender studies called attention to channeling forces that diverted women from the marketplace and left men ill-equipped for caregiving responsibilities (Nash, 1965; Pleck & Sawyer, 1974). Two decades may have relaxed such gender-based regimentation; yet the expression of role reversal is tempered by the same gender-based division of experience.

The transition to role reversal usually involves a switch in the relative caretaking responsibilities of mothers and fathers and is not a mere continuation of the preseparation child-rearing pattern (Maccoby & Mnookin, 1992). Counter to stereotypes about role reversal families, the nonresidential mother often maintains an active, although diminished, role while the father shoulders additional parenting responsibilities.

Studies of role reversal families reveal varying histories of paternal participation in the care of children. Caretaker fathers view themselves as "child oriented" (Watson, 1981). Some studies report that fathers have a record of active caretaking (Keshet & Rosenthal, 1978; Smith & Smith, 1981), although this is not a universal finding (George & Wilding, 1972). At least from the fathers' perspective, the gap in parental participation is smaller between mothers and fathers who reverse parental roles. Fathers' retrospective ratings of maternal involvement in the two-parent household are relatively lower among role reversal families and closer to the fathers' account of his own participation in child rearing (Maccoby & Mnookin, 1992).

Following the breakup, mothers in role reversal families often maintain considerable, although not primary, responsibility for their children. Nonresidential mothers are far more likely than nonresidential fathers to have frequent contact with their children (Furstenberg et al., 1983; Greif & Pabst, 1988). Compared with nonresidential fathers, they visit more frequently, assume more parenting functions, are less likely to cease contact over time, and are more likely to ultimately assume the primary parenting role (Maccoby & Mnookin, 1992). Nonresidential mother participation is particularly strong when the reasons for the breakup are mutual and when the mother endorses the residential placement (Greif & Pabst, 1988).

Across all residential arrangements, fathers earn higher wages and are better educated than mothers (Maccoby & Mnookin, 1992), and this gap is accentuated in role reversal families (Chang & Dienard, 1982; Depner, Maccoby, & Mnookin, 1988). Nonresidential mothers are less likely than their male counterparts to be ordered to pay child support (Christensen, Dahl, & Rettig, 1990; Greif & Pabst, 1988; Pearson & Thoennes, 1988). Since equivalence of maternal and paternal income is more common in low socioeconomic strata, the probability that mothers are ordered to pay is affected by both the absolute and relative income of the two parents (Maccoby & Mnookin, 1992).

The Etiology of Parental Role Reversal

Is it possible to isolate particular dynamics and decision-making processes that increase the likelihood of parental role reversal? Some of the reasons for parental role reversal parallel the causal bases of mother caretaking. Desire to maintain a close relationship with a child is one reason for seeking the role of primary caretaker (Turner, 1984). Children may choose to live with their fathers (Giles-Sims & Urwin,

1989; Maccoby et al., 1988; Mendes, 1979; Victor & Winkler, 1977). Such decisions may be based on the father-child relationship, triggered by tensions in the maternal household, or based on attractions to the paternal home. "Runaway" parents of both genders abandon their children to the care of the other parent (Gersick, 1979; Greene, 1978; Todres, 1978; Watson, 1981).

Concerns that mothers are being dislodged forcibly from the primary caretaker role are the impetus for careful scrutiny of the way in which role reversal comes about. Some fathers report seeking custody assertively (Chang & Dienard, 1982; Greif, 1985), whereas others claim to have the children only because their wives voluntarily relinquished custody (Chang & Dienard, 1982; Gersick, 1979; Greene, 1978). Mendes (1976) labels these two groups as *seekers* and *assenters*. This section reviews the effects of family dynamics and decision-making processes on residential placement.

The Influence of the Legal and Social Context

Custody Standards

How do custody standards affect residential determination? The expressive function of the law should not be discounted. The nature of the laws and the outcomes of high-profile cases may influence a parent's assessment of the chances of gaining formal custody. A lifetime of gender-based stratification creates dramatic differences in the bargaining endowments of mothers and fathers (Forer, 1991; Minow, 1990). Mothers build stronger credentials as primary caretakers, but fathers accumulate career and financial assets (Weitzman, 1985). A review of the literature suggests that, in the absence of custodial standards that assign a clear advantage to a particular parent, risk-aversive mothers or fathers can feel that the other parent has superior claims to custody and fail to challenge leveraged demands.

Role reversal can be the product of gender-neutral custody standards. Some theorists argue that women capitulate to custody and/or financial demands because they feel that the law accords them no special entitlement to the children. According to this line of reasoning, gender-neutral custody standards nullify mothers' primary parenting experience while fathers retain economic leverage (Polikoff, 1983). Lonsdorf (1991) argues that family law is predicated on the assumption that the child has equal rights to the emotional resources of both parents, but denies the child equal access to financial resources. She suggests that contemporary custody standards may force mothers to relinquish custody to maintain their children's financial security.

At the same time, however, there is evidence that the law discourages some fathers from seeking legal custody despite the fact that they have been enacting the primary caregiver role (Bartz & Witcher, 1978; Mendes, 1979; O'Brien, 1980). Advocates for fathers insist that the law is neutral in theory only and that examination of actual custody outcomes reveals the perpetuation of a strong and unjustifiable maternal bias (Bartz & Witcher, 1978; Giles-Sims & Urwin, 1989; Keshet & Rosenthal, 1978).

An analysis of the outcomes of most legal processes shows that few fathers pursue their rights to custody under gender-neutral standards. Two studies report that, although more than half of the fathers privately express an interest in having custody, only a small proportion actually petition for custody in court. Weitzman (1985) reported that 57% of the fathers in her study said that they were interested in having custody of their children, but only 13% requested custody in a divorce petition. Her comparison of court records across the period from 1968 to 1977 revealed a general decrease in the number of fathers who requested sole physical or legal custody. Mnookin, Maccoby, Albiston, and Depner (1990) found that only 37% of fathers who wanted sole custody petitioned for it.

Private Deliberations Between Parents

In most families, decisions about the residence of the children are made privately between parents and not in the courts (Mnookin & Kornhauser, 1979). Custody law permits parents wide latitude in determining arrangements in their children's best interests. It is assumed that parents, rather than a third party unfamiliar with the family, are in the best position to evaluate what is best for their particular offspring (Mnookin, 1975). Criteria are deliberately amorphous (Forer, 1991). Very little is known about the private decision-making process, but there is concern about undue impact of inappropriate criteria or power imbalances between parents (Longsdorf, 1991; Weitzman, 1985). Available data cannot establish how commonly such process dangers materialize.

Some role reversal families are characterized by distinctively bitter and acrimonious marital breakups (Chang & Dienard, 1982; Gersick, 1979; Greene, 1978; Katz, 1979; Orthner, Brown, & Ferguson, 1976), in which fathers express hostile and sometimes vindictive feelings (Woody, 1978) or seek custody in an effort to motivate the mother to reconcile (Turner, 1984). Indeed, Gersick (1979) concluded that a father's motivation to seek custody was heightened by feelings of sexual betrayal or abandonment. Weitzman (1985) reported that some mothers relinquished claims to custody because of intimidation and coercion.

The few studies of the mother's perspective commonly state that role reversal was elected because it was best for the children (Fischer & Cardea, 1984; Greif & Pabst, 1988; Todres, 1978). In some cases, this has to do with the parenting skills of the father. In others, it is attributed to criteria that the law would deem inappropriate—such as financial considerations.

Advocates of both mothers and fathers raise concerns about the causal role of finances in parental role reversal. Compared with other fathers, those who assume the primary caretaker role are more likely to be mature, highly educated, and high wage earners. Nonetheless, there are not dramatic differences in the socioeconomic status of fathers across residential arrangements (Depner et al., 1988). Fathers' advocates claim a financial double standard that requires men to demonstrate a certain level of affluence in order to be seriously considered as prospective caretakers (Orthner, Brown, & Ferguson, 1976).

Mothers' advocates raise further concerns that financial disparities affect the process itself. Because men generally have more resources than their wives, they are in the position to threaten protracted custody battles (Polikoff, 1982). By withholding financial assistance, fathers have the power to coerce financially dependent mothers to relinquish custody (West & Kissman, 1991). There are no data to establish how commonly such intimidation occurs.

From the vantage point of nonresidential mothers, financial resources influence residential placement (Paskowicz, 1982; Greif & Pabst, 1988). It is unknown how many women relinquish their children because they cannot meet the financial demands of single parenthood or because the father alone is able to maintain the children in the marital household, without disruption in schools or peer relationships. Mendes' (1976) study of fathers revealed situations in which roles were reversed to permit the mother time either to retrain or to establish herself in the workplace.

Litigation

Parental role reversal is rarely the product of litigation. Protracted legal battles for sole custody are uncommon. Weitzman found only 15 such cases in her 1977 Los Angeles sample. Contested cases rarely result in parental role reversal (Giles-Sims & Urwin, 1989; Greif & Pabst, 1988; Phear, Beck, Hauser, Clark, & Whitney, 1984). Of the 15 cases isolated by Weitzman, fathers were awarded custody by a judge in 5. She cited corroborative data from a Northern California county in which fathers obtained custody in 5 of the 13 contested custody trials during 1979. In a sample of 1,124 families, Mnookin et al. (1990) found that only 5 fathers won sole physical custody when mothers also wanted sole custody. Chang and Dienard's (1982) review of Minnesota custody records showed that about 11% of the fathers were awarded sole, split, or joint custody. Custody was awarded to the father by the courts in only 25 cases (1%). In all other cases, the father's petition was uncontested (8%) or the parents stipulated to the agreement outside court (2%).

Alternative Dispute Resolution

With the emergence of alternative forums for crafting parenting arrangements, aggressive litigation is not the only forum for seeking custody. Despite the popularity of mediation and other alternative dispute resolution techniques, some critics (Grillo, 1991) are concerned that women's relational nature may induce them to unwisely forego primary parenting. Role reversal arrangements are, however, no more common in mediation than in other fora (Depner, 1992). Facchino and Aron (1990) found that fathers reported similar outcomes, regardless of whether they obtained custody through mutual agreement, mediation, or litigation.

Family Functioning in Role Reversal Families

Role reversal families function in a relatively normless context dominated by powerful stereotypes (Katz, 1979; Mendes, 1976). It is not unreasonable to anticipate that such families will face the double stigma of single parenting (Levitin, 1979) and gender role reversal.

Parental Role Adjustment

Up to one-third of the 516 noncustodial mothers in a study by Greif (1987) identified no major problems in adjustment to the role. Among those who experienced difficulties, areas of clinical focus included low self-esteem, lack of clear role definition, victimization, and rejection by the children. In role reversal families, it is the nonresidential parent who faces the challenge of entering the work force (Little, 1982). Nonresidential mothers also encounter many of the difficulties of non-residential parenting that are documented in studies of nonresidential fathers (Hetherington & Camara, 1984; Jacobs, 1982).

Social stigma is a particular challenge to the adjustment of nonresidential mothers (West & Kissman, 1991). Mothers who become nonresidential parents defy powerful gender-based social conventions (Walters, 1988) and also must grapple with deeply entrenched social stereotypes. Those who relinquish custody have been cast as self-centered, and those who lose custody are presumed unfit (Paskowicz, 1982; West & Kissman, 1991).

Transition to the nonresidential role marks unique discontinuities in the parent-child relationship. Like other women, nonresidential mothers assumed major caretaking responsibility before the parental breakup, but role reversal demands that they adapt to a dramatic diminution of their contact with and responsibility for their children. Although many nonresidential mothers express the opinion that the children are better off residing with their fathers, most voice particular pain in being parted from their children (Greif & Pabst, 1988).

The central challenge for role reversal fathers appears to be less linked to stigma than to acquisition of primary parenting skills. In research conducted in the 1970s, residential fathers reported discrimination (Schlesinger & Todres, 1976), but in a more recent study (Nieto, 1990), most fathers feel comfortable in the caretaker role and experience positive reactions from others.

Like their female counterparts, residential fathers face the demands of single parenting, yet most do so with less experience in the role of primary caretaker. Fathers who assume primary caretaking report an array of transitional tasks, including household organization, setting up rules and routines for children, arranging child care, dealing with children's response to the transition, and adjusting to the pressures of primary parenting (Gasser & Taylor, 1976; George & Wilding, 1972; Katz, 1979; Mendes, 1976; Nieto, 1990; Orthner et al., 1976; Schlesinger, 1979; Smith & Smith, 1981; Todres, 1975; Weiss, 1975). Comparative research is rare but tends to confirm that, regardless of gender, residential parents face many similar issues. Defrain and Eirick (1981) found no sex differences on a battery of items about role adjustment of residential parents. Mothers and fathers who assumed primary caretak-

ing experienced comparable issues of child rearing, household management, interparental relationships, and needs for adaptation.

Unlike their female counterparts, residential fathers usually have
substantial experience in the work force, but face the new challenge of
integrating caretaking with an established work role. Domestic responsibilities constrain the time that fathers can devote to work, and they,
like caretaker mothers, express concern that this adversely affects job
security and opportunities for advancement (Chang & Dienard, 1982;
Greene, 1978; Schlesinger, 1979). Like caretaker mothers, they report
that it is difficult to find and maintain adequate services (Schlesinger
& Todres, 1976), and many discover that their jobs offer little flexibility
to meet caregiving demands (Chang & Dienard; Keshet & Rosenthal,
1978). Some caretaker fathers feel that employers are particularly
hesitant to accord flexibility to male workers, and at least one study
underscored fathers' feelings that their role was not legitimized by
co-workers and employers (Keshet & Rosenthal, 1978).

Little is known about the co-parental relationship in role reversal
families. Maccoby, Depner, & Mnookin (1990) found that residential
arrangements were not distinctive with respect to patterns of co-parental cooperation and conflict. Nonetheless, residential fathers were distinctive in that they preferred to minimize communications between
parents.

Child Adjustment

Primary caretaker fathers report satisfying relationships with their
children (Orthner et al., 1976; Pichitino, 1983) and good child adjustment. There is little direct assessment of children in the role reversal
literature (Lewis, 1978). To an amazing degree, the focus of the literature
is on the struggle between parents, and their claims and counterclaims
about outcomes. Some comparisons of the functioning of children in
different family structures show no difference in the adjustment of children
reared primarily by fathers or mothers (Luepnitz, 1982; Rosen, 1979).
Rarely is the potentially salubrious effect of heightened nonresidential
parent involvement addressed.

A few studies suggest that children may function better under the
primary care of a parent of the same gender (Camara & Resnick, 1987).
Some research shows that fathers are better able to control behavioral
problems, particularly with boys (Ambert, 1982; Lowery & Settle,
1985; Maccoby et al., 1988; Santrock & Warshak, 1979). Orthner et al.

(1976) contend that the courts question the ability of fathers to raise daughters. Two studies included fathers who were concerned about dealing adequately with their daughters' emerging sexuality (Mendes, 1976; Orthner et al., 1976), although this concern is not widely reported in the literature.

Other scholars have attributed these gender advantages to factors that differentiate the circumstances of mothers and fathers who are residential parents. Differences ascribed to gender pairing of child and residential parent may in fact be explained by the fact that residential fathers have access to greater financial resources (Schnayer & Orr, 1989) or that role reversal children enjoy more extensive involvement of nonresidential parents (Camara & Resnick, 1987).

Particular advantages of maintaining a sound relationship between the child and the nonresidential mother are illustrated in Camara & Resnick's (1987) comparison of children's social development in three household configurations. Children's self-esteem, aggressive behavior, and behavioral problems were linked to a good relationship with the nonresidential mother. In father-custody families, a good relationship between the nonresidential parent and the child could buffer adverse effects of a strained bond between the child and the residential parent. In both mother-custody and father-custody families, a positive relationship between the child and the nonresidential parent was also linked to more frequent and lengthy visits.

There are unique challenges to assessing outcomes for role reversal families. Because such families are more likely to have experienced multiple domestic arrangements, it is misleading to associate outcomes with any one domestic arrangement. Adjustment problems could be the impetus for shifting to paternal residence. If this is the case, the situation may look poorer on outcome measures. Conversely, adjusting the residential arrangements may ameliorate problems, resulting in more favorable outcome measures. Tenure in the arrangement may also affect outcome measures (Schnayer & Orr, 1989), reflecting either a "honeymoon" period or transitional difficulties.

Directions for Further Research

The corpus of research about parental role reversal offers rich descriptive material about the concerns of mothers and fathers. Future research should continue to focus on such themes as legal entitlements, financial disparities, parental functioning, and their implications for cooperative functioning between parents. The issues are highly complex and value-laden. It is clear that role reversal families are a heterogeneous group and that there is substantial variability over time in this residential arrangement. This situation presents serious challenges to future research on role reversal families, yet several important contributions can be made.

The variability and heterogeneity of role reversal families impose important demands on research. Because children in role reversal households are likely to experience multiple living arrangements, categorical research designs that classify children on the basis of their living arrangements at a static point in time could misclassify many families and yield misleading information about role reversal's causes and consequences. Measures of the duration and timing of role reversal are necessary. The heterogeneity of role reversal families also demands sample sizes that are large enough to take within-group variation into account.

In fact, several advantages could be realized from larger, more heterogeneous samples. The small samples of convenience most characteristic of this field present serious impediments to generalization. Culture, religion, and social class are likely to be important factors in understanding the development and functioning of different family forms, yet the literature is devoted primarily to the middle class and overrepresents its concerns and situations (Bartlett & Stack, 1991). New research must extend to the wider spectrum of families who face custody issues. Large representative samples will also be required to develop sound prevalence data that speak to concerns about unintended consequences of the laws as currently structured.

Multimethod investigation should be assigned high priority on the agenda for role reversal research. Investigations must draw information from the perspectives of multiple family members, gather independent assessments of children, and track the progress of role reversal families over time. The contributions of family systems theory would be particularly helpful in guiding research that considers factors both affecting and affected by all family members.

There is also strong need for comparative data. Because most role reversal research does not include a control group, it is difficult to evaluate whether such families are distinctive or are experiencing issues common to families in which the mother assumes the primary caretaker role. Designs that specify equivalence in the timetable since the parental breakup would also facilitate a comparative understanding of role reversal families. There is a high degree of variability across subjects in any given study with respect to the length of time the children have lived in a particular domestic arrangement. This factor affects the comparability of retrospective reports, making some more subject to recall error and post hoc reconstruction of events.

It is also time for some basic rethinking of the conceptual framework of research in this area. Parental role reversal appears to be a shift in a couple's established division of parental roles, one that for many families is temporary. The arrangement is usually struck by private deliberations between parents and there is an incomplete understanding of the decision-making considerations and dynamics. Future research should extend the time frame to identify the changing dynamics of the family over time. Such an approach would incorporate antecedents of residential arrangements that may be powerful forces in long-range outcomes. For example, the literature suggests that the origins of a paternal caretaker arrangement may be highly consequential for its viability. Concern about outcomes for children must weigh the relative impact of residential history against the circumstances and dynamics that set the trajectory for family relationships.

Policy Issues

Empirical investigation of role reversal families takes place in a highly charged political climate (Depner, 1987). Advocacy scholarship is common, and research findings may be distorted to endorse a particular policy position. Nonetheless, the concurrent evolution of research and legal policy deliberation points out particular vulnerabilities of fathers and mothers and potential abuses of parental role reversal. There is certainly cause for concern that some mothers feel coerced into relinquishing claims to the primary caretaker role. At the same time, it is clear that few fathers successfully attain the primary caretaker role, regardless of the decision-making forum. Research can play an important role in challenging stereotypes and accurately describing role reversal families and the driving forces in their determination and ongoing viability.

The literature also points out several interventions that may be particularly helpful in facilitating the adjustment of role reversal families. Fathers express the need for information about child rearing-practices and single parenting (Mendes, 1976; Schlesinger & Todres,

1976). In addition, education for both parents can make them aware of successful models for negotiating their particular arrangement (Smith & Smith, 1981; Woody, 1978). Katz (1979) recommends that parent education be available as an adjunct to the court. Indeed, some states are making such programs available (Lehner, 1991). Community-based agencies have unique potential to connect mothers and fathers with local resources for support and information. Planned communities designed to accommodate the needs of single-parent caretakers are envisioned by Schlesinger (1979). Some national organizations, such as Mothers Without Custody, provide useful support to nonresidential mothers.

Rigid job schedules and personnel policies make it difficult to meet simultaneous responsibilities for work and family caregiving. Caretaker fathers sometimes face the added burden of sexist bias in the workplace when they attempt to meet care-giving responsibilities (Chang & Dienard, 1982; Katz, 1979).

Hanson and Bozett (1987) emphasize the widespread need for social institutions to acknowledge and facilitate fathers' involvement as parents. For example, they call for school-based policies that bolster a norm to include fathers in activities and conferences and to provide equal parental access to school records.

In many respects, the policy solutions that make sense for role reversal families would be helpful to all families in that they are directed toward supporting both parents in their efforts to create arrangements in the best interests of their children.

References

Albiston, C. R., Maccoby, E. E., Mnookin, R. H. (1990). Does joint legal custody matter? *Stanford Law & Policy Review, 167-179.*

Ambert, A. (1982). Differences in children's behavior toward custodial mothers and custodial fathers. *Journal of Marriage and the Family, 44,* 73-86.

Bartlett, K. T., & Stack, C. B. (1991). Joint custody, feminism, and the dependency dilemma. In J. Folberg (Ed.), *Joint custody and shared parenting* (2nd ed., pp. 63-88). New York: Guilford Press.

Bartz, K., & Witcher, W. (1978). When father gets custody. *Children Today, 7*(5), 2-35.

Benedek, E. P., & Benedek, R. A. (1974). New child custody laws: Making them do what they say. *American Journal of Orthopsychiatry, 42,* 825-834.

Bishop, J. P. (1881). *Commentaries on the law of marriage and divorce* (Vol. 2). Boston: Little, Brown.

Bray, J. H. (1991). Psychosocial factors affecting custodial and visitation arrangements. *Behavioral Science and the Law, 9,* 419-437.

Camara, K. A., & Resnick, G. (1987). Marital and parental subsystems in mother-custody, father-custody and two-parent households: Effects on children's social development. In J.P. Vincent (Ed.), *Advances in family intervention, assessment and theory* (Vol. 4, pp. 165-196). Greenwich, CT: JAI Press.

Chang, P. N., & Dienard, A. S. (1982). Single-father caretakers: Demographic characteristics and adjustment processes. *American Journal of Orthopsychiatry, 52*, 236-243.

Chesler, P. (1986). *Mothers on trial.* New York: McGraw-Hill.

Christensen, D. H., Dahl, C. M., & Rettig, K. (1990). Noncustodial mothers and child support: Examining the larger context. *Family Relations, 39*, 421-432.

Clingempeel, W. G., & Reppucci, N. D. (1982). Joint custody after divorce: Major issues and goals for research. *Psychological Bulletin, 91*, 102-127.

Depner, C. E. (1987, August). *Value dilemmas in divorce research and practice.* Paper presented at the annual meeting of the American Psychological Association, New York City.

Depner, C. E. (1992, June). Trends in characteristics of users of juvenile and family courts: Child custody, visitation, and family court service. In G. Melton (Chair), *Children, families, and the justice system in the 21st century.* Symposium sponsored by the Family and Juvenile Court Committee, Commission on 2020 Vision: A Plan for the Future of the California Courts, San Francisco.

Depner, C. E., Maccoby, E. E., & Mnookin, R. H. (1987, August). *Child residence in the post-divorce family.* Paper presented at the annual meeting of the American Psychological Association, New York City.

Depner, C. E., Maccoby, E. E., & Mnookin, R. H. (1988, August). *Assessing father participation in the post-divorce family.* Paper presented at the annual meeting of the American Psychological Association, Atlanta.

Defrain, J., & Eirick, R. (1981). Coping as divorced single parents: A comparative study of fathers and mothers. *Family Relations, 30*, 265-274.

Facchino, D. & Aron, A. (1990). Divorced fathers with custody: Method of obtaining custody and divorce adjustment. *Journal of Divorce, 13*(3), 45-56.

Fischer, J. L., & Cardea, J. M. (1984). Mother-child relationships of mothers living apart from their children. *Family Relations, 32*, 351-357.

Folberg, J. (1991). Custody overview. In J. Folberg (Ed.), *Joint custody and shared parenting* (2nd ed., pp. 3-10). New York: Guilford Press.

Forer, L. G. (1991). *Unequal protection: Women, children, and the elderly in court.* New York: Norton.

Foster, H. H., Jr., & Freed, D. (1978). Life with father. *Family Law Quarterly, 11*, 321.

Furstenberg, F. F., Nord, C. W., Peterson, J. L., & Zill, N. (1983). The life course of children of divorce: marital disruption and parental contact. *American Sociological Review, 48*(5), 656-668.

Furstenberg, F. F., & Spanier, G. (1984). *Recycling the family: Remarriage after divorce.* Beverly Hills, CA: Sage.

Gasser, R. D., & Taylor, C. M. (1976). Role adjustment of single parent fathers with dependent children. *The Family Coordinator, 25*, 397-401.

George, V., & Wilding, P. (1972). *Motherless families.* London: Routledge & Kegan Paul.

Gersick, K. (1979). Fathers by choice: Divorced men who receive custody of their children. In G. Levinger & O. Moles (Eds.), *Divorce & separation* (pp. 307-323). New York: Basic Books.

Giles-Sims, J., & Urwin, C. (1989). Paternal custody and remarriage. *Journal of Divorce, 13*(1), 65-79.

Greene, R. S. (1978). Custodial single fathers. *Conciliation Courts Review, 16*(2), 18-79.

Greif, G. L. (1985). *Single fathers*. Lexington, MA: Lexington Books.

Greif, G. L. (1987). Mothers without custody. *Social Work, 32*, 11-16.

Greif, G. L., & Pabst, M. S. (1988). *Mothers without custody*. Lexington, MA: Lexington Books.

Grillo, T. (1991). The mediation alternative: Process dangers for women. *Yale Law Journal, 100*(6), 1545-1610.

Hanson, S.M.H., & Bozett, F. W. (1987). Fatherhood: A review and resources. *Family Relations, 36*, 333-340.

Hetherington, E. M., & Camara, K. A. (1984). Families in transition: The process of dissolution and reconstitution. In R. Parke (Ed.), *Review of child development research* (Vol. 7, pp. 398-439). Chicago: University of Chicago Press.

Hochschild, A. (1989). *The second shift*. New York: Avon.

Jacobs, J. W. (1982). The effects of divorce on fathers: An overview of the literature. *American Journal of Psychiatry, 139*, 1235-1241.

Katz, A. J. (1979). Lone fathers: Perspectives and implications for family policy. *Family Coordinator, 28*(4), 521-527.

Keshet, H. F., & Rosenthal, K. M. (1978). Single-parent fathers: A new study. *Children Today, 7*, 13-17.

Lehner, L. (1991). Mediation parent education programs in the California Family Courts. *Family and Conciliation Courts Review, 30*(2), 207-216.

Levitin, T. E. (1979). Children of divorce: An introduction. *Journal of Social Issues, 35*, 1-25.

Lewis, K. (1978). Single-father families: Who they are and how they fare. *Child Welfare, 57*(10), 643-651.

Little, M. (1982). *Family breakup*. San Francisco: Jossey-Bass.

Lonsdorf, B. J. (1991). The role of coercion in affecting women's inferior outcomes in divorce: Implications for researchers and therapists. In C. A. Everett (Ed.), *The consequences of divorce: Economic and custodial impact on children and adults* (pp. 69-106). New York: Haworth.

Lowery, C. R., & Settle, S. A. (1985). Effects of divorce on children: Differential impact of custody and visitation patterns. *Family Relations, 34*(4), 455-464.

Luepnitz, D. A. (1982). *Child custody: A study of families after divorce*. Lexington, MA: Lexington Books.

Maccoby, E. E., Depner, C. E., & Mnookin, R. M. (1988). Custody of children following divorce. In E. M. Hetherington & J. Arasteh (Eds.), *The impact of divorce, single-parenting and step-parenting on children* (pp. 91-114). Hillsdale, NJ: Lawrence Erlbaum.

Maccoby, E. E., Depner, C. E., & Mnookin, R. M. (1990). Co-parenting in the second year after divorce. *Journal of Marriage and the Family, 52*(2), 141-155.

Maccoby, E., & Mnookin, R. H. (1992). *Dividing the child: The social and legal dilemmas of custody*. Cambridge, MA: Harvard University Press.

Mendes, H. A. (1976). Single fatherhood. *Social Work, 21*, 308-312.

Mendes, H. A. (1979). How divorced fathers obtain custody—a review of research. *Conciliation Courts Review, 17*(1), 27-30.

Miller, J., & Schreiner, T. (1992, January 20). Single dads lead more families. *The San Francisco Chronicle*, pp. 1, 4.

Minow, M. (1990). *Making all the difference: Inclusion, exclusion, and American law.* Ithaca, NY: Cornell University Press.

Mnookin, R. H. (1975). Child custody adjudication: Judicial functions in the face of indeterminacy. *Law and Contemporary Problems, 39*, 226-293.

Mnookin, R. H., & Kornhauser, L. (1979). Bargaining in the shadow of the law: The case of divorce. *Yale Law Journal, 88*, 950-997.

Mnookin, R. H., Maccoby, E., Albiston, C. R., & Depner, C. E. (1990). Private ordering revisited: What custodial arrangements are parents negotiating? In S.D. Sugarman & H. Hill Kay (Eds.), *Divorce reform at the crossroads* (pp. 37-74). New Haven, CT: Yale University Press.

Nash, J. (1965). The father in contemporary culture and current psychological literature. *Child Development, 36*, 261-297.

Nieto, D. S. (1990). The custodial single father: Who does he think he is? *Journal of Divorce, 13*(3), 27-43.

O'Brien, M. (1980). Lone fathers: Transition from married to separated state. *Journal of Comparative Family Studies, 9*(1), 115-127.

Orthner, D. K., Brown, T., & Ferguson, D. (1976). Single-parent fatherhood: An emerging life style. *The Family Coordinator, 25*, 429-437.

Paskowicz, P. (1982). *Absentee mothers*. New York: Universal Books.

Pearson, J., & Thoennes, N. (1988). Supporting children after divorce: The influence of custody on support levels and payments. *Family Law Quarterly, 22*, 319-339.

Phear, W.P.C., Beck, J. C., Hauser, B. B., Clark, S. C., & Whitney, R. A. (1984). An empirical study of custody arrangements: Joint versus sole legal custody. In J. Folberg (Ed.), *Joint custody and shared parenting* (pp. 142-158). Washington, DC: BNA Books.

Pichitino, J. P. (1983). Profile of the single father: A thematic integration of the literature. *Personnel and Guidance Journal, 61*(5), 295-300.

Pleck, J. H., & Sawyer, J. (1974). *Men and masculinity*. Englewood Cliffs, NJ: Prentice-Hall.

Polikoff, N. D. (1982). Why are mothers losing: A brief analysis of criteria used in child custody determinations. *Women's Rights Law Reporter, 7*(3) 2-10.

Polikoff, N. D. (1983). Gender and child custody determinations: Exploding the myths. In Diamond, I. (Ed.), *Families, politics and public policies: A feminist dialogue on women and the state* (pp. 195-218). New York: Longman.

Rosen, R. (1979). Some crucial issues concerning children of divorce. *Journal of Divorce, 3*, 19-25.

Santrock, J. W., & Warshak, R. A. (1979). Father custody and social development in boys and girls. *Journal of Social Issues, 35*, 112-125.

Schlesinger, B. (1979). Single parent fathers: A research review. *Children Today, 8*(5), 12-19, 37-39.

Schlesinger, B., & Todres, R. (1976). Motherless families: An increasing societal pattern. *Child Welfare, 55*(8), 553-558.

Schnayer, R., & Orr, R. R. (1989). A comparison of children living in single-mother and single-father families. In S. A. Wolchik & P. Karoly (Eds.), *Children of divorce: Developmental and clinical issues* (pp. 171-184) New York: Haworth.

Smith, R. M., & Smith, C. W. (1981). Child rearing and single-parent fathers. *Family Relations, 30,* 411-417.

Spanier, G. B., & Glick, P. C. (1981). Marital instability in the United States: Some correlates and recent changes. *Family Relations, 30,* 329-338.

Stack, C. (1976). Who owns the child? Divorce and child custody decisions in middle-class families. *Social Problems, 23,* 505-523.

Todres, R. (1975). Motherless families. *Canadian Welfare, 51,* 11-13.

Todres, R. (1978). Runaway wives: An increasing North-American phenomenon. *Family Coordinator, 27*(1), 17-21.

Turner, J. R. (1984). Divorced fathers who win contested custody of their children: An exploratory study. *American Journal of Orthopsychiatry, 54*(3), 498-501.

Victor, I., & Winkler, W. A. (1977). *Fathers and custody.* New York: Hawthorn.

Wallerstein, J. S., & Kelly, J. B. (1980). *Surviving the breakup: How children actually cope with divorce.* New York: Basic Books.

Walters, M. (1988). Moving to the front of the bus. In M. Walters, B. Carter, P. Papp, & D. Silverstein (Eds.), *The invisible web: Gender patterns in family relationships* (pp. 306-313). New York: Guilford Press.

Warshak, R. A., & Santrock, J. W. (1983). Children of divorce: Impact of custody disposition on social development. In E. J. Callahan & K. A. McCluskey (Eds.), *Life-span developmental psychology* (pp. 241-263). New York: Academic Press.

Watson, M. A. (1981). Custody alternatives: Defining the best interests of the children. *Family Relations, 30,* 474-479.

Weiss, R. (1975). *Marital separation.* New York: Basic Books.

Weitzman, L. J. (1985). *The divorce revolution: The unexpected social and economic consequences for women and children in America.* New York: Free Press.

West, B., & Kissman, K. (1991). Mothers without custody: Treatment issues. In C. A. Everett (Ed.), *The consequences of divorce: Economic and custodial impact on children and adults* (pp. 229-237). New York: Haworth.

Woody, R. H. (1978). Fathers with child custody. *The Counseling Psychologist, 7*(4), 60-63.

PART II

Using Social Science Research in Policy and Practice

4

The Economics of Parenting Apart

JAY D. TEACHMAN
KATHLEEN PAASCH

Parenting apart and its implications have drawn attention with the increased likelihood that individuals may spend at least some part of their lives in a single-parent family as either a parent or a dependent. And, while there are many long-term consequences of growing up in a single-parent family, especially for children (e.g., early marriage and childbearing, less education—see McLanahan, 1985; McLanahan & Bumpass, 1988), the purpose of this chapter is to examine a more immediate dimension of single parenting—the economic consequences. We note, however, that the long-term consequences of living in a single-parent family may be traced, at least in part, to the poor economic health of single-parent families.

In "traditional" or two-parent families, there is usually a division of labor involving the socialization of and provision for children. When marriages are disrupted or when only one parent lives with the child, both care of children and economic provision must be shouldered disproportionately by the single parent, responsibilities that traditionally have been shared by two parents. For single parents, the number of hours that can be worked is limited by the expense and availability of child care. At the same time, child care is limited by the amount of income brought in. The situation is exacerbated by the fact that most

AUTHORS' NOTE: Support was provided by Grant No. SES-8812215 from the National Science Foundation.

single parents are women who face limited economic opportunities in the labor market. Even if they are able to work full-time, full-year, women are paid only 70% of what comparable male workers earn (U.S. Bureau of the Census, 1991b).

We begin by outlining changes that have occurred in household and family structure in the United States and show how this has changed the composition of the population in poverty. We then outline various forms of economic assistance available to single parents. In conclusion, we discuss policy options that may help alleviate the economic distress associated with living in a single-parent family.

The Demographic Transformation of Living Arrangements for Children

During the past few decades, the United States has witnessed dramatic changes in the structure of families and households. For families, the most remarkable change has been the decline of the two-parent family and in its place the rising number of single-parent families. Soaring divorce rates are most often cited as the reason so many children live with one parent. Divorces have risen from 9 per 1,000 married women in 1960 to 21 per 1,000 married women in 1988 (U.S. Department of Health and Human Services, 1991a). Although the divorce rate appears to have stabilized or even declined slightly in recent years, almost two-thirds of recently contracted marriages (1970-1985) are likely to end in separation or divorce (Martin & Bumpass, 1989). While divorce is the main demographic force, concurrent rises in age at marriage and outside-of-marriage births have also contributed to the increase in single-parent families, especially among African-Americans. The median age at first marriage for women rose from about 20 years in 1960 to 24 years in 1990. At the same time, outside-of-marriage births rose to almost 27% of all births in 1989 (U.S. Department of Health and Human Services, 1991c) up from only 5% in 1960 (U.S. Bureau of the Census, 1980). Note that the rise in the proportion of births occurring to women outside of marriage cannot be attributed solely to increases in rates of illegitimacy. Indeed, among African-American women, rates of illegitimacy have declined over the past three decades. Rather, the increasing proportion of outside-of-marriage births can be attributed to substantial delays in marriage combined with significant reductions in marital fertility. That is, the rate at which marital births has declined is greater than the rate at which nonmarital births has declined, leading to a greater proportion of births occurring outside of marriage.

The percentage of births to unmarried women varies considerably by race. About 19% of Caucasian births were to unmarried mothers, compared to approximately 66% of African-American births (U.S. Department of Health and Human Services, 1991b). The percentage of Hispanic births to unmarried mothers, 34%, fell between these two figures in 1988 (U.S. Bureau of the Census, 1991).

All three trends—rising age at marriage, increased likelihood of divorce, and greater proportions of births occurring outside of marriage—have resulted in dramatic changes in living arrangements for children (see Table 4.1). In 1990 approximately one-quarter of all children under 18 years old lived with only one parent—up from 9% in 1960. Reflective of trends in outside-of-marriage childbearing and custody settlements of divorced parents, the majority of children living with one parent lived with their mother. One in five children were living with only their mother in 1990.

Striking differences are apparent in the living arrangements of African-American and Caucasian children. Despite high divorce rates, in 1990 the majority of Caucasian children still lived with both parents (76%). African-American children, on the other hand, were much more likely to live with one parent—more than half lived with their mothers only. African-American children are also more likely than Caucasians to live with other relatives, although the prevalence of this household type seems to be declining.[1] The data for Hispanics indicate figures that are again between those for African-Americans and Caucasians.

For both races and Hispanics, the percentage of children living with fathers only is very small. Because single parenting most often involves single mothers and their children, our discussion will be confined mainly to these families. It is not our intent to dismiss father-only families, and where possible, we include findings on these families. However, little information is available.

Cross-sectional views of living arrangements, as presented in Table 4.1, can be misleading. In actuality, a much greater portion of children will spend at least some part of their lives in a single-parent family. Bumpass and Sweet (1989) estimate that approximately one-half of all children born between 1970 and 1984 will spend some time in a mother-only family. Again, the numbers are quite different for African-Americans and Caucasians, with 80% of African-American children likely to experience life in a female-headed family, compared to 36%

Table 4.1 Living Arrangements of Children Under 18 Years Old (in Percents)

	1960	1970	1980	1990
All Races				
Two Parents	87.7	85.2	76.7	72.5
One Parent	9.1	11.9	19.7	24.7
Mother Only	8.0	10.8	18.0	21.6
Father Only	1.1	1.1	1.7	3.1
Other Relatives	2.5	2.2	3.1	2.2
Nonrelatives	0.7	0.7	0.6	0.5
Children < 18 yrs. (in 1,000s)	63,727	69,162	63,427	64,137
Caucasians				
Two Parents	90.9	89.5	82.7	76.0
One Parent	7.1	8.7	15.1	19.2
Mother Only	6.1	7.8	13.5	16.2
Father Only	1.0	0.9	1.6	3.0
Other Relatives	1.4	1.2	1.7	1.4
Nonrelatives	0.5	0.6	0.5	0.4
Children < 18 yrs. (in 1,000s)	55,077	58,790	52,242	51,390
African-Americans				
Two Parents	67.0	58.5	42.2	37.7
One Parent	21.9	31.8	45.8	54.8
Mother Only	19.9	29.5	43.9	51.2
Father Only	2.0	2.3	1.9	3.5
Other Relatives	9.6	8.7	10.7	6.5
Nonrelatives	1.5	1.0	1.3	1.0
Children < 18 yrs. (in 1,000s)	8,650	9,422	9,375	10,018
Hispanics				
Two Parents	na	77.7	75.4	66.8
One Parent	na	na	21.1	30.0
Mother Only	na	na	19.6	27.1
Father Only	na	na	1.5	2.9
Other Relatives	na	na	3.4	2.5
Nonrelatives	na	na	0.1	0.8
Children < 18 yrs. (in 1,000s)	na	4,006	5,459	7,174

SOURCE: U.S. Bureau of the Census, 1991c.

of Caucasian children. In addition, Bumpass and Sweet report that time spent in single-parent families is likely to be substantial, as only 44% of Caucasian mothers and 23% of African-American mothers are likely to marry within 5 years of becoming a single parent. London (1990) reports slightly higher percentages of remarriages within 5 years (50% for Caucasians; 25% for African-Americans), but does not separate mothers from women without children.

The changing composition of families is an interesting phenomenon by itself. However, the issue becomes considerably more important when the economic situation of these different types of families is evaluated. As we indicate below, there are dramatic differences in the economic well-being of families according to the number of parents living in the household.

Poverty and the Changing Composition of Families

The composition of all families by type and of families living in poverty by type is shown in Table 4.2. Not surprisingly, the composition of all families is not equal to the composition of families living in poverty. For example, female-headed families with children comprised 48% of families living in poverty in 1990, but constituted only 12% of all families. Conversely, married couples with children comprised only 28% of poor families, while they made up 38% of all families. Over the past 30 years, these two types of families have exchanged places as the predominant type among poor families. As the percentage of two-parent families has declined with respect to female-headed families, female-headed families have increased as a percentage of all poor families. Married couple families without children also represent a smaller percentage of poor families today than in 1960 (14% versus almost 30%), even though they make up a larger share of the total population.

Another perspective on the relationship between family type and poverty is given in Table 4.3. While Table 4.2 shows the composition of all families and families living in poverty by type, Table 4.3 shows the risk of being in poverty by family type. It is immediately apparent that mother-only families have been, and continue to be, the most likely to experience poverty. Despite the fact that the percentage of female-headed households living in poverty has declined somewhat from 1960, due to federal aid programs, approximately half of all such families remain poor. Although data by race is available only for the past two

Table 4.2 Composition of Families in Poverty and Composition of All Families

	1960		1970		1980		1990	
	Poor	All	Poor	All	Poor	All	Poor	All
Married couple (with children)	47[a]	53	34[a]	49	32	43	28	38
Married couple (without children)	30[a]	34	28[a]	36	17	39	14	40
Female-headed family (with children)	18	6	32	7	43	10	48	12
Female-headed family (without children)	6	4	5	4	4	5	5	5
Male-headed family (with children)	-	1	-	1	2	1	4	2
Male-headed family (without children)	-	2	-	2	1	2	-[b]	2

[a] Data not available separately, includes percentage of married couples in poverty as well as male-headed families in poverty.
[b] Less than 1% in poverty
SOURCE: U.S. Bureau of the Census, 1991d.

decades, the figures in Table 4.3 clearly show that female-headed families have been the most disadvantaged group, with African-American and Hispanic families of this type being more likely to experience poverty than Caucasians.

In addition to being more likely to be living in poverty at a given point in time, families headed by women are likely to remain poor longer. Bane and Ellwood (1982) find that during the late 1970s, female-headed families experienced an average poverty spell of 7 years, in contrast to a less than 2-year spell experienced by others in poverty (Duncan, Coe, & Hill, 1984). Thus, poverty among families headed by women is not only more prevalent, it is more likely to be chronic.

Tables 4.2 and 4.3 summarize what has come to be known as the feminization of poverty: Over the past three decades, poverty has become increasingly concentrated among female-headed families. The feminization of poverty also holds implications for the poverty status of children. Eggebeen and Lichter (1991) have examined shifts in family structure from 1960 to 1988 with respect to changes in child poverty. They find that, had the proportions of children in married-couple, female-headed, and male-headed households remained the same as in 1960, the child poverty rate in 1988 would be one-third less than the child poverty rate actually observed. Analyses conducted by race indicate that changes in African-American family structure during the 1980s were responsible for 65% of the increase in the official poverty of African-American children, while changing family structure among Caucasians accounted for 37% of the rise in official child poverty. Eggebeen and Lichter also note that while children are at greater risk of poverty because they are more likely to live in single-parent families, one should also recognize that nonpoor families are having fewer children, which results in proportionately more children living in poor families.

Reasons for Poverty in Mother-Headed Families

The above discussion documents the substantial differences in poverty associated with family type. Clearly, living in a female-headed family substantially increases the risk of experiencing poverty. However, the data on poverty status and family type only outline the demographic parameters of the issue. Such data tell us little about why families headed by women are so economically vulnerable. It is to this question that we now turn our attention.

Table 4.3 Percent of Families With Children Living in Poverty by Type

	1960	1970	1980	1990
All Races				
All families with children	19.7	11.6	14.7	16.4
Children residing with:				
Both parents	na	na	7.7	7.8
Mother	56.3	43.8	42.9	44.5
Father	na	na	18.0	18.8
Families with children (1,000s)	27,102	30,070	32,773	34,503
Caucasians				
All families with children	15.3	8.5	11.2	12.6
Children residing with:				
Both parents	na	na	6.8	7.1
Mother	47.1	36.9[a]	35.9	37.9
Father	na	na	16.0	16.0
Families with children (1,000s)	na	26,256	27,416	28,117
African-Americans				
All families with children	na	34.9	35.5	37.2
Children residing with:				
Both parents	na	na	15.5	14.3
Mother	na	60.0[b]	56.0	56.1
Father	na	na	24.0	27.3
Families with children (1,000s)	na	3,470	4,465	5,069
Hispanics				
All families with children	na	24.5[c]	27.2	31.0
Children residing with:				
Both parents	na	na	na	20.8
Mother	na	na	60.0[d]	58.2
Father	na	na	na	28.1
Families with children (1,000s)	na	1,700c	2,409	3,497

[a] 1970 figures not available, 1971 data shown.
[b] 1960 figures not available, 1961 data shown.
[c] 1970 figures not available, 1972 data shown.
[d] 1980 figures not available, 1981 data shown.
SOURCE: U.S. Bureau of the Census, 1991d.

Despite media myths about ex-wives who strip husbands of assets, divorce brings with it substantial economic setbacks for the majority of women and their children. After divorce, two households are formed and the previous family income is rarely divided equally. A number of researchers have examined living standards of spouses after divorce; all find a decline in living standards for women following divorce. Duncan and Hoffman (1985, 1988) find that family income for women divorcing or separating falls by approximately 34%, and size-adjusted family income falls by 25%.[2] For men, family income falls by only 15%, while their size-adjusted family income increases by 3%. Size-adjusted family income rises for men because they rarely have custody of children. David and Flory (1989) and Burkhauser, Duncan, Hauser, and Berntsen (1991) report similar changes following divorce.

To cope with this decline in income, many women either newly enter or reenter the labor force after divorcing. Duncan and Hoffman (1985) find that while only 51% of mothers worked 20 hours or more a week before divorcing, 73% worked this amount after divorcing. While increasing work hours would appear at first glance to improve living standards, it often has mixed results for families. Because many women are new labor force entrants or are returning to work after being absent for some time, it is difficult for them to secure jobs that pay enough to support families. Many times these women must take shift work in order to earn sufficient wages or to be home with their children at least some of the time.

Presser (1986) reports that unmarried mothers are almost twice as likely as married mothers to work non-day shifts, and that the biggest work constraint on these women is the availability and affordability of child care. Presser and Baldwin (1980) and O'Connell and Bloom (1987) also report that the lack of affordable child care prevents many single mothers from working. Moreover, it is the young, African-American, poorly educated, low-income mothers who are most constrained by child care costs—the very women most in need of work. Unfortunately, it is often more expensive for these women to work and pay for child care than it is to stay at home and receive welfare (McLanahan & Garfinkel, 1986; Sawhill, 1976).

The situation is similar for never-married mothers. Although fewer of these women must deal with a substantial drop in income from previous levels, they must deal with the same stresses of balancing employment and child care as divorced women. If anything, the economic situation of never-married mothers is worse due to their even more tenuous ties to the labor force. Never-married mothers are more likely than ever-married mothers to possess characteristics negatively valued in the labor force. That is, never-married mothers are more likely to be young, African-American, and poorly educated.

We have outlined how the dire economic circumstances faced by single mothers are related to their tenuous position in the labor market. We next consider various income transfers that influence the well-being of female-headed families. Two basic types of transfers are considered: welfare and child support. We pay particular attention to the latter, given recent policy initiatives and the likely form of future policy developments.

Public Assistance and Single Mothers

Economic circumstances are such that a large number of female-headed families, both divorced and never-married, are eligible to receive welfare assistance. This aid can take many forms, but most common are Aid to Families with Dependent Children (AFDC), Supplemental Security Income (SSI), food stamps, housing assistance, and school lunches. As shown in Table 4.4, the majority (69%) of female-headed families participate in one or more of these programs. Slightly less than one-half of women receiving welfare receive cash assistance or food stamps. One-fifth of the women receiving assistance live in public or subsidized housing.

Reflecting race differences in poverty rates discussed earlier, there are large differences by race in the receipt of public assistance. Nearly 82% of African-American female-headed families receive some kind of assistance, compared to 60% of Caucasian families of the same type. More than half of African-American female-headed families are recipients of cash assistance or food stamps.

The impact of public assistance on families is substantial. If it were not for government transfers, the percentage of all female-headed families in poverty would rise from approximately 48% to 54% (U.S. Bureau of the Census, 1991f). By race, the percentage of poor, Caucasian, female-headed families would rise from 40% to more than 46%, while for African-Americans it would rise from 58% to 65% in poverty.

The effect of government programs on poor female-headed families can be further realized by adding the estimated cash value of transfers to recipients' income. Such transfers are not included when calculating official measures of poverty. Using the Census Bureau's income definition 14,

Table 4.4   Mother-Headed Families[a] Receiving Means-Tested Assistance

	Number (in 1,000s)	Percent
All Races		
Total mother-headed families	13,793	
In household that received means-tested assistance	9,464	68.6
Types of assistance received:[b]		
In household that received cash assistance	6,085	44.1
In household that received food stamps	6,474	46.9
Lived in public or subsidized housing	3,130	22.7
Caucasians		
Total mother-headed families	7,840	
In household that received means-tested assistance	4,666	59.5
Types of assistance received:[b]		
In household that received cash assistance	2,791	35.6
In household that received food stamps	3,025	38.6
Lived in public or subsidized housing	1,194	15.2
African-Americans		
Total mother-headed families	5,475	
In household that received means-tested assistance	4,478	81.8
Types of assistance received:[b]		
In household that received cash assistance	3,099	56.6
In household that received food stamps	3,279	59.9
Lived in public or subsidized housing	1,833	33.5

[a] Families with female householder, no spouse present, and related children under 18 years.
[b] Percentages do not add to 100 because households may receive more than one type of assistance. Also, the families may receive types of assistance not listed here.
SOURCE: U.S. Bureau of the Census, 1991d.

the percent of all female-headed families living in poverty declines to about 34%.[3] Under this income definition, only 29% of Caucasian female-headed families live in poverty, while the percentage of African-American female-headed families living in poverty declines to 43%.

Although government transfers serve to lessen poverty, their main intent is assistance in the short term, not long range payments for raising children. Moreover, public assistance is aimed at lessening the impact of poverty, not eliminating it. This fact is reflected in the large percentage of families headed by women that remain in poverty after public transfers are taken into account. In the United States, it is assumed that financial, as well as social, responsibility for children should rest with parents.

Thus, we turn our attention to child support as a means to increase the economic well-being of single-parent families. As we shall see, many female-headed families receive little or no support from the nonresidential father. Child support is important not only because of its impact on single-parent families but also because of its potential impact on welfare costs. Garfinkel (1988) estimates, based on data from Wisconsin, that a child support program that would assure the collection of child support would more than pay for itself with savings in welfare expenditures. He also argues that for these poor female-headed families, dollars paid in child support are more beneficial than AFDC payments because child support would be less likely to reduce labor force activity. AFDC payments are reduced for earned income and provide little incentive to work. On the other hand, child support dollars not only would not be reduced if the recipient worked but also would represent a net gain in income. We now turn our attention to child support and the factors that determine its award and receipt.

Child Support

Historically, child support, in the form of a cash transfer from fathers to mothers, has evolved as the primary mechanism whereby nonresidential fathers are legally required to support their children.[4] Unfortunately for female-headed families, child support awards are generally small, and all too often payments do not arrive regularly (cf. Peterson & Nord, 1990). However, because single mothers have relatively low incomes, the receipt of child support payments can make a substantial difference. Child support payments comprised almost 19% of the total income for mothers who received support in 1989. For women below the poverty level, payments made up a much larger proportion—37% of their total income (U.S. Bureau of the Census, 1991e). From these figures, it is apparent that child support payments have the capacity to make quite a difference in the living standards of these families. Because incomes are so low, the failure to receive child support may force many female-headed families into poverty or keep them from rising out of poverty (Lerman, 1987).

Because of increasingly strong public opinion that nonresidential parents should be financially responsible for their children, recent decades have witnessed several policy initiatives aimed at improving the rate of the award and receipt of child support. In 1975 the Child Support Enforcement program was enacted. It provided federal reimbursement to states of up to 70% of the cost of establishing paternity, locating absent parents, and collecting child support. Use of Internal Revenue Service data to collect child support was authorized for mothers receiving AFDC benefits. In 1980 the right to use Internal Revenue Service data was extended to cover non-AFDC families.

In 1984 even tougher legislation went into effect. This program required states to devise a system to withhold child support from the wages of parents who fail to pay. It also required states to institute statewide standards for setting the amount of child support awards. More recently, the Family Support Act of 1988 was enacted to revise public assistance programs so that work, child support, and AFDC benefits are all emphasized. The child support provisions of greatest importance cover establishing paternity (more of the costs are covered by the federal government, and states are required to establish paternity in a proportion of cases), withholding of wages (beginning in 1994, all new support orders will be paid through wage withholding), and setting guidelines for size of awards (guidelines set in the 1984 legislation will now become binding on judges) ("Family Support Act," 1989).

The Family Support Act of 1988 sets guidelines and minimal requirements for states. Each state then devises programs for implementation. As such, the success of such programs may differ by state, depending on the level of commitment and program effectiveness. However, all state programs must be federally approved and reviewed periodically. Garfinkel, Oellerich, and Robins (1991) provide an indication of the diversity that occurs between states with respect to provisions meeting the standards of the Family Support Act of 1988.

Child Support Outcomes

Table 4.5 shows the percent of mothers with absent partners who were awarded and received child support from 1978 to 1989. For this period, slightly less than 60% of single mothers were awarded child support. Of these mothers, about 71% to 75% received payments. Thus, less than 50% of mothers actually received child support from the nonresidential father. Only about 25% of mothers receive the full amount of child support awarded.

The figures for mothers (those living both above and below the poverty level) indicate a slight increase over time in the proportion receiving child support payments. The percentages for those mothers awarded support and who received the full amount did not change greatly nor in a consistent manner. The biggest changes have occurred among women living below the poverty level. This is probably due to federal programs targeting men whose ex-partners (both formerly married and never married) receive AFDC payments. For these women, the percentage who were due child support but did not receive payments declined from 41% in 1978 to 32% in 1989. At the same time, the percent who were awarded child support increased slightly—from 38% to 43%.

The per annum amounts of child support due and received for selected years are shown in Table 4.6. The amounts involved are relatively small. On average, women were due less than $3,500 yearly in child support and received less than $2,500.

For each year, the amount received is considerably lower than the amount due, although the gap is shrinking slightly. In 1978 women received, on average, 64 cents of every dollar they were owed by nonresidential fathers. By 1989 the situation had improved somewhat, as women received 68 cents of every dollar they were owed. It should be noted, though, that the gap between the amount received and the amount owed is not closing because female-headed families are receiving more child support. In fact, the average amount received has decreased over time. The improvement in the ratio of the amount due to the amount received is attributable to the fact that the mean payment *due* has decreased even more rapidly than the mean payment *received* when adjusted for inflation. So, despite the fact that more mothers are receiving a greater percentage of the amount due, the average amount awarded has declined. Not only are fathers failing to meet their child support obligations, but courts are also failing to award child support that keeps pace with inflation. The declining size of awards may also be due to the fact that more low-income fathers are being ordered to pay child support.

Because the above figures are based on reports from either the custodial parent (most often the mother) or court records, there is almost certainly a downward bias in the reported amount of support received. Braver, Fitzpatrick, and Bay (1991) match payment reports from fathers

Table 4.5 Child Support: Percent Awarded and Receipt

All Mothers[a]	1978	1981	1983	1985	1987	1989
Awarded child support	59.1	59.2	57.7	61.3	59.0	57.7
Received payments	71.7	71.8	76.0	74.0	76.1	75.2
Received full amount	48.9	46.7	50.5	48.2	51.3	51.4
Due but did not receive payments	28.3	28.2	24.0	26.0	23.9	24.8

Mothers Below Poverty Level	1978	1981	1983	1985	1987	1989
Awarded child support	38.1	39.7	42.5	40.4	44.3	43.3
Received payments	58.9	61.4	62.0	65.7	71.9	68.3
Due but did not receive payments	41.1	38.6	38.0	34.3	28.1	31.7

[a] Mothers below the poverty level are also included in these figures.
SOURCE: U.S. Bureau of the Census, 1991e.

with receipt reports from mothers and find fathers' reports to be much higher, which suggests that both reports may be biased. Additionally, they find that court data underestimate the amount of child support received, since only payments through the court clerk are recorded. Apparently, noncustodial parents often bypass the clerk and make payments directly to the mother. In light of this, one must recognize that most reports of the receipt of support will be downwardly biased. However, unless reports from both parents are matched with complete court records, we have no way of knowing the degree of bias.

The Award and Receipt of Child Support

The issue of child support has attracted considerable attention from researchers seeking to understand why so many mothers are not awarded support and why so many fathers do not pay. While it may appear intuitive that the factors influencing awards would affect receipt, it seems that the two are only partially correlated. That is, the factors that determine award of support are not necessarily those that determine receipt of support.

The single most important determinant of whether a mother receives child support from a nonresidential father is the presence of a court-

Table 4.6   Child Support Payments Due and Received[a]

	1978	1981	1983	1985	1987	1989
Mothers Due Support (1,000s)	3,424	4,043	3,995	4,381	4,829	4,953
Mean Payments Due ($)	3,680	3,382	3,139	2,877	3,293	3,292
Mean Payments Received ($)	2,370	2,080	2,215	1,892	2,252	2,252
Due–Received ($)	1,310	1,302	924	985	1,041	1,040

[a] In 1989 dollars
SOURCE: U.S. Bureau of the Census, 1991e.

ordered award (Peterson & Nord, 1990). As shown earlier in Table 4.5, only 58% of all single mothers with nonresidential fathers were awarded support. This proportion varies widely according to the socioeconomic characteristics of both parents, the nature of their relationship, and characteristics of the legal system (Beller & Graham, 1986).

Perhaps the most important factor in determining whether an award is made is marital status—the effects of which remain after socioeconomic and legal characteristics are controlled. Beller and Graham find never-married women are 73% less likely than ever-married women to have an award. Table 4.7 provides figures on the award of child support by marital status of the mother. It is immediately apparent that a much greater percentage of ever-married mothers are awarded child support (72%) than are never-married mothers (24%). The percentages of mothers due support are even lower: 62% of ever-married mothers and only 20% of never-married mothers. The number due support is generally less than the number awarded support because several factors may change after the initial award, which may result in the renegotiation of the award. For example, mothers may remarry and relinquish their right to receive child support, or children may reach age 18.

The difference in award of child support by marital status occurs for a variety of reasons. Mothers who are divorcing are likely to have a lawyer and are already dealing with the legal system. For these mothers, seeking a child support award is often simply an extension of divorce proceedings. Additionally, the father has more than likely supported the children during marriage, making acknowledgement of financial responsibility more likely. Never-married mothers would have to initiate legal proceedings, something that many are reluctant to do, given the time and expense involved. Also, many never-married mothers, especially if young or with little education, may not know how to go about initiating such proceedings. Establishing paternity is an additional barrier. When a couple divorces, the husband is assumed to be the father. Never-married mothers must prove paternity. This is often difficult, especially if the father is unwilling to contribute to the child's welfare.

Although about the same percentage of ever-married and never-married mothers who are due child support receive payments, a much smaller percentage of all never-married mothers receive child support: 15% versus 48%. Ever-married mothers are also better off in terms of both average amount of child support received and total income. The smaller amount of child support received by never-married mothers likely reflects the less-favorable economic situation of never-married men as well as the larger family size of ever-married mothers—the greater the number of children, the greater the child support award. To a lesser degree, it also likely reflects less commitment on the part of never-married fathers.

The greater amount of child support received by ever-married mothers does not entirely account for the difference in mean total income between ever- and never-married mothers. If income from child support is subtracted from total income, ever-married mothers still have an income more than $6,200 greater than never-married mothers. This difference reflects the more advantageous set of background characteristics possessed by ever-married mothers.

A number of other background characteristics are also important in determining the award of child support. Race has a significant effect, with African-Americans being much less likely to receive an award independent of other factors. Beller and Graham (1986) find that African-Americans are less than half as likely as Caucasians to be awarded child support. This is primarily due to the fact that African-Americans are less likely to be married, and if they do marry, they are more likely to be separated rather than divorced. Educational attainment, age, place of residence, and number of children are also related to award of child support, and differences in composition on these variables help to explain some, but not all, of the lower rate of awards for African-Americans (Beller & Graham). Women who are older and have more education are more likely to receive an award. Also, awards are positively associated with having younger children and having been married longer. Teachman (1990) reports similar findings but finds that the effect of race is insignificant when socioeconomic resources are controlled.

Table 4.7 Child Support Awarded and Received by Marital Status of Mother: 1989

	Ever-Married[a]	Never-Married
Awarded Child Support	72%	23.9%
Due Child Support	62%	20%
Received Support Among Due Support	75.4%	73.2%
Received Support Among All Women	48%	15%
Mean Child Support Received	$3,138	$1,888
Mean Total Income	$16,964	$9,495
Child Support as Percent of Total Income	18.5%	19.9%

[a] Includes divorced, separated, and divorced women who have remarried.
SOURCE: Based on calculations from U.S. Bureau of the Census, 1991e.

While the award of child support depends on a wide variety of characteristics, the determinants of the receipt of support are more select. A few studies have found the receipt of child support to be affected by characteristics of mothers and children. Robins and Dickinson (1984), using data from the 1979 *Current Population Survey,* find that receipt of child support is positively related to the age and education of the mother, and negatively related to having young children and duration since divorce. Robins and Dickinson include one characteristic of fathers—income—which they find to be positively correlated with receipt of child support.

Peterson and Nord (1990), using data from the *Survey of Income and Program Participation* (SIPP), find that having a voluntary child support agreement and the amount of the award positively affect the likelihood of receiving support. However, they found characteristics of the mother to have no effect (e.g., race, education, marital status, number of children). Father characteristics were not available in the SIPP data set. More recently, using data containing information on both fathers and mothers, as well as child support arrangements (the *National Longitudinal Study of the High School Class of 1972*), Teachman (1991a) finds that the receipt of child support is mostly dependent on the circumstances of fathers. When fathers' characteristics are controlled, the characteristics of mothers and children have no direct impact on receipt of support.

Somewhat unexpectedly, Teachman (1991a) found that fathers who have remarried are more likely to pay child support than other fathers. This finding is consistent with those reported earlier by Hill (1984), who suggests that remarried fathers are more "family oriented" and so are more motivated to pay support. A closer physical proximity and visits with children are both positively related to the receipt of child support likely reflecting father's involvement with children. Other important factors affecting the receipt of support are the amount of the award and whether it was made voluntarily, which both have positive effects, and the length of time since divorce, which negatively affects child support receipt.

Seltzer (1991) also finds the receipt of child support associated with father characteristics but also examines their indirect effects through child custody. Using data from Wisconsin divorce cases, she finds that fathers with higher incomes are more likely to acquire joint custody of their children. As such, families with joint custody tend to have higher than average award amounts due to the higher incomes of fathers. Surprisingly, however, families with joint legal custody and those with sole custody do not differ in the level of support paid after divorce. Seltzer speculates that children are probably benefiting informally from joint custody arrangements because they have more contact with fathers than children in mother-custody families.

It appears that fathers' motivation and ability to pay child support are the most important determinants of the receipt of child support (Chambers, 1979). Unlike the award of support that is decided in a more public environment, subject to normative and legal constraints in favor of providing child support, the decision to send child support is less public and rests primarily with the father. Hence, the attributes of the mother have little effect on receipt of support.

Other Types of Child Support

Since child support is the primary mechanism by which nonresidential parents make contributions to the well-being of their children, most research has focused on the determinants of support awards and the receipt of payments. However, although child support payments are the predominant means of contribution, fathers may also help support their children in other, less formal ways. There has been some speculation that nonresidential fathers may substitute other means of support for the more formal child support in order to have more control over the way the contribution is utilized (Stack, 1974; Teachman, 1991b).

Teachman (1991b) and Paasch and Teachman (1991) have examined other means by which nonresidential fathers may contribute to their children. Both Teachman and Paasch and Teachman examine whether, and with what regularity, single mothers receive from nonresidential fathers contributions such as payment for children's clothes, presents, vacations, dental care, medical insurance, help with homework, and attending school events. Teachman (1991), using data from the *National Longitudinal Study of the High School Class of 1972*, finds that the majority of nonresidential fathers seldom or never make contributions to their children (see Table 4.8). Among fathers who contribute, the most frequent ways are through child support, medical insurance, and dental care. Fathers are more likely to provide contributions requiring outlays of money rather than time. Very few fathers do time-intensive activities, such as helping their children with homework or attending school events.

In addition, the evidence does not suggest that fathers substitute other forms of assistance for cash payments of child support. That is, a negative correlation between paying child support and providing other forms of assistance does not occur. However, fathers who provide at least one type of assistance are more likely to provide other types of assistance. This pattern indicates the presence of a small group of fathers dedicated to the overall well-being of their children.

Paasch and Teachman extend this work on informal types of support by examining differential provision according to gender of children. Drawing on an earlier study by Morgan, Lye, and Condran (1988), which finds that couples with at least one son are less likely to divorce, they hypothesize that nonresidential fathers will be more likely to make contributions to sons than to daughters. Contrary to initial expectations, results indicate that fathers are no more likely to contribute to the well-being of sons and, in some cases, are more likely to extend support to daughters, particularly in the form of medical insurance and dental care.

Although the reason for such findings is not clear, it is possible that divorced fathers with sons are a selective group who, on average, are likely to be less involved with their sons than are divorced fathers with daughters. Since those with daughters are more committed on average, they will be slightly more likely to make contributions to their daughters. However, such arguments remain at the level of speculation since other studies appear to have conflicting results. Hetherington, Cox, and Cox (1982) found that fathers visited sons more frequently and for longer durations than daughters after divorce. Hess and Camara (1979) report similar results. It should be noted that both of these studies used very small sample sizes. (Hess and Camara studied 32 families; Hetherington, Cox, and Cox examined 72 children and their parents.) Using a larger sample (more than 2,000 households), Furstenberg, Nord, Peterson, and Zill

Table 4.8   Percent of Nonresidential Fathers Providing Each Contribution
($n = 644$)

Form of Assistance	Never to Very Regularly				
	1	*2*	*3*	*4*	*5*
Pays for clothes	65.1	15.4	11.6	2.6	5.2
Pays for presents	40.1	19.1	20.1	8.0	12.7
Takes the children on vacation	65.2	11.3	11.4	4.1	8.0
Pays for routine dental care	74.5	4.6	5.2	3.1	12.6
Carries medical insurance	61.1	3.6	4.9	2.6	27.8
Pays for uninsured medical expenses	75.7	4.1	5.9	2.6	11.6
Helps the children with homework	84.9	6.2	4.9	1.6	2.3
Attends school events	74.8	11.8	6.9	2.9	3.6

	Never	Seldom	Occasionally	Regularly
Child Support Payments	28.0	18.0	11.0	43.0

SOURCE: Teachman, 1991b.

(1983) found no difference in visitation of sons and daughters. Due to the lack of consensus in this area, additional research is needed.

Discussion

The data paint a consistent portrait of the economics of parenting apart. Single parents, the majority of whom are women, are economically vulnerable. Whether the proximate demographic cause was divorce or outside-of-marriage childbearing, female-headed households are much more likely to experience poverty than households consisting of two parents. While a substantial proportion of mother-headed families receive public assistance, such transfer payments are not designed to be permanent and are insufficient to remove recipients from poverty. Indeed, in recent years there has been increasing pressure to place the responsibility of outside support on nonresidential fathers.

Only a minority of female-headed families receive child support from nonresidential fathers. And the amount of support received is minimal. The existing evidence suggests that the provision of child support depends on the motivation of the absent fathers. While characteristics of mothers and children are important factors determining whether an award is made, they are not important in determining receipt of support. This pattern is crucial in understanding the importance of recent legislation concerning child support.

Until relatively recently, there was little in the way of public pressure to award child support in sufficient amounts to reduce the likelihood of child poverty. That has changed, at least on the surface. Over the past decade legislation has been passed that attempts to remove the burden of support from public assistance and place it with nonresidential fathers. Pressure also has been put on the legal system to make more awards and to standardize size of awards. The Family Support Act of 1988 substantially increases the strength of such efforts.

The Family Support Act of 1988 also seeks to increase the flow of support from nonresidential fathers to their children by ensuring that court-ordered payments are made. New regulations stipulate that delinquent cases be subject to immediate wage withholding. And starting in 1994, all new child support orders will operate through wage withholding. These provisions attempt to remove any element of discretion in the payment of child support.

It is not clear whether legislation such as the Family Support Act of 1988 will be successful. Some research suggests that child support legislation can be effective—to a degree, that is (Garfinkel, 1988; Garfinkel, Oellerich, & Robins, 1991). Experience with the Wisconsin system suggests that strong guidelines for awarding child support, along with wage withholding, can increase the flow of income to single parents (Garfinkel). Secondary evidence pertaining to the Family Support Act of 1988 indicates that the new guidelines will increase child support payments by about 50% (Garfinkel, Oellerich, & Robins). However, the evidence to date is weak, and more research with better data is necessary before drawing firm conclusions. The leeway that states have in designing child-support programs to fulfill the requirements of the Family Support Act of 1988 will likely yield opportunities for comparative research that will sharpen our understanding of how policy initiatives affect behavior in the arena of child support. Unfortunately, it will be several years before the full impact of such policies will be evident.

While evaluation of the Family Support Act of 1988 is of crucial importance, the literature suggests continuing avenues for the development of policy designed to increase the flow of resources from absent parents to their children. As noted above, the motivation of absent fathers appears to play a crucial role in determining whether child support is received by the mother. These findings suggest that policies aimed at increasing the father's motivation to pay child support would be effective in increasing the flow of resources to children. One possible route to increase such motivation would be to design programs improving the relationship between former spouses, perhaps through mediation at the time of divorce. Several studies indicate that father's motivation to pay child support is linked to the quality of the relationship between the mother and father (Teachman, 1991a; Wright & Price, 1986).

Of particular importance for the development of new policy is the potential impact on family-related behaviors that may indirectly affect socioeconomic welfare. What are the implications of legislation such as the Family Support Act of 1988 for migration, marriage, divorce, and remarriage? By changing the calculus by which parents may negotiate their relationships, there may exist indirect but far-reaching implications for the way in which individuals form their life course, and such changes may substantially affect the well-being of children. To date, there has been no research of which we are aware that examines the impact of actual or simulated child support regimes on subsequent life-course behavior.

Finally, we note the almost complete lack of knowledge about noncustodial parents. While there is some evidence to suggest that they can pay more child support, there is little specific information about their financial situation nor how changes in child support payments would affect their economic and family-related behaviors. Such a lacuna in the literature makes it difficult to assess the potential impact of social policy on a substantial portion of the U.S. population. While there exists considerable speculation about the impact of child support obligations on the behavior of noncustodial parents, there is too little information to justify policy development. Indeed, the available evidence appears to run counter to popular conception. For instance, noncustodial parents who remarry are more likely to pay child support than are noncustodial parents who remain single (Teachman, 1991a). Thus, the additional constraints imposed by starting a new family do not appear to reduce support to absent children. Only additional research can help us sort out the mechanisms generating such behavior.

Notes

1. The race difference in this category is probably a reflection of the higher African-American rates of teenage childbearing. Care of the children is often taken over by other relatives. The rate of African-American teenage childbearing is declining, which may explain the decline in the number of children living with other relatives.

2. Size-adjusted income takes into account the size and composition of families and so more accurately reflects a decline or rise in living standards.

3. The Census Bureau's income definition 14, in addition to standard income, includes the Earned Income Tax Credit (a refundable tax credit for persons who qualify), the estimated cash value of Medicare, Medicaid, noncash transfers, and both means- and nonmeans-tested cash transfers. Means-tested cash transfers are based on need (i.e., AFDC payments) while nonmeans-tested transfers are based on other criteria (i.e., Social Security payments, Pell Grants).

4. We recognize that nonresidential mothers may also be required to pay child support. However, the vast majority of nonresidential parents are fathers, and our terminology reflects this fact.

References

Bane, M. J., & Ellwood, D. (1982). *Slipping into and out of poverty: The dynamics of spells*. Unpublished paper, Harvard University.

Beller, A., & Graham, J. (1986). Child support awards: Differences and trends by race and marital status. *Demography, 23*, 231-245.

Braver, S., Fitzpatrick, P., & Bay, C. (1991). Noncustodial parent's report of child support payments. *Family Relations, 40*, 180-185.

Bumpass, L., & Sweet, J. (1989). Children's experience in single-parent families: Implications of cohabitation and marital transitions. *Family Planning Perspectives, 21*, 256-260.

Burkhauser, R., Duncan, G., Hauser, R., & Berntsen, R. (1991). Wife or frau, women do worse: A comparison of men and women in the United States and Germany after marital dissolution. *Demography, 28*, 353-360.

Chambers, D. (1979). *Making fathers pay: The enforcement of child support*. Chicago: University of Chicago Press.

David, M., & Flory, T. (1989). Changes in marital status and short-term income dynamics. In the U.S. Bureau of the Census (Ed.), *Individuals and families in transition: Understanding change through longitudinal data* (pp. 15-22). Washington, DC: U.S. Bureau of the Census.

Duncan, G., Coe, R., & Hill, M. (1984). The dynamics of poverty. In G. Duncan (Ed.), *Years of poverty, years of plenty* (pp. 33-70). Ann Arbor: University of Michigan Press.

Duncan, G., & Hoffman, S. (1985). A reconsideration of the economic consequences of marital dissolution. *Demography, 22*, 485-497.

Eggebeen, D., & Lichter, D. (1991). Race, family structure, and changing poverty among American children. *American Sociological Review, 56*, 801-817.

Family Support Act of 1988, The. (1989). *Focus, 11,* 15-18. Madison: University of Wisconsin-Madison Institute for Research on Poverty.

Furstenberg, F., Nord, C. W., Peterson, J. L., & Zill, N. (1983). The life course of children of divorce: Marital disruption and parental contact. *American Sociological Review, 48,* 656-668.

Garfinkel, I. (1988). Child support assurance: A new tool for achieving social security. In A. Kahn & S. Kamerman (Eds.), *Child support* (pp. 328-342). Newbury Park, CA: Sage.

Garfinkel, I., & McLanahan, S. (1986). *Single mothers and their children.* Washington, DC: Urban Institute.

Garfinkel, I., & Oellerich, D. (1989). Noncustodial fathers' ability to pay child support. *Demography, 26,* 219-233.

Garfinkel, I., Oellerich, D., & Robins, P. (1991). Child support guidelines: Will they make a difference? *Journal of Family Issues, 12,* 404-429.

Hess, R., & Camara, K. (1979). Postdivorce family relationships as mediating factors in the consequences of divorce for children. *Journal of Social Issues, 35,* 79-96.

Hetherington, E. M., Cox, M., & Cox, R. (1982). Effects of divorce on parents and children. In M. Lamb (Ed.), *Nontraditional families* (pp. 233-288). Hillsdale, NJ: Lawrence Erlbaum.

Hill, M. S. (1984). *PSID analysis of matched pairs of ex-spouses: Relation of economic resources and new family obligations to child support payments.* Unpublished manuscript, Institute for Social Research, University of Michigan.

Hoffman, S., & Duncan, G. (1988). What are the economic consequences of divorce? *Demography, 25,* 641-645.

Lerman, R. (1987). *Child support and dependency.* Report prepared for U.S. Department of Health and Human Services under contract HHS-CS-100-86-0021.

London. K. (1990). Cohabitation, marriage, marital dissolution, and remarriage: United States, 1988. *Advance data from vital and health statistics, No. 194.* Hyattsville, MD: National Center for Health Statistics.

Martin, T., & Bumpass, L. (1989). Recent trends in marital disruption. *Demography, 26,* 37-51.

McLanahan, S. (1985). Family structure and the reproduction of poverty. *American Journal of Sociology, 90,* 873-901.

McLanahan, S., & Bumpass, L. (1988). Intergenerational consequences of family disruption. *American Journal of Sociology, 94,* 130-152.

Morgan, S.P., Lye, D., & Condran, G. (1988). Sons, daughters, and the risk of marital disruption. *American Journal of Sociology, 94,* 110-129.

O'Connell, M., & Bloom, D. (1987). Juggling jobs and babies: America's child care challenge. *Population Bulletin, No. 12.* Population Reference Bureau.

Paasch, K. M., & Teachman, J. D. (1991). Gender of children and receipt of assistance from absent fathers. *Journal of Family Issues, 12,* 450-466.

Peterson, J., & Nord, C. W. (1990). The regular receipt of child support: A multi-step process. *Journal of Marriage and the Family, 52,* 539-552.

Presser, H. (1986). Shift work among American women and child care. *Journal of Marriage and the Family, 48,* 551-563.

Presser, H., & Baldwin, W. (1980). Child care as a constraint on employment: Prevalence, correlates, and bearing on the work and fertility nexus. *American Journal of Sociology, 85,* 1202-1213.

Robins, P. K., & Dickinson, K. P. (1984). Receipt of child support by single-parent families. *Social Service Review, 58*, 622-641.

Sawhill, I. (1976). Discrimination and poverty among women who head families. *Signs, 2*, 201-211.

Seltzer, J. (1991). Legal custody arrangements and children's economic welfare. *American Journal of Sociology, 96*, 895-929.

Stack, C. (1974) *All our kin*. New York: Harper & Row.

Teachman, J. D. (1990). Socioeconomic resources of parents and award of child support in the United States: Some exploratory models. *Journal of Marriage and the Family, 52*, 689-700.

Teachman, J. D. (1991a). Who pays: The receipt of child support in the United States. *Journal of Marriage and the Family, 53*, 759-772.

Teachman, J. D. (1991b). Contributions to children by divorced fathers. *Social Problems, 38*, 358-371.

U.S. Bureau of the Census. (1980). *Statistical abstract of the United States: 1980*. Washington, DC: Government Printing Office.

U.S. Bureau of the Census. (1991a). *Statistical abstract of the United States: 1991*. Washington, DC: Government Printing Office.

U.S. Bureau of the Census. (1991b). Money income of households, families and persons in the United States: 1990. *Current Population Reports* (Series P-60, No. 174, August 1991). Washington, DC: Government Printing Office.

U.S. Bureau of the Census. (1991c). Marital status and living arrangements: March 1990. *Current Population Reports* (Series P-20, No. 450, May 1991). Washington, DC: Government Printing Office.

U.S. Bureau of the Census. (1991d). Poverty in the United States: 1990. *Current Population Reports* (Series P-60, No. 175, August 1991). Washington, DC: Government Printing Office.

U.S. Bureau of the Census. (1991e). Child support and alimony: 1989. *Current Population Reports* (Series P-60, No. 173, September 1991). Washington, DC: Government Printing Office.

U.S. Bureau of the Census. (1991f). Measuring the effect of benefits and taxes on income and poverty: 1990. *Current Population Reports* (Series P-60, No. 176, August 1991). Washington, DC: Government Printing Office.

U.S. Department of Health & Human Services. (1991a). *Monthly vital statistics report* (Vol. 39, No. 12, Supp. 2). Washington, DC: Government Printing Office.

U.S. Department of Health & Human Services. (1991b). *Monthly vital statistics report: Advance report of final natality statistics, 1989* (Vol. 40, No. 8). Washington, DC: Government Printing Office.

Wright, D., & Price, S. (1986). Court ordered child support: The effect of former spouse relationship on compliance. *Journal of Marriage and the Family, 48*, 869-874.

5

A Social Exchange Model of Nonresidential Parent Involvement

SANFORD L. BRAVER
SHARLENE A. WOLCHIK
IRWIN N. SANDLER
VIRGIL L. SHEETS

The past two decades have seen an unprecedented increase in the proportion of families experiencing divorce. This increase in prevalence has not been matched by a corresponding understanding of the nature of post-divorce familial relationships. One problem that has hampered this understanding is the lack of a coherent theory to guide the development of programmatic research. While theorizing is plentiful concerning the intact nuclear family (Burr, Hill, Nye, & Reiss, 1979), and there is substantial conceptual work on why adult relationships dissolve (Duck, 1982; Guttentag & Secord, 1983; Levinger, 1976), there is very little theoretical writing on the structure of family relationships after divorce.[1]

One potentially fruitful approach is to divide the post-divorce family into dyadic units for purposes of empirical and conceptual analysis. There are at least three dyadic relationships available for study post-divorce: the mother-father relationship, the residential parent-child

AUTHORS' NOTE: The writing of this chapter was facilitated by Grant 1RO1HD/MR19383, titled "Non-Custodial Parents: Parents Without Children," from the National Institute of Child Health and Human Development, and by Grant 1PC50MH39246, titled "Center for the Prevention of Child and Family Stress," from the National Institute of Mental Health.

dyad, and the nonresidential parent-child dyad. There also may be a fourth, sibling-sibling relationship in multichild families.[2]

The Importance of the Nonresidential Parent-Child Dyad

Of these, the nonresidential parent-child dyad[3] has received the least attention, though it seems especially worthy of theoretical development for three reasons. First, the nonresidential parent-child relationship is very likely to change substantially post-divorce, and explaining this change will require theory. Second, this relationship appears the most variable across families. Many fathers maintain extremely strong bonds with their children post-divorce,[4] and many become even more involved with their children post-divorce than they were before the divorce (Hetherington, Cox, & Cox, 1978; Wallerstein & Kelly, 1980a). However, most nonresidential parents gradually discontinue their relationships with their children after the divorce and eventually cease to play an active role in their children's lives (Fulton, 1979; Furstenberg & Nord, 1985; Furstenburg, Nord, Peterson, & Zill, 1983; Seltzer, 1991; Wallerstein & Kelly, 1980a). Although there are some recent data that indicate this tendency is diminishing,[5] there is little doubt that the assertion still applies to many fathers. This kind of variability and heterogeneity call for theoretical explanation.

Third, the strength of the nonresidential parent-child bond post-divorce is important because it has several crucial ramifications for the child. A poor-quality or low-quantity nonresidential parent-child relationship frequently has been shown to be detrimental to the child's psychological well-being, social adjustment, and academic performance (Camara & Resnick, 1987; Guidibaldi, Cleminshaw, Perry, & McLaughlin, 1983; Hess & Camara, 1979).[6]

Nonresidential parents with weak bonds to their children may also abandon their children financially by failing to pay court-ordered child support, thus imposing economic hardship on their children (Seltzer, Schaeffer, & Charng, 1989; Teachman & Paasch, this volume). Although estimates of the scope of the nonpayment problem vary considerably (e.g., Braver, Fitzpatrick & Bay, 1991; Peterson & Nord, 1990; Seltzer, 1991; Sonenstein & Calhoun, 1988; U.S. Bureau of the Census, 1980), there is little doubt that child support nonpayment remains a serious, highly variable, and poorly understood issue.

For these reasons, development of a theoretical model to elucidate the post-divorce nonresidential parent-child relationship seems critical. But what would such a model look like? This chapter proposes such a theory and evaluates its usefulness by relating the theory to existing findings.

A Social Exchange Perspective

We propose that the social exchange approach, a social psychological theory with an economic perspective, provides a useful perspective in predicting the nonresidential parent's involvement with the child. The social exchange approach, pioneered by Homans (1961), Blau (1964), and Thibaut and Kelley (1959), has been used frequently by past theorists to explain and predict general dyadic relationship formation, maintenance, and dissolution. More recently, the approach has been applied to the analysis of family and divorce issues (e.g., Levinger, 1976; Nye, 1979). Invariably, however, the approach was used to explain adult relationships, such as relationships between spouses or prospective spouses. It rarely has been applied to a parent-child dyad (specifically, as we attempt here, the nonresidential parent-child dyad), perhaps because the model stresses rational decision making and decision alternatives. While these concepts are of obvious utility in analyzing adult relationships and even have relevance to childbearing (e.g., Hoffman & Manis, 1982), they have not appeared compelling concepts to use in analysis of parent-child relationships, which are usually seen to involve little choice about whether to remain in the relationship. Indeed, we agree that in an intact family there is little reason to employ decision/choice concepts.

We argue, however, that the decision-making framework is indeed powerful and applicable in analyzing the nonresidential parent's involvement in the child's life post-divorce. The ending of the marital relationship may or may not simultaneously imply the end of the nonresidential parent-child relationship. The extent of the nonresidential parent's involvement with the child becomes an open question for the parent to consider at the time of separation, and reconsideration appears frequent. Evidence shows, for example, that visitation is a very mutable and fluid matter in the early post-divorce period (Bray & Berger, this volume; Hetherington, 1987).

Perceived Rewards Versus Costs

According to the social exchange approach, the concepts of perceived rewards and costs are critical in determining choices. As Nye (1979) has stated:

> The general principle . . . of the theory . . . is that humans avoid costly behavior and seek rewarding statuses, relationships, interactions, and feeling states to the end that their profits are maximized. Of course, in seeking rewards they voluntarily accept some costs; likewise in avoiding costs, some rewards are foregone, but the person . . . will choose that best outcome available, based on his perceptions of rewards and costs. (p. 12)

The theory implies that the individual assesses both the potential rewards and the potential costs of any relationship. Whether to maintain a given relationship is a rational decision based upon the person's evaluation of the reward-to-cost balance, as opposed to that of alternative relationships. People implicitly "compute" the estimated psychological "profit" (i.e., the psychological "rewards" less the "costs") of a potential or actual relationship, in deciding whether to enter into it or remain in it. Our central hypothesis is that the nonresidential parent evaluates whether to maintain a relationship with the child after divorce in terms of the relationship's anticipated costs versus its perceived rewards. *The greater the perceived rewards and the less the perceived costs of the parent-child relationship, the greater the parental involvement is predicted to be.*

To proceed further, it is useful to adapt Levinger's (1976) analogous formulation in elaboration of the rewards and costs implicitly considered by spouses evaluating the marital relationship. According to Levinger's analysis, a reward may be of two varieties: *an advantage of continuing the relationship* or *a disadvantage of terminating it.* Similarly, costs have two varieties: a disadvantage of maintaining involvement in the relationship or an advantage of terminating it. He further conceptualizes rewards and costs as three types: Affectional or Interpersonal; Material or Tangible; and Symbolic or Moral (e.g., obligations). The social exchange model we propose uses the same typology. Our model proposes that as either the affectional/interpersonal, material/tangible, and/or symbolic/moral rewards increase, the nonresidential parent's involvement with the child should increase, leading to more visitation and better child-support compliance. Conversely, as affectional/interpersonal, material/tangible, and/or symbolic/moral costs increase, the involvement with the child should decrease, leading to less visitation and less compliance with child-support obligations.

Two rather minor points of clarification are needed. The first concerns the issue of decision alternatives. In many versions of the theory, any contemplated action within a relationship is referred to a comparison value, for example Thibaut and Kelley's (1959) "comparison level for alternatives." Thus, the theory specifies that the individual will select the "most profitable" relationship from the alternatives available. In the application to the post-divorce nonresidential parent-child relationship, however, it does not seem reasonable to posit that the nonresidential parent compares this relationship to relationships with individuals other than the child, as might be appropriate for the decision of whether to divorce, for example.[7] Instead, the relevant decision alternatives include either remaining involved with or terminating the relationship with the child. Even more reasonably, we may regard the "level of involvement" as a set of alternative relationships with more or less continuous gradations. Under the latter formulation, the nonresidential parent chooses the particular level of involvement that maximizes the anticipated reward-to-cost balance.

The second point is that the assessment of rewards and costs may well occur at a rather low level of consciousness, according to recent social exchange theorists (e.g., Giles-Sims, 1987; Guttentag & Secord, 1983). Individuals may not consciously engage in deliberate or constant calculation of benefits, and they may be only dimly aware of the costs and/or rewards; even without conscious awareness, however, individuals should choose in such a way that their rewards are maximized and their costs minimized.

Specifying the Rewards and Costs
of the Nonresidential Parent-Child Dyad

To be useful in any kind of predictive way, the model must proceed beyond these generalities to specify what exactly constitutes the rewards and costs of the post-divorce relationship with the child. This is problematic, since, as Levinger (1982) notes, "the theory itself offers no special basis for analyzing the value of the varying rewards" in a relationship (p. 101). Thus, a task of the theorist is to construct what Nye (1980) calls *minitheories*[8] for specific relationships; that is, to elaborate upon the general nature of the potential rewards and costs available by enumerating a comprehensive list of the specific rewards and costs operative in specialized types of dyadic relationships. Thus, for example, when social exchange theorists Nye (1978), Scanzoni (1972), and Levinger (1976) began applying the theory to the marital relationship, potential rewards such as sexual satisfaction and child-rearing assistance were specified, rewards that had not been considered when earlier theorists (Homans, 1961; Thibaut & Kelley, 1959) applied the theory to workplace, business, or friendship relationships.

In the following sections, we enumerate the types of rewards and costs applicable in evaluating the value of post-divorce relationship with the child. These rewards and costs may be considered the social exchange minitheory of the post-divorce nonresidential parent-child relationship.

The full list of the reward-cost factors predicted to impact level of involvement with child is contained in Table 5.1, divided into our 3×2 classification scheme. As we discuss them below, we review extant studies that help assess the importance of the respective reward/cost factor in predicting involvement. While child support payment and visitation are the two observable manifestations of the level of involvement construct according to our model, we do not predict that all specific rewards and costs affect the two manifestations equally. Some may apply more to visitation, others primarily to child support. Our discussion below focuses on whichever of the two manifestations of involvement is most frequently addressed in the empirical literature.[9]

Affectional or Interpersonal Costs

This category includes aspects of the interpersonal circumstances of the nonresidential parent that make it affectively costly to continue a strong level of support and contact with the child. These interpersonal circumstances include the post-divorce relationship with the child (including stressful interactions within visits), with the residential parent, and with other people, such as a new spouse and/or (step)children. Social psychologists have often recognized the importance of interpersonal affect as critical to an individual's decision to maintain any relationship. We hypothesize that for nonresidential parents, the negative feelings elicited by interactions with their ex-spouses or their children can serve to diminish their efforts to maintain a strong, healthy relationship with their children. Specifically, we predict that the cost of the relationship with the child to the nonresidential parent increases as each of the following increases:

Visitation Awkwardness

Many commentators (e.g., Dudley, 1991; Greif, 1979; Kruk, 1992; Wallerstein & Kelly, 1980a) have found that the visiting parent role lacks a well-defined prescription. It is consistent with this finding to hypothesize that this confusion affects nonresidential parents' willingness to maintain a bond with their children. "Disengaged" fathers in Kruk's (1992) study expressed an inability to adapt to the constraints of the "visiting" relationship. They reported feeling like "observers" rather than participants in their children's lives and found it easier to give up than to continue on unsure ground. Wallerstein and Kelly (1980a) report that nonresidential parents visit more when their children express pleasure during their visits and when they show no anger toward the nonresidential parent.

Visitation Painfulness

Nonresidential parents may experience much suffering about the breakup and loss of the family, which is made more acute by sporadic contact with the child. Limiting the contact may alleviate the nonresidential parent's suffering. In several studies, the brief and superficial nature of being a weekend parent reminded many nonresidential parents of their painful loss, and many report being unable to continue this type of relationship (Greif, 1979; Hetherington, Cox, & Cox, 1978; Wallerstein & Kelly, 1980a). This appears especially true for those who had been strongly involved with their children before divorce (Wallerstein & Kelly, 1980b).

Anger Toward, Conflict With, and Denigration by the Residential Parent

Since visitation is normally an occasion for contact with the residential parent, negative affect (anger) toward and/or overt conflict with the residential parent should increase the negative side effects (i.e., costs) of visiting. There is little empirical research assessing the relationship of visiting with anger; however, at least one researcher (Ahrons, 1983) found no correlation between the nonresidential parent's anger at the ex-spouse and visitation.[10]

Interparental conflict, however, has been consistently associated with low levels of visitation (Greif, 1979; Kruk, 1992).[11] In fact, Dudley (1991) found that conflict with the ex-spouse was the most common

Table 5.1 The Factors in the Social Exchange Model Predicted to Impact Nonresidential Parent's Involvement With the Child

Affectional or Interpersonal Costs	*Affectional or Interpersonal Rewards*
• Visitation experienced as awkward, stressful, disturbing, or unpleasant. • Limited relationship to the child and family is regarded by the nonresidential parent as painful. • Anger at the ex-spouse. • Conflict with the ex-spouse. • Denigration by the ex-spouse. • Visitation discouraged, interfered with, prevented or threatened by the residential parent. • Relationship with child interferes with or prevents interaction in other enjoyable interpersonal relationships, such as with friends or family. • Relationship with the child interferes with interaction with a new partner or spouse, or new children or stepchildren. • If the new partner opposes or is irritated by the relationship between the nonresidential parent and child • If there is friction between the new partner and child • If there is friction between the child and new children introduced as the result of new romantic relationships.	• Visitation relieves loneliness. • Visiting relationship regarded as beneficial for the child. • Relationship supported by significant others such as important family and friends.
Material or Tangible Costs	*Material or Tangible Rewards*
• Perceived or actual privation or economic hardship of meeting the child support obligation. • The financial costs of visitation. • The competing nonsocial time demands upon the nonresidential parent, such as work demands and household tasks.	• The perceived costs in time and money of discontinuing child support.

Symbolic or Moral Costs	*Symbolic or Moral Rewards*
• Child support is considered abused by the residential parent. • Child support obligation considered unfair. • Dissatisfied with the divorce settlement (e.g., property settlement, custody arrangement) or divorce system considered unfair. • Nonresidential parent's lack of control over aspects of the post-divorce relationship with the child.	• The symbolic commitment to the parent role. • Guilt over marital disruption. • Moral obligation to honor agreements.

reason given by fathers for infrequent visits, cited by one-third of the sample. Of course, it is possible that much of this conflict results from blocked visitation, rather than being a cause for the nonresidential parent to reduce visitation.

Also, visitation may directly expose the nonresidential parent to derogatory personal remarks ("bad-mouthing") made to others (including the children) by the residential parent. While nonresidential parents commonly offer the bad-mouthing they experience as a reason for their limited contact with their children (Dudley, 1991), there is little confirming evidence of the effect, either via residential parents' reports or via correlations between contact and derogation.

The costs listed above illustrate the need for an important theoretical caveat. Normatively, anger at the ex-spouse constitutes a cost of involvement. But there may be idiographic exceptions, such as the nonresidential parent who visits primarily because doing so will irritate the ex-spouse. For such an individual, counter to the normative prediction, as anger subsides, visitation will decrease. Similarly, derogation may, contrary to normative prediction, be a spur to more visitation as a means of proving the allegations false. In these scenarios, the normative identification of a cost or reward may be reversed in individual cases.

Similar exceptions are possible with all of the costs or rewards listed below. These scenarios exemplify the problems of minitheory construction within the social exchange perspective. To the degree that such idiographic construals of rewards and costs cumulate, they will reduce the strength of the hypothesized associations. If they are the rule rather than the exception, there is cause to change the characterization of the factor from cost to reward. On the other hand, if the factor relates significantly in the direction hypothesized despite the possibility in principle of such idiographic exceptions, support is provided for the minitheory in particular and for the social exchange perspective in general.

Discouraged or Blocked Visitation

Obviously, literal visitation interference or denial by definition impedes the nonresidential parent's relationship with the child. Braver et al. (1991) found that one-quarter to one-third of the residential mothers in their sample actively impeded visits by the nonresidential parent (see also Dudley, 1991; Johnston, this volume; Wallerstein & Kelly, 1980a).

Less forceful discouragement or threat also should increase the costs of visiting. Several researchers (Arditti, 1991; Braver & Bay, in press; Koch & Lowery, 1984; Kruk, 1992; Tepp, 1983) have found that lack of encouragement for visiting by the residential parent diminishes the nonresidential parent-child relationship. In contrast, a positive relationship between the ex-spouses may be critical to the development of a durable nonresidential parent-child bond (Ahrons, 1983; Camara & Resnick, 1987, 1988; Dudley, 1991; Koch & Lowery, 1984; Kruk, 1992; Wallerstein & Kelly, 1980a).

Effects of Involvement on Other Interpersonal Relationships

Another affectional cost is the degree to which the relationship with the child interferes with other desirable social activities, such as socializing with friends. Of special interest is interference with interaction with a new romantic partner or spouse, or with new children or stepchildren. This tends to arise when the new partner either opposes or is irritated by the relationship between the nonresidential parent and child; when there is friction between the new partner and child; or when there is friction between the child and new children introduced by new romantic relationships. In social exchange language, the cost here is that of foregoing or avoiding alternative rewards.

While few nonresidential parents admit that they fail to visit or support their children because of competing social demands (Dudley, 1991), there is some evidence that this happens. For instance, Braver and Bay (in press) found that the existence of a new love relationship diminished visiting. Bray and Berger (this volume) review a number of studies that show similar tendencies for reduced contact among remarried nonresidential parents (e.g., Tepp, 1983). There is also evidence that child support is reduced when the payer remarries or supports new children (Cassety, 1978; Pearson & Thoennes, 1986; Wallerstein & Huntington, 1983), although this finding is not replicated in recent nationwide research (Seltzer, Schaefer, & Charng, 1989).

Affectional or Interpersonal Rewards

This category concerns the ways in which the nonresidential parent benefits interpersonally from a close and supportive relationship with the child. For example, the relief from loneliness experienced while visiting, and the social approval received from significant others for involvement, are interpersonal rewards. Specifically, we predict that the reward value of the relationship with the child increases as each of the following increases:

The Relief From Loneliness

Wallerstein and Kelly (1980a) report that for some nonresidential parents, visitation is regarded explicitly as a means of relieving the loneliness they might otherwise experience. Hence, we predict that lonelier nonresidential parents should visit more.

The Belief That Involvement is Beneficial for the Child

Tepp (1983) found a significant positive correlation between nonresidential fathers' beliefs that visits are good for their children and the frequency of their visitation. Camara and Resnick (1987) found that nonresidential fathers who felt competent as parents were more likely to have frequent visits. Dudley (1991) noted that many nonresidential parents who do not visit their children report this to be in their children's best interests. Indeed, about 25% of such parents reported having substance abuse or emotional problems that could have interfered with their parenting, lending some credence to their claims.

Receiving Social Approval for Involvement

To the degree that the relationship with the child is supported and promoted by significant others, such as grandparents (Hetherington, 1989) and other important family and friends, we would expect more involvement and support. The current social climate promotes more father involvement (Lamb, 1976) and more strongly condemns child-support noncompliance (Braver, Fitzpatrick, & Bay, 1991) than previously. We expect involvement to increase for those nonresidential parents more strongly subjected to such social approval and disapproval.

Material Costs

In this category are the tangible costs in time or money required for the nonresidential parent to maintain a close relationship with the child. Economic privations and competing nonsocial demands on the nonresidential parent's time are examples of material costs. Specifically, we predict that the cost to the nonresidential parent of the relationship with the child increases as each of the following increases:

Perceived and/or Actual Economic Hardship of Child Support

A nonresidential parent who experiences difficulty paying child support is more likely to terminate both child support payment (Beller & Graham, 1986; Braver, Fitzpatrick, & Bay, 1991; Chambers, 1979; Peterson & Nord, 1990) and the visiting relationship with the child (Wallerstein & Kelly, 1980a). However, the causal sequence of this relation is unclear and awaits additional research (Seltzer, 1991; Seltzer, Schaeffer, & Charng, 1989).

Financial Costs of Visitation

Visits frequently involve considerable financial outlays for food and recreation. Sleepover visitation requires additional space in the home and possibly child-care expenses. Long-distance visitation involves expensive transportation costs, particularly if the child is too young to travel alone. The higher these material costs, the lower the level of involvement is expected to be.

There is considerable support for this factor in the empirical literature. One of the most important predictors of visitation is the distance between the nonresidential parent's and the residential parent's homes (Furstenberg et al., 1983). Dudley (1991) also found that 15% of nonresidential parents who have infrequent contact with their children report that it is the physical distance and the cost of overcoming it that constrain their visitation. Equally important, most of these nonresidential parents reported visiting more frequently when they lived closer to their children. The validity of such reports is also supported by Seltzer, Schaeffer, and Charng (1989), who found that nonresidential parents who live in different states than their families are much less likely to visit the children or to pay child support.

Competing Nonsocial Time Demands

The expenses of visitation are not measured in money alone. Competing temporal demands also have been suggested to diminish the regularity of nonresidential parents' visits. Dudley (1991) found that several nonresidential parents reported that job demands conflicted with court-decreed visitation periods, and that visitation often lost out to job concerns. Tepp (1983) noted that frequency of visits is highly correlated with their convenience; those nonresidential parents who have other commitments tend to visit less.

Material Rewards

This category includes those factors that might be considered the benefits, in time or money, of maintaining a close and supportive relationship with the child. It is difficult to envision direct versions of such gains. Remaining involved with a child doesn't save time or money; ordinarily, it costs them. However, the social exchange perspective considers *costs foregone or avoided as rewards*. Thus, the rewards considered here are actually the avoidance of material costs of terminating the relationship; in other words, the costs (in time or money) of not paying support.[12]

Avoiding the Costs of Not Paying Child Support.

These costs would accrue to the extent that if child support were reduced or discontinued, action would be taken, such as prosecution and wage garnishment, that would entail loss of the nonresidential parent's time and/or money. For instance, Chambers (1979), Peterson and Nord (1990), and Seltzer (1991) suggest that aggressive child support collection practices, including incarceration for nonpayment, are more likely to sustain a nonresidential parent's good payment performance than are nonaggressive approaches.

Symbolic Costs

Symbolic costs pertain to violations of the individual's value system. These factors concern the moral or symbolic costs of maintaining a supportive relationship with the child.

How might such a relationship violate moral principles? An example is the belief that child support monies are not being used for the child's benefit or are not actually unnecessary. To the degree that the nonresidential parent considers these arrangements wrongful, a moral cost would be borne by continuing to abide by them. Specifically, we predict that the cost of the relationship with the child increases as each of the following increases:

Perceived Child Support Abuse

The nonresidential parent may feel that the residential parent is not using child support for the child's benefit, but rather to benefit the residential parent. Such beliefs about "child support abuse" are one of the chief complaints of fathers' groups. According to Silver and Silver (1981) (one of whom is president of Fathers' Rights of America): "Since there generally is no accounting of how [child support] is spent, what happens in actual practice is that women spend it on their own personal needs rather than on the children" (p. 151). Indeed, Haskins (1988) found that a belief that residential parents would spend the money on themselves rather than on their children is a common justification for nonpayment.

Child Support Obligation Considered Unfair

That nonresidential parents may refuse to pay child support when they consider it to be unfair is suggested in the self-reports of nonresidential parents who do not comply with their court orders. Greif (1985) noted that nonresidential fathers offered unfair court judgments (in which residential mothers received awards that were unreasonably high) and obstruction of visitation by the mother as chief reasons for failing to pay support.

The Divorce System or Settlement Considered Unfair

To the degree that the nonresidential parent considers the system or the divorce settlement (e.g., property settlement, custody arrangement) wrongful or is dissatisfied with them, the nonresidential parent would bear a moral cost by abiding by them. Kruk (1992) has found that nonresidential parents who fail to visit their children report feeling treated unfairly by the system more than did nonresidential parents who remained involved with their children.

Lack of Control

Reactance theory (Brehm, 1966) predicts that loss of control leads to negative arousal. Thus, the nonresidential parent's feeling of lack of control over aspects of the relationship with the child can be seen as a symbolic cost of continuing involvement with the child. Kruk (1992) reported that nonresidential parents who "disengaged" themselves from their children tended to feel less control about visits occurring than did nonresidential parents who remained involved. In particular, the disengaged nonresidential parents reported that visits depended on the whim of the residential parent, regardless of the visitation specified in their decrees.

Symbolic Rewards

This last category refers to moral rewards that accrue by continuing involvement with and support of the child. To the degree that the nonresidential parent has values that can be expressed by more involvement with the child, such as a symbolic commitment to the parent role, involvement is predicted to increase. Specifically, we predict that the rewards of the relationship with the child increase as each of the following increases:

Symbolic Commitment to the Parent Role

The more important the role of parent in the nonresidential parent's system of values, the more continuing the relationship with the child benefits the nonresidential parent symbolically. We are aware of only one researcher who has explicitly considered this possibility. Tepp (1983) found that a sense of responsibility to their children was significantly correlated with nonresidential fathers' reports that they visit their children.

Guilt About Divorce

To the degree that the nonresidential parent feels culpable in the marital dissolution, guilt can be exculpated by continuing to function as an active parent. Several researchers have documented that the relationship between feelings of guilt and nonresidential parents' visitation patterns is in fact negative (Ahrons, 1983; Tepp, 1983; Wallerstein & Kelly, 1980a).

Moral Obligation to Honor Agreements

If the nonresidential parent has the belief that it is morally right to maintain agreements voluntarily made, involvement is expected to increase. This presupposes that any agreement concerning visitation and child support was willingly entered into, rather than forced upon the nonresidential parent by litigation. There is substantial evidence to suggest that nonresidential parents who voluntarily enter into child-support agreements pay more support than those who do not (Beller & Graham, 1986; Peterson & Nord, 1990; Seltzer, Schaeffer, & Charng, 1989), as we hypothesized.

Evaluation of the Model

Overall, the extant evidence discussed here is generally consistent with the hypotheses generated from our model. These analyses suggest that our model is both plausible and useful in terms of organizing the existing data. However, several limitations concerning this evidence temper our conclusions. In particular, the data we have presented are frequently of limited scope; few researchers have obtained a representative sample of nonresidential parents. Similarly, the questionable validity of the measures precludes firm conclusions. Perhaps the most important weakness of past research, however, is that it was unable to address the dynamic and changing nature and interplay of the factors in the model. The analyses undertaken have almost always been cross-sectional rather than longitudinal. This precludes an examination of how the factors change and interact over time. An example is the nonresidential parent's guilt over the marital breakup; the literature cited found that less guilt predicted more involvement, contrary to our model. It might be that in the early post-divorce period, guilt leads to increased visitation, as we predicted. However, over time, substantial visitation may relieve guilty feelings, and involved parents thus may later report less guilt than less involved parents.

Causal orderings are another problem in evaluating the model. For instance, does visitation lead to a sense of parental competency? Or does parental competency lead to visitation? The latter two problems can best be clarified by conducting longitudinal studies, in which the changing nature of the factors and the interplay between them can be sorted out.

To rectify these shortcomings, the present authors are engaged in a large-scale effort to evaluate the model more definitively (Braver, Fitzpatrick, & Bay, 1991). All the factors listed in the model have been carefully measured on a representative sample of nonresidential parents.

We also employ a longitudinal design, with assessments pre-divorce, shortly after divorce, and 3 years post-divorce. Preliminary results suggest substantial support for most of the hypotheses.

Implications for Research, Policy, and Practice

A number of additional questions for future research need to be addressed. How does the system of rewards and costs combine; do some factors within a category count more than others; and do some categories of rewards/costs (e.g., symbolic) have more impact than others? Also, are all the relationships linear, as implied, or do they deviate at the extremes (for example, for parents who are a risk for their children)?

The scope of application of the model will also require investigation. Does this perspective apply equally well for female as for male nonresidential parents, for never-married parents, and for parents of various ethnicities or cultural backgrounds?

Similarly, the changing cultural and legal milieus undoubtedly affect the applicability of the model. Cultural norms regarding parenting and divorce are rapidly shifting and are accompanied by sweeping legal changes, especially in child support enforcement. What implications do these changes have for the theory? One possibility is that child support payments, which federal law will soon require to be routinely withheld from wages, will cease to be as strong a manifestation of the sense of involvement with the child, and the relation of support with visitation will be reduced.

The various factors in the model and the literature reviewed in its support also have implications for policy and practice. The two factors in the preliminary analysis of our own data set that have emerged as most powerful are the nonresidential parents' perceived lack of control over both the dissolution process and the child's activities, and the discouragement of involvement received from the ex-spouse. Both of these factors strongly predict diminished visitation and child support noncompliance longitudinally. The finding on control suggests that practice interventions that facilitate the nonresidential parents' perceptions of control, such as divorce mediation rather than litigation of the divorce settlement, should lead to increased involvement. Interestingly, we have also found (Bay & Braver, 1990) that the father's and mother's sense of control is not a zero-sum game; indeed, the two are moderately positively correlated, suggesting that the "win-win" outcome painted by mediation theory is indeed realistic.

Policy applications might be directed at enhancing both parents' sense that the divorce system is fair and just. Educational efforts for residential parents that are designed to diminish overt conflict and encourage more nonresidential parent involvement may be successful as well. Finally, the model and empirical results suggest that child support compliance can be enhanced by aggressive child support enforcement practices, as well as by policies that lessen the economic hardship to the nonresidential parent of child support payment and visitation, such as job training and enhancement programs.

Notes

1. Notable exceptions are Hetherington and Camara (1984) and Ahrons and Rodgers (1987).

2. The role of extended kin, such as grandparents, in the post-divorce family has been neglected until recently. See Bray and Berger (1990); Gladstone (1989); and Hetherington (1989).

3. In about 90% of American families, the nonresidential parent is the father (Glick, 1989).

4. This appears especially true where joint legal custody prevails (Maccoby, Depner, & Mnookin, 1988; Pearson & Thoennes, 1990).

5. In our own data set, for example (Bay & Braver, 1990; Braver & Bay, in press; Braver, Fitzpatrick, & Bay, 1991; Braver, Wolchik, Sandler, Fogas, & Zvetina, 1991), at the third year post-divorce, only 11% of the nonresidential parents reported that they had not seen their children at all in the past year.

6. However, investigators (Healy, Malley, & Stewart, 1990; Johnston, Kline, & Tschann, 1989) have found that when the level of conflict between the parents is excessive, high levels of contact with the nonresidential parent can be equally detrimental to the child.

7. The choice between alternative relationships formulation may be appropriate, however, when stepchildren or subsequent children are present.

8. Huesman and Levinger (1976) use the term *sub-theories.*

9. It should be noted, however, that our model predicts the two manifestations, having a common cause, will substantially covary. Such a relationship has frequently been found (Arditti, 1991; Fox, 1985; Pearson & Thoennes, 1986; Peterson & Nord, 1990; Seltzer, 1991; Seltzer, Schaeffer, & Charng, 1989; Wallerstein & Huntington, 1983).

10. Interestingly, the anger of residential parents was predictive of visitation in Ahrons' (1983) study.

11. This might be in the child's best interests, however. See note 6.

12. In principle, this category should also consider the material or tangible rewards of maintaining visitation. However, while not paying child support does engender such tangible rewards, not visiting ordinarily does not, except in those states where statutes permit the child support obligation to be reduced by abundant visitation. Accordingly, we make a prediction for child support but not visitation.

References

Ahrons, C. R. (1983). Predictors of paternal involvement postdivorce: Mothers' and fathers' perceptions. *Journal of Divorce, 6*, 55-69.

Ahrons, C. R., & Rodgers, R. H. (1987). *Divorced families: A multidisciplinary developmental view.* New York: Norton.

Arditti, J. A. (1991). Child support noncompliance and divorced fathers: Rethinking the role of paternal involvement. *Journal of Divorce and Remarriage, 14*, 107-118.

Bay, R. C., & Braver, S. L. (1990). Perceived control of the divorce settlement process and interparental conflict. *Family Relations, 39*, 382-387.

Beller, A. H., & Graham, J. W. (1986). The determinants of child-support income. *Social Science Quarterly, 67*, 353-364.

Blau, P. M. (1964). *Exchange and power in social life.* New York: John Wiley.

Braver, S. L., & Bay, R. C. (in press). Assessing and compensating for self-selection bias (nonrepresentativeness) of the family research sample. *Journal of Marriage and the Family.*

Braver, S. L., Fitzpatrick, P., & Bay, R. C. (1991). Non-custodial parents' report of child-support payments. *Family Relations, 40*, 180-185.

Braver, S. L., Wolchik, S., Sandler, I., Fogas, B. S., & Zvetina, D. (1991). Frequency of visitation by divorced fathers: Differences in reports by fathers and mothers. *American Journal of Orthopsychiatry, 61*, 448-454.

Bray, J. H., & Berger, S. H. (1990). Noncustodial parent and grandparent relationships in stepfamilies. *Family Relations, 39*, 414-419.

Brehm, J. W. (1966). *Psychological reactance: A theory of freedom and control.* New York: Academic Press.

Burr, W., Hill, R., Nye, F. I., & Reiss, I. (Eds.), (1979). *Contemporary theories about the family* (Vol. 2). New York: Free Press.

Camara, K. A., & Resnick, G. (1987). The interaction between marital and parental subsystems in mother-custody, father-custody, and two-parent households: Effects on children's social development. In J. P. Vincent (Ed.), *Advances in family intervention, assessment and theory* (Vol. 4, pp. 165-196). Greenwich, CT: JAI Press.

Camara, K. A., & Resnick, G. (1988). Interparental conflict and cooperation: Factors moderating divorce, single-parenting and step-parenting on children. In E. M. Hetherington & J. Arasteh (Eds.), *The impact of divorce, single-parenting, and step-parenting on children* (pp. 169-196). Hillsdale, NJ: Lawrence Erlbaum.

Cassety, J. (1978). *Child support and public policy.* Lexington, MA: Lexington Books.

Chambers, D. L. (1979). *Making fathers pay: The enforcement of child support.* Chicago: University of Chicago Press.

Duck, S. (1982) (Ed.). *Personal relationships, 4: Dissolving personal relationships.* New York: Academic Press.

Dudley, J. R. (1991). Increasing our understanding of divorced fathers who have infrequent contact with their children. *Family Relations, 40*, 279-285.

Fox, G. L. (1985). Noncustodial fathers. In S. M. Hanson & F. W. Bozett (Eds.), *Dimensions of fatherhood* (pp. 393-415). Beverly Hills, CA: Sage.

Fulton, J. A. (1979). Parental reports of children's post-divorce adjustment. *Journal of Social Issues, 35*, 126-139.

Furstenberg, F. F. & Nord, C. W. (1985). Parenting apart: Patterns of child-rearing after divorce. *Journal of Marriage and the Family, 47*, 893-904.

Furstenberg, F. F., Nord, C. W., Peterson, J. L., & Zill, N. (1983). The life course of children of divorce: Marital disruption and parental contact. *American Sociological Review, 48*, 656-668.

Giles-Sims, J. (1987). Social exchange in stepfamilies. In K. Pasley & M. Ihinger-Tallman (Eds.), *Remarriage and step-parenting: Current research and theory* (pp. 141-163). New York: Guilford Press.

Gladstone, J. W. (1989). Grandmother-grandchild contact: The mediating influence of the middle generation following marriage breakdown and remarriage. *Canadian Journal on Aging, 8*, 355-365.

Glick, P. (1989). Remarried families, step-families, and step-children: A brief demo-graphic profile. *Family Relations, 38*, 24-27.

Greif, G. (1979). Fathers, children, and joint custody. *American Journal of Orthopsychiatry, 49*, 311-319.

Greif, G. (1985). *Single fathers*. Lexington, MA: Lexington Books.

Guidibaldi, J., Cleminshaw, H. K., Perry, J. D., & McLaughlin, C. S. (1983). The impact of parental divorce on children: Report of the nationwide NASP study. *School Psychology Review, 12*, 300-323.

Guttentag, M., & Secord, P. (1983). *Too many women? The sex-ratio question*. Beverly Hills, CA: Sage.

Haskins, R. (1988). Child support: A father's view. In S. Kamerman & A. Kahn (Eds.), *Child support: From debt collection to social policy* (pp. 306-327). Newbury Park, CA: Sage.

Healy, J. M., Malley, J. E., & Stewart, A. J. (1990). Children and their fathers after parental separation. *American Journal of Orthopsychiatry, 60*, 531-543.

Hess, R. & Camara, K. (1979). Post-divorce family relationships as mediating factors in the consequences of divorce for children. *Journal of Social Issues, 35*, 79-96.

Hetherington, E. M. (1987). Family relations six years after divorce. In K. Pasley & M. Ihinger-Tallman (Eds.), *Remarriage and step-parenting: Current research and theory* (pp.185-205). New York: Guilford Press.

Hetherington, E. M. (1989). Coping with family transitions: Winners, losers, and survivors. *Child Development, 60*, 1-14.

Hetherington, E. M., & Camara, K. A. (1984). Families in transition: The processes of dissolution and reconstitution. In R. D. Parks (Ed.), *Review of child development research: Vol. 7. The family* (pp. 398-439). Chicago: University of Chicago Press.

Hetherington, E. M., Cox, M., & Cox, R. (1978). The aftermath of divorce. In J. H. Stevens & M. Mathews (Eds.), *Mother/child, father/child relationships* (pp. 110-155). Washington, DC: National Association for the Education of Young Children.

Hoffman, L. W., & Manis, J. D. (1982). The value of children in the United States. In F. I. Nye (Ed.), *Family relationships: Rewards and costs* (pp. 143-170). Beverly Hills, CA: Sage.

Homans, G. C. (1961). *Social behavior: Its elementary forms*. New York: Harcourt Brace Jovanovich.

Huesman, L. R., & Levinger, G. (1976). Incremental exchange theory: A formal model for progression in dyadic social interaction. In L. Berkowitz & E. Walster (Eds.), *Advances in experimental social psychology* (pp. 191-229). New York: Academic Press.

Johnston, J., Kline, M., & Tschann, J. (1989). Ongoing post-divorce conflict: Effects on children of joint custody and frequent access. *American Journal of Orthopsychiatry, 59*, 576-592.

Koch, M. A., & Lowery, C. R. (1984). Visitation and the noncustodial father. *Journal of Divorce, 8*, 47-65.

Kruk, E. (1992). Psychological and structural factors contributing to the disengagement of noncustodial fathers after divorce. *Family and Conciliation Courts Review, 30*, 81-101.

Lamb, M. (Ed.). (1976). *The role of the father in child development.* New York: John Wiley.

Levinger, G. (1976). A social-psychological perspective on marital dissolution. *Journal of Social Issues, 32*, 21-47.

Levinger, G. (1982). A social exchange view on the dissolution of pair relationships. In F. I. Nye (Ed.), *Family relationships: Rewards and costs* (pp. 97-122). Beverly Hills, CA: Sage.

Maccoby, E., Depner, C., & Mnookin, R. (1988). Child custody following divorce. In E. M. Hetherington & J. D. Arasteh (Eds.), *Impact of divorce, single-parenting, and step-parenting on children* (pp. 91-114). Hillsdale, NJ: Lawrence Erlbaum.

Nye, F. I. (1978). Is choice and exchange theory the key? *Journal of Marriage and the Family, 40*, 219-233.

Nye, F. I. (1979). Choice, exchange, and the family. In W. Burr, R. Hill, F. I. Nye, & I. Reiss (Eds.), *Contemporary theories about the family* (Vol. 2, pp. 1-41). New York: Free Press.

Nye, F. I. (1980). Family mini-theories as special instances of choice and exchange theory. *Journal of Marriage and the Family, 42*, 479-489.

Pearson, J., & Thoennes, N. (1986). Will this divorced woman receive child support? *Minnesota Family Law Journal, 3*, 65-71.

Pearson, J., & Thoennes, N. (1990). Custody after divorce: Demographic and attitudinal patterns. *American Journal of Orthopsychiatry, 60*, 233-249.

Peterson, J. L., & Nord, C. W. (1990). The regular receipt of child support: A multistep process. *Journal of Marriage and the Family, 52*, 539-551.

Scanzoni, J. (1972). *Sexual bargaining.* New York: Free Press.

Seltzer, J. A. (1991). Relationships between fathers and children who live apart: The father's role after separation. *Journal of Marriage and the Family, 53*, 79-101.

Seltzer, J. A., Schaeffer, N. C., & Charng, H. (1989). Family ties after divorce: The relationship between visiting and paying child-support. *Journal of Marriage and the Family, 51*, 1013-1032.

Silver, G. A., & Silver, M. (1981). *Weekend fathers: For divorced fathers, second wives, and grandparents.* Los Angeles: Stratford Press.

Sonenstein, F. L., & Calhoun, C. A. (1988). *Survey of absent parents: pilot results.* Paper presented to the Western Economic Association, Los Angeles.

Tepp, A. V. (1983). Divorced fathers: Predictors of continued paternal involvement. *American Journal of Psychiatry, 140*, 1465-1469.

Thibaut, J. W., & Kelley, H. (1959). *The social psychology of groups.* New York: John Wiley.

U. S. Bureau of the Census. (1980). Child-support and alimony: 1978. *Current population reports* (Series P-23, No. 106). Washington, DC: Government Printing Office.

Wallerstein, J. S., & Huntington, D. S. (1983). Bread and roses: Nonfinancial issues related to fathers' economic support of their children following divorce. In J. Cassety (Ed.), *The parental child-support obligation* (pp. 135-156). Lexington, MA: Lexington Books.

Wallerstein, J. S., & Kelly, J. B. (1980a). Effects of divorce on the visiting father-child relationship. *American Journal of Psychiatry, 137*, 1534-1539.

Wallerstein, J. S., & Kelly, J. B. (1980b). *Surviving the break up: How children and parents cope with divorce.* New York: Basic Books.

6

Children of Divorce
Who Refuse Visitation

JANET R. JOHNSTON

In the United States, more than one million children experience the divorce of their parents each year. The majority of these children (85% to 90%) will reside primarily with their mothers; and their fathers, in general, will have visitation rights (Glick, 1988). Estimates vary of the extent to which, for whatever reasons, visitation rights are not exercised, with the result that the child no longer has any contact with the nonresidential parent. In their national study, Furstenberg and his colleagues estimated that in almost one-half of divorcing families, there was no contact between one parent and the child 2 years following the divorce (Furstenberg, Nord, Peterson, & Zill, 1983). More recent studies suggest the rate of failure to visit is somewhat lower, that is, one-tenth to one-third (Braver, Wolchik, Sandler, & Sheets, this volume; Bray & Berger, this volume; Maccoby & Mnookin, 1992). It is not known whether these varying estimates reflect sampling biases or geographical and cohort differences.

Children's reluctance or refusal to visit a noncustodial parent has rarely been investigated in the prominent studies of divorce (e.g., Furstenberg & Nord, 1985; Hetherington, Cox, & Cox, 1982; Maccoby & Mnookin, 1992). Hence the contribution of the child to the nonresidential parent's diminished involvement or failure to maintain contact has not

AUTHOR'S NOTE: The research on which this chapter is based was made possible by grants from the San Francisco Foundation, the Morris Stulsaft Foundation, the Van Loben Sels Foundation, the Zellerbach Family Fund, and the Gerbode Foundation.

been adequately considered. In fact, it is probably difficult to estimate the extent to which disengagement results from voluntary withdrawal of the parent or from being pushed out or excluded by the child (as well as by the residential parent), because the dropping out is likely to be a subtle process of reaction and counterreaction to the mutual disappointment inherent in a failed relationship.

A small proportion of nonresidential parents apparently do not disappear from their children's lives without protest, as is evidenced when the child's refusal to visit becomes the subject of litigation in the family courts. In these cases, judges are called upon to arbitrate, while mediators and therapists are called upon to resolve the problem through negotiation and counseling. Police may be asked to enforce court-ordered visitation between a reluctant child and his or her parent. Within the polemics of court litigation, the residential parent is often blamed for a child's refusal to visit: The parent may be accused of aiding and abetting the child's noncompliance, of "brainwashing" the child on behalf of the parent's own agenda. This all results in a plethora of ethical, legal, and family dilemmas that are usually regarded as being extremely difficult to resolve. The key problems are, first, whether and under what conditions visitation should be encouraged, facilitated, enforced, or denied; and, second, what the prognosis is for resolution of the problem, given alternative intervention strategies.

It is surprising that such a perplexing and serious problem as children's refusal to visit has received so little systematic attention by researchers. The purpose of this chapter is to propose some etiological factors that lead to a child's reluctance or refusal to visit a nonresidential parent, using as a database two samples of children who are the subjects of ongoing post-divorce conflict and litigation. It is not known whether these observations can be generalized to all families where the child is resisting visitation, because there are no systematic data from non-litigating families with which to compare these high-conflict families. Furthermore, inasmuch as the data analysis is exploratory, these findings are preliminary, and the explanations offered are theoretical speculations intended to stimulate more thorough investigation.

Previous Research and Clinical Observations

In previous studies and clinical reports, reluctance of a child to visit with a nonresidential parent has often been used interchangeably with, and hence confounded with, parent-child alignment (or parent-child alignment). Distinctions need to be made between these two sets of phenomena. Reluctance to visit includes a broad range of observable behavior in which the child, for any reason, verbally or gesturally complains about and resists spending time with the nonresidential parent. The resistance may be manifested only at the time of transition from one home to the other, or it may involve intermittent or ongoing complaints about visits. In extreme cases, it can encompass a complete refusal to have any contact with the other parent. It is interesting to note that, among this broadly defined category of reluctance to visit, the child may or may not be hostile or negative to the parent he or she is resistant to visiting, although, in extreme cases, there is often expressed fear and negativity.

On the other hand, parent-child alignment and its counterpart, parent-child alienation, are defined as the child's making an overt or covert attitudinal or behavioral preference for one divorced parent and, to varying degrees, denigrating and rejecting the other parent. By definition, then, this phenomenon involves a negative, conflictual, or avoidant relationship between the child and the rejected parent, whether that is the residential or the nonresidential parent. In extreme cases of a strong alignment with a residential parent, the child usually refuses to visit with the nonresidential, alienated parent. Hence, reluctance to visit and alignment/alienation are empirically overlapping but distinct phenomena.

Only one community study of divorce has provided any detailed account of children's reluctance or refusal to visit. Wallerstein and Kelly (1980) studied 131 children from 60 mother-custody families in one county in Northern California at the time of filing for divorce, with follow-ups 18 months and 5 years later. This sample was not considered to be a high-conflict litigating group. The researchers' observations were that the majority of these children were eager to visit their noncustodial fathers and often wanted more time than the usual every-other-weekend visits allowed. Those children who had infrequent visits longed for more contact and were often painfully hurt by the apparent lack of interest shown by their fathers. However, a minority, about 20% of the 131 children, were "in considerable conflict about the visits" (p. 144) and another 11% were "genuinely reluctant to visit" (p. 146); most notable were those between 9 and 18 years of age. The reasons varied: A number of children appeared to have empty, ungratifying relationships with their fathers; they did not have a warm or secure attachment to him. Visiting in the father's home was lonely, boring, alienating, and sometimes anxiety provoking; he did not comfort, soothe, or provide for their interests. Others appeared to be responding angrily in counter-rejection to an uninvolved father.

The authors of this study, however, attributed the reluctance to visit among a subset of 25 (19%) of these children to an extreme identification with one parent, referred to as "an alignment." This alignment was defined as "a divorce-specific relationship that occurs when a parent and one or more children join in a vigorous attack on the other parent" (p. 77). The alignment was seen to be fed by an angry parent who felt rejected, betrayed, and often abandoned for another partner by the separating spouse. Parent and child shared moral outrage over the deserting parent's conduct, and this evolved into "a complexly organized strategy aimed at harassing the former spouse and sometimes at shaming him or her into returning to the marriage . . . the unspoken agenda was revenge" (p. 78).

In the Wallerstein and Kelly sample, twice as many children united with the mother as with the father, and most of the aligned children were in the 9-to-12-year age range. While alignments with the noncustodial parent did not appear to last past the first postseparation year, maternal alignments were remarkably stable through the 18-month follow-up. This is possibly because all of these children were in primary custody of the mother. Children in these alignments were clinically assessed to be less psychologically healthy; their mothers were disturbed, angry women, who appeared to be using the child's allegiance in a campaign to ward off their own depression. Cross-gender alignments appeared to be most common.

Gardner (1987), whose clinical practice largely involved court evaluations on behalf of parents litigating custody and visitation of their children, coined the term *parent alienation syndrome* to describe the phenomenon of children's stubborn refusal to visit. He estimated that 90% of protracted custody conflicts involve this syndrome, in which the child is preoccupied with deprecation and criticism of a parent, which may be exaggerated or unjustified. Gardner believes that the etiology of the disorder is predominantly with the behavior and attitudes of the aligned parent, usually the mother. The mother is either involved consciously in a systematic programming of the child to denigrate the father or is unconsciously transmitting her own angry, hurt, humiliated, vengeful attitudes to the child.

Gardner does acknowledge that child attributes partially account for the condition. He notes that some of these children are basically more psychologically bonded with the aligned parent and become even more so as the parental conflict threatens that bond. Other children are actually afraid of the intensity of one parent's rage and align with that parent through fear of being rejected or abandoned themselves. Fear of loss of love hence underlies an anxious attachment to the aligned parent. Gardner has not considered age and gender effects in such alignments, though he does make passing reference to age-appropriate Oedipal conflicts that can exacerbate the problem. Other "situational factors" are noted; specifically, primary residence with the aligned parent is seen to consolidate the alignment.

Gardner recommends radical treatment in extreme cases of the parent-alienation syndrome by forcibly removing the child from the custody of the aligned parent and placing him or her with the "hated" other parent. When the conflict is played out in the courtroom, where attorneys and therapists are involved in litigation of these cases, this radical intervention stance has resulted in the major portion of the blame for the problem being placed upon the parent who is believed to fuel the child's alienation. That is, less attention is being paid to what the child brings to the situation, whereas the hated parent is viewed entirely as the victim.

Method

Two separate studies were undertaken of divorcing families who represent the more ongoing and entrenched disputes over custody and visitation. The first sample consisted of 80 divorcing parents disputing custody and visitation of 100 children (ages 1 to 12 years), about which we have published extensively elsewhere (e.g., Johnston & Campbell, 1988). They were referred by four family courts in the San Francisco Bay Area for counseling and mediation between 1982 and 1984. The parents had either failed to reach agreements in court-mandated mediation, or they were still disputing after a stipulation by the parties or an order imposed by the court. The sample was multiethnic: 64% Caucasian, 13% Hispanic, 8% African-American, 8% Asian, and 8% other. Socioeconomic status was varied and they had individual low-middle incomes (median $10,000 to $15,000 per annum). The parents had been separated, on average, for more than 2 years after a mean marriage duration of almost 7 years. Six percent had never been married to each other. Almost one-third were involved in post-decree litigation.

The second sample comprised 60 divorcing parents with 75 children (ages 3 to 12 years), who were referred from two family courts in the San Francisco Bay Area during 1989-1990 because of violence between the parents and/or ongoing conflict of a nonviolent kind over custody and visitation (Johnston, 1992). On average, parents had been separated for more than 3 years after 8 years of marriage. Fifteen percent had never been married to each other. Half were involved in post-decree litigation. The ethnic composition of this sample was 80% Caucasian, 3% African-American, 8% Hispanic, 3% Asian, and 5% other. Socioeconomically, they were very diverse, with median individual incomes of $18,000 to $25,000 per annum.

In the first study, 56% of the children were in the physical custody of their mothers, 14% were in father custody, and 30% were in the joint custody of their parents. Children in mother custody spent an average of 5 days per month and those in father custody spent an average of almost 7 days per month visiting the noncustodial parent. Those in the sole custody of either parent made an average of one to two transitions per week. Children in joint custody spent an average of 12 days each month with the least-seen parent and made two to three transitions each week between parental homes.

In the second study, sole physical custody to mother was in effect for 57% of the children, who saw their fathers on the average of 6 days each month and made two transitions each week between parents. Sole father custody was in effect for 7% of the children, who spent a mean of 9 days per month with mother and made one transition each week. Thirty-six percent of the children were in the joint custody of their parents, and they had contact with the least-seen parent on the average of 15 days each month and made two transitions between parental homes each week.

Procedures and Measures

In both samples, parents were interviewed separately at intake to obtain a full history; were administered a battery of standardized measures; and were seen in structured observation with their children, all of which has been described in detail elsewhere (Johnston, 1990, 1992). Children were also interviewed separately and assessed with standardized projective measures. Subsequently, all family members participated in counseling sessions, amounting to a total of about 25 hours of direct contact with the clinician per family over a 3- to 6-month period.

Parents in both studies evaluated their children, using the Child Behavior Checklist (CBCL) (Achenbach & Edelbrock, 1983), and evaluated the interparental relationship, using the Conflict Tactics Scale (CTS) (Straus, 1979). In the second study, the parents' own emotional dysfunction was assessed, using the Brief Symptom Inventory (BSI) (Derogatis & Spencer, 1982), and the teachers evaluated the children, using the Teacher-Child Rating Scale (TRS) (Hightower, Work, Cowan, Lotyczewski, Spinell, & Guare, 1986). Clinicians had the opportunity to evaluate the children, parents, and parent-child relationships in both studies, using factor-derived clinical rating scales (CRS) (Tschann, Johnston, Kline, & Wallerstein, 1989).

Two specific measures were used to assess children's resistance to visitation and the kinds of alignments children had with their disputing parents. The "Child's Reactions to Transitions Between Parents" was a 21-item checklist of symptoms that are commonly manifested among children in response to moving between parental homes. Four of these items involved resistance to visitation: (1) separation problems, clingy; (2) whiny, crying, fretful, weepy; (3) verbally resistant, complains about leaving/coming back; and (4) physical resistance, screams and holds on, won't leave, hides. In both studies, mothers and fathers were interviewed at intake by the clinician and asked about their child's current reactions to transitions. The clinician classified parents' responses using the checklist.

In the first study only, the counselors rated the child's attitude and behavior towards the disputing parents in terms of five possibilities: (1) acceptance of both/avoidance or preference; (2) temporary reactions; (3) shifting allegiances; (4) loyalty conflicts; (5) alignment. In both studies mild and strong alignments were distinguished. Two independent raters classified the responses, and any discrepancies in their judgments were resolved by discussion and consensus among three clinicians.

Principal Findings and Discussion

Children's resistance or refusal to visit a nonresidential parent after separation and divorce is an overt behavioral symptom that can have its roots in multiple and often interlocking psychological, developmental, and family systemic processes. Six different themes among children who are reluctant to visit are described here with accompanying empirical evidence. These are: (1) the child's basic anxiety about separating from the primary attachment figure, especially when parents are overtly conflictual with one another; (2) the child's limited cognitive capacity to be aware of both divorcing parents' opposing viewpoints and feelings, so that an alignment is a resolution to painful loyalty conflicts; (3) the intensity and longevity of parental disputes, which also make alignments more likely; (4) the child's inability to extricate his or her feelings and ideas from an emotionally distressed residential parent; (5) the child's exposure to traumatic emotional abuse and physical violence between parents; and (6) the child's sense of counter-rejection and retaliation by the rejected parent and others. It is interesting to note that the first two of these themes are developmentally appropriate responses of children. The next three themes are related to pathological parent-child and family relationships. The last theme is a tertiary, systemic process, a compounding of the problems that may arise from any one or more of the first five processes. In the analysis and intervention with any one case, it is important to consider that the child's resistance or refusal to visit can be, and often is, multidetermined.

Normal Separation Anxiety in Young Children

In both studies, which included only children 12 years of age and under, there were very high levels of resistance to visitation manifested in symptomatic behavior at the time of transition from one parental home to another, as reported by both parents. Two findings are noteworthy here.

First, younger children were markedly more resistant compared to older children, as shown by significant correlations between age and the resistance measure (see Table 6.1). Specifically, younger children were likely to manifest more separation anxiety when leaving either parent than were older children. However, younger children in general were likely to manifest more whining, crying, verbal complaints, and physical resistance to visits when separated from their mothers, compared to their fathers; that is, these children resisted transitions to the father, whereas reluctance to return to the mother was rare. There were no gender differences, except that girls tended to be more physically resistant than boys when leaving their fathers. However, the relatively small sample sizes may have precluded establishing statistical significance.

Second, there was more resistance to visitation among children in families where there was more overt verbal and physical aggression between parents. This was shown in significant correlations between the CTS scores and the resistance measure and also by the observation that resistance to visitation was generally higher in the second study, which was characterized by more severe physical violence compared to the first study (see Table 6.1).

The primary explanation for these findings—that resistance to visitation occurs more frequently among younger children mostly irrespective of gender—is that young children are more likely to react with anxiety and to protest being separated from the parent with whom they have a primary psychological attachment, and that parent is more likely to be the mother. The transition from one parent to the other commonly sets off developmentally expectable anxieties about safety and survival, especially among children younger than 3 or 4 years, who have not yet internalized an image of the primary attachment figure (Bowlby, 1969; Main, Kaplan, & Cassidy, 1985); that is, they cannot for any length of time visualize or keep in mind a memory of the absent parent, so that visitation to the nonresidential parent creates separation or abandonment anxieties. Children of this age also have not obtained object-constancy (Mahler, Pine, & Bergman, 1975); that is, they do not have a concept of self that is independent or separate from the primary parent. Instead, the young child's primitive affective-cognitions of human relations are of two kinds: There is the good, gratifying parent-me and the bad, frustrating parent-me; it is these combined images that are split off from one another. The threat of separation from the gratifying mother or primary attachment person, necessitated by the visitation schedule, activates the opposite, negative cognitive-affective experience, and the child feels frustrated, angry, bad, and alienated. These feelings are also anxiety-provoking if not frightening. Children older than 3 or 4 years may continue to have difficulty if they have had repeated distressing separations and maintain an anxious attachment to the parent. It is also possible that children under the ages of 4 or 5 do not have a sufficient understanding of the concept of time (Piaget, 1960) and, for this reason, are confused about the particular visitation schedule. Consequently, they are anxious about when they will be reunited with the primary or residential parent.

Younger children's resistance to leaving their parents may also reflect an Oedipal theme. It has been commonly observed that from about 4 through 6 years, boys become libidinally or sexually attracted to their mothers and girls to their fathers, and both are competitive with the same-gender parent. Parents' separation and divorce offer the possibility

Table 6.1   Resistance to Visitation* by Age of Child

| | Number and Percent of Children | | | | |
	2-3 years	4-5 years	6-8 years	9-12 years	Total
Study No. 1 N = 92	17 (74%)	15 (60%)	12 (63%)	14 (56%)	58 (63%)
Study No. 2 N = 63	—	15 (100%)	14 (70%)	16 (57%)	45 (71%)

NOTE: *Resistance to visitation includes separation problems, verbal complaints, and physical resistance to leaving on visits.

to children that their fantasies of possessing the mother or father could be realized. This arouses conflicts in children, anxieties about their impulses, and fears of reprisal from the same-gender parent, which may manifest in resistance to transitions between parents.

The fact that, in both studies, resistance to visitation at the time of transition between parents was greater when there had been ongoing conflict and overt aggression between parents suggests that fright engendered by overt parental quarrels may contribute to the child's resistance to visitation. Conversely, parents are more likely to be worried and dispute with each other if the child is symptomatic and reluctant to make the transition between parental homes. It appears less likely that parents' emotional dysfunction contributes to children's resistance to visitation that is manifested at the time of transition. In these studies, resistance was unrelated to the parents' degree of emotional disturbance (as measured by the BSI); neither were children who resisted visitation seen to be significantly more disturbed (as measured by the CBCL and the TRS) than those who did not resist. However, many of the high-conflict parents in this litigating population were ambivalent or skeptical of the value of visitation, especially when the child was symptomatic and resistant at transitions; these parents were not well suited to soothing the child and making the child feel safe and competent in handling the changes. The fact that children were often symptomatic at transitions but were not seen as being significantly disturbed, in general, supports the view that resistance to visitation is a developmentally expectable divorce-specific separation anxiety, which is made more intense by overt conflict between parents.

The Child's Cognitive Understanding of Parental Disputes

Reluctance or refusal to visit a nonresidential parent was found to be more common among children who had made an alignment with the residential parent. Alignment has been defined as occurring when the child, to varying degrees, shares the attitudes and opinions of the aligned parent and avoids or actively rejects the other parent. The most striking findings in this respect indicated that older children were significantly more likely to be in an alignment compared to younger children; that children were more likely to be aligned with the parent with whom they spent the majority of their time (usually the mother); and that boys were more likely to be aligned than were girls.

Figure 6.1 shows the age-specific attitudes and behavior of children in response to both disputing parents in the first study. Note that temporary reactions, which were defined as affective and behavioral distress in the immediate presence of disputing parents and acceptance of both parents at other times, predominated among 2-3-year-olds, was less frequent among 4-8-year-olds, and was absent among 9-12-year-olds. The incidence of shifting allegiances, defined as inconsistent preferences for first one parent and then the other, with corresponding swings in positive and negative affect, were most frequent among the 4-5-year-old group, less frequent among 6-8-year-olds, and relatively infrequent in the youngest and oldest children in the sample. Loyalty conflicts, defined as affective ambivalence and distress about hurting either parent, were highest in incidence among the 6-8-year-olds and were less frequent after that age. Alignments, which were defined as verbal and behavioral preference for one parent over the other, either overt or covert, showed an increased frequency with age in this sample, with three-fourths of the 9-12-year-olds in alignments, in contrast to only about one-tenth of the 2-3-year-olds. These findings were based on ratings by the clinicians who counseled the children in the first study for several months. Two-thirds of the children could be easily classified in one of the primary categories. The remaining third had mixed responses during the counseling period, especially the older children, who wavered between loyalty conflicts, alignments, and attempts to avoid a preference for either parent.

Age at separation varied greatly among the children in this study, so that clinicians were able to obtain from both mothers and fathers a

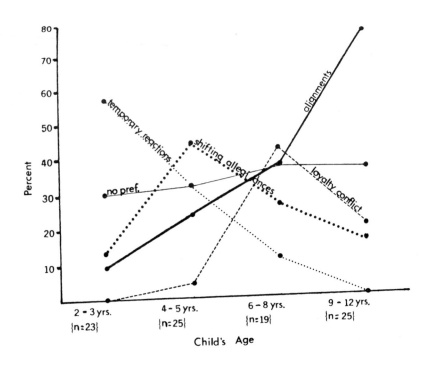

Figure 6.1. Children's Attitudes Toward Their Disputing Parents

SOURCE: Johnston, J. R., & Campbell, L. E. G. (1987). Instability in the networks of divorced and disputing families. *Advances in Group Process, 4,* 243-269. Reprinted with permission of JAI Press, New York, NY.

history of the change in children's attitudes and behavior towards their disputing parents. Clinicians were also able to follow about one-fourth of this sample over the decade that has elapsed since these data were collected. From these retrospective and longitudinal observations, there is reason to believe that the patterns in the findings were based on the children's growing and changing cognitive capacities to understand the disputes between their parents and their parents' attitudes to each other, and to infer their parents' attitudes to themselves.

To summarize, the expectable developmental trends for children in their attitudes and responses to their chronically disputing parents are temporary reactions (2-4-year-olds), shifting allegiances (4-7-year-olds), loyalty conflicts (7-9-year-olds), and alignments (9-12-year-olds). The case of a child followed for more than a decade illustrates these changes.

Christie was 3 years old when her parents separated. At this time, she showed temporary resistance to visiting her father on alternate weekends. She clung to her mother and cried, especially when her parents were overtly hostile toward one another at transitions. However, she quickly settled into the visits, as she was attached to the warm, loving grandmother who lived in her father's home. When Christie was 5 years old, her father remarried, and the hostility increased between her parents, mostly instigated by the new stepmother. During the next several years, Christie seemed to shift allegiances from one parent to the other: She told negative stories to both parents that aimed to please, placate, and confirm her parents' separate views. As she approached the age of 9, Christie seemed to become increasingly anxious, confused, and guilty about her divided loyalties. Unfortunately, the conflict between her two parents remained intense, and the child was increasingly pressured to take sides. When she was 9 years old, Christie entered into an alignment with her mother that gradually became entrenched. She became more and more covertly hostile toward her father and stepmother, complained about them, and tried to avoid visiting them. By the time she was 12 years old, she was overtly verbally abusive to her father and adamantly refused to visit, despite her mother's pleas that she had no choice "because the visits are court-ordered."

This intriguing pattern of developmental trends is largely explained by children's perspective-taking abilities in social relationships, in the context of a disputing social network (Johnston & Campbell, 1987). Social-cognitive developmental theorists (e.g., Flavell, Fry, Wright, & Jarvis, 1968; Piaget, 1965; Selman, 1980) have shown that children have an evolving capacity to hold in mind one perspective or more at a time, in relation to their own. They also have an advancing ability to differentiate self and others, in increasingly psychological terms and less in behavioral terms.

Early Preschoolers (2-4 years). Very young children are immediately reactive to witnessing overt parental conflict. This is so because their capacity to take a perspective in social relations is limited to a recognition of concrete and observable distinctions between people; they have little awareness that people can feel differently than they act. Further, at this age children are egocentric, in that they assume that others perceive and feel just as they do, and that they themselves cause the actions of others. Therefore, in response to their parents' conflict, these children seem to believe that parents are angry with each other only if the anger is overtly demonstrated in some observable manner. These littlest ones experience tension and stress when they are in the physical presence of their actively hostile parents. At such times, they typically cry and cling to one parent and they may temporarily avoid and reject the other parent. As soon as they are alone with the rejected parent, they can rapidly change and behave as though there is no issue. When their parents converse amicably, they respond happily to both, appearing delighted at the truce ("Daddy likes Mommy 'cause he talks nice to her"; or, conversely, "Daddy hates Mommy 'cause he talks mean"). Note, however, that if left alone with an angry parent who is distressed by a fight with the ex-spouse, these little ones are likely to misconstrue the reason for the parent's anger and to feel they are to blame for the upset ("I made Mommy mad 'cause I made too much noise").

Late Preschool–Early School Age (4-7 years). Children at this age have a budding capacity to take another person's viewpoint. The child can now take one parent's perspective at a time, but not both simultaneously. Although they are better able to understand that parents have internal or subjective feelings different from their overt behavior, and that their parents' feelings may be different from their own, all feelings are seen as simple, unitary ones. Mixed or ambivalent feelings are difficult for them to comprehend. For these reasons, it is not uncommon, at this age, for children of high-conflict divorce to have unstable, shifting allegiances, first taking one parent's viewpoint, and later taking the other's. (At home with mother they hear and believe one story, "Daddy didn't pay Mommy any money"; at father's house they are quickly convinced that "Mommy wasted all the money.") They become easily confused and can excite concern and chaos in their parents by telling different stories to each. Likewise, these young children have very simplistic notions of how to mend the quarrel ("Daddy says he's sorry, so can he come back home now?"). It is not possible for them to understand that mother may feel differently about father's change of heart.

Early Latency Age (7-9 years). By this age, children have begun to develop the capacity for self-reflexive thinking ("I know that she knows that I know"). They can also simultaneously hold more than one perspective at a time, for example, both their parents' viewpoints. They can even imagine how their parents view them, though their capacities are still limited in this respect. At this age, children begin to recognize the existence of mixed feelings, and that they may continue over time. Hence, children may begin to make judgments about the sincerity of parents' behavior ("He says he's sorry, but I don't think he really means it"). These new cognitive capacities mean that children of this age can experience acute loyalty conflicts for the first time because they can comprehend the complexity and incompatibility of their parents' opposing views. Furthermore, with their newly acquired self-consciousness and concreteness of operations, they are worried about how parents may view their actions ("Will Dad feel I don't love him as much as Mom if I spend more time with her?"). This may, in part, be an explanation for the considerable pain, sadness, and powerlessness typically seen in younger latency-age children in reaction to their parents' quarrels and divorce. In response, they want very much to be fair to both sides and to remain equidistant from each; they may try assiduously to avoid situations in which they are simultaneously in the presence of both parents, whether or not the parents are overtly fighting. Moreover, there is still a tendency to blame the self for parents' problems at this age (cf. Wallerstein & Kelly, 1980). This may be a defense against the perceived consequences of being angry at parents upon whom they are wholly dependent, or it may reflect the vestige of their younger egocentric perspective.

Late Latency Age (9-13 years). Loyalty conflicts in intensely disputing divorcing families do not appear to be sustained for very long by children at this age, probably because they are too painful and hence unbearable. Instead, children in later latency typically begin to make alignments with one or the other parent, and with varying degrees of intensity begin to exclude or reject the other parent. Many of these alignments waver between somewhat mild, secret preferences and wishes not to hurt or anger the rejected parent; or they may represent the child's attempt to maintain a distance and not get involved in the parental battles. A significant proportion of children, however, make strong alliances, these being overtly hostile, unshakeable stances in which the child may stridently reject and refuse to see or visit one parent.

The alignments seen at this age appear to result from a convergence of developmental and family-interactional factors: the child's capacity to conceptualize the whole system of conflictual relationships in the family; his or her tendency to adopt a polarized moral view of the situation; and pressure to take a more active role in the parental fight from family members who perceive the child as being "old enough to take a stand."

Early-Middle Adolescence (13-15 years). Our studies did not initially include adolescents, but a follow-up of the first sample of children, 2 to 3 years later, suggests that these alliances typically last several years into middle adolescence. About that time, the teenager develops the capacity for third-person perspective-taking (a more objective stance, in which they can view each parent's position as well as their own from a greater distance and can make more independent judgments). Under the best of circumstances, this greater objectivity allows them to use their cognitive skills to withdraw strategically from the parental fights.

Unfortunately, it appears that a significant proportion of children are not able to do this, and remaining caught up in the parental fight is associated with their having more emotional and behavioral difficulties (Buchanan, Maccoby, & Dornbusch, 1991; Johnston, Kline, & Tschann, 1989). In general, boys are more likely than girls to be behaviorally and emotionally symptomatic in response to parental conflict and violence, a finding which is confirmed by a large body of research (Emery, 1982; Jaffe, Wolfe, & Wilson, 1990; Zaslow, 1989).

Intensity and Longevity of Parental Disputes

There are factors other than the child's age and cognitive perspective-taking ability that contribute to the formation of parent-child alignments, and in turn, to children's refusal to visit. First, our studies showed that alignments made by the older children were more common in those families where the litigation was chronic and the hostility between parents unremitting. In fact, from both the retrospective histories of these children and from prospective longitudinal observations of those children who have been followed over time (as illustrated by the case of Christie, above), we have hypothesized that it is highly likely that children will move into alignments as they approach early adolescence, if the parental conflict is ongoing.

It is evident, however, in comparing the estimates of alignments in different samples, that when conflicts are overt and involve the children, and when the disputes are intense and prolonged, the children are more likely to submit to this alignment mode of defending and coping. Wallerstein and Kelly's (1980) community study of recently separated parents found that one-fifth of the children were in alignments; most of these were among the 9-12-year-old group and most of the alignments were not sustained. In the two studies described above, which involved custody and visitation disputes of divorcing families referred from the courts, almost one-third of the total sample of children were in alignments more than 2 to 3 years postseparation. Moreover, note that among the 9-12-year-olds, three-fourths were in alignments. Gardner (1987), who acts as an expert witness in custody evaluations and trials, estimates that nine-tenths of the children he sees are in entrenched alignments, which he terms the *parent alienation syndrome.*

Contribution of Emotionally Disturbed Parents to Parent-Child Alignments and Children's Refusal to Visit

While the changes in attitudes and behavior toward disputing parents, shown in Figure 6.1 and described above, appear to constitute the general developmental trend, there is a great deal of deviation from these patterns. Some children seem never to separate psychologically from a parent in the first place, or they enter into alignments early on (at 7 or 8 years). Some try to remain loyal to both parents and avoid alignment or alienation by becoming withdrawn and distanced from both. Some children nurture mild, covert preferences for one parent; others enter into strong alliances with the parent who is perceived as "all good," while the "all bad" parent is stridently rejected and even persecuted. Moreover, children may align with a parent even if there is relatively mild estrangement and an absence of overt conflict between the divorced parents, which suggests that parental conflict is not a necessary condition for the formation and maintenance of alignments.

To have a more complete understanding of the variation observed among these children, it is important to consider the intensity, consistency, and apparent irrationality of the parent-child alignment, and the degree to which the child has developed the capacity to psychologically separate (individuate) from his or her parent. Table 6.2 distinguishes between strong and mild alignments. A strong alignment is defined as a definite, consistent, overtly verbal and behavioral preference for one parent, together with rejection and denigration of the other. It is accompanied by affect that is unequivocally hostile and negative toward the rejected parent. A mild alignment is defined as a more moderate verbal and behavioral preference for one parent, often private or covert. It is accompanied by affect that is mildly negative and sometimes ambivalent.

As shown in Table 6.2, strong alignments were more common in older children than in younger: One-fourth to two-fifths of the children ages 9-12 years were in strong alignments. In these cases, the child consistently denigrated and rejected the other parent. Often, this was accompanied by an adamant refusal to visit, communicate, or have anything to do with the rejected parent. In extreme cases, the child's reality distortion and negative construal of the behavior and character of the

Table 6.2   Strong and Mild Alignments* by Age of Child

| | Number and Percent of Children | | | | |
	2-3 years	4-5 years	6-8 years	9-12 years	Total
Study No. 1 (N = 92)					
Mild Alignment	2 (9%)	6 (24%)	7 (37%)	12 (48%)	27 (30%)
Strong Alignment	0 (0%)	0 (0%)	0 (0%)	7 (28%)	7 (7%)
Study No. 2 (N = 63)					
Mild Alignment	—	4 (27%)	6 (30%)	8 (29%)	18 (29%)
Strong Alignment	—	1 (7%)	4 (20%)	12 (43%)	17 (27%)

NOTE: *Mild alignment is defined as moderate verbal and behavioral preference for one parent, usually covert. Strong alignment is a consistent, overt verbal and behavioral preference for one parent together with rejection of the other.

nonaligned parent took on a bizarre quality. Strong alignments are probably most closely related to the behavioral phenomenon Gardner (1987) referred to as *parent alienation syndrome*, which typically creates considerable consternation among parents, mental health professionals, and the courts.

In our studies of high-conflict litigating families, the children who were in extreme alignments with one parent were likely to be viewed as more psychologically disturbed by mothers, fathers, teachers, and clinicians (as measured by the CBCL, TRS, and CRS). In addition, children made stronger alliances when the parents were more emotionally dysfunctional (as measured by the BSI). Note that strongly aligned parents were more likely to be mothers (or residential parents), and alienated parents were more likely to be fathers (or nonresidential parents).

This brings us to the fourth major factor contributing to children's refusal to visit, which involves the psychological health of the aligned parent and the nature of the relationship between the child and that parent. The theories that contribute to this explanation are object-relations theory (Kernberg, 1975; Kohut & Wolf, 1978; Mahler et al., 1975; Winnicott, 1971) and attachment theory (Bowlby, 1969; Main et al., 1985). This literature draws attention to the way in which psychological disturbance in the parent, especially borderline and psychotic conditions as well as anxiety and depression, can affect the child.

The early origins of disorders in attachment and separation are believed to occur among very young children (especially from 12 to 24 months), when the child is psychologically separating from the mother and attaining a sense of object constancy and a separate self. Secure attachments, a sense of autonomy, and the beginnings of a separate self are believed to be the outcome of parenting by the primary caretaker that is empathic and emotionally attuned to the child's developmental strivings for independence and control. The parent must also be sensitive to the child's anxieties about survival, separation, and abandonment, which are a consequence of the child's tentative venturing out "into the world." The parent should know when to offer encouragement and applaud the toddler's autonomous efforts and when the child needs comfort, soothing, and constraints upon overwhelming stimuli and impulses. Graduated failure of the mother's special attunement to the child is developmentally appropriate as the child grows older, because it helps the child to internalize the mother-child relationship in order to gain an autonomous self. It also helps the child fuse the images of the "good and bad me" and the "good and bad mother" and thereby attain self and object constancy.

Separation and divorce for the parent is typically experienced as loss (with accompanying feelings of anxiety, sadness, and fear of being alone) and rejection (together with feelings of shame and failure). Divorcing individuals differ in their ability to manage and integrate these divorce-engendered emotions (Johnston & Campbell, 1988). Some especially vulnerable parents can become acutely or chronically distressed, anxious, or depressed. They may show increased characterological disturbance, even to the point of psychosis. Such disturbed parents, especially mothers (who are usually the primary attachment figures), are unable to sustain the emotional attunement and responsiveness necessary to provide for or sustain the child's psychological separation. Instead, they may use the child on behalf of their own need for nurturance and companionship, or as an ally against the world. Children of such parents, in order to have their own needs met to any extent, have to reflect whatever the parent needs and wants. Consequently, they become vigilant and highly attuned to the parent and mold themselves to preserve this tie. In so doing, the child does not have the opportunity to experience and acknowledge his or her own separate feelings and ideas. The child fears that disappointing or abandoning mother, physically, emotionally, or ideologically, may result in being ignored, abandoned, rejected, punished, or even destroyed by the angry, depressed, anxious, or emotionally volatile parent. Alternately, sensing an apparent omnipotence in caring for a distressed parent, the child acts as though the parent's survival depends on his or her constant vigilance and caretaking. For these reasons, the child may find it extremely difficult, if not impossible, to leave willingly for visits to the nonresidential parent, for fear of what might happen to the residential parent during his or her absence, or out of anxiety at disappointing and betraying that parent by "going over to the other side."

The Child's Exposure to Traumatic Emotional Abuse and Physical Violence Between Parents

Vulnerability to separation/individuation difficulties is not limited to young children. Recent developments in post-traumatic stress theory have shown that children who have witnessed traumatic violence between parents (Pynoos & Eth, 1986), those who have observed or been subject to terrorizing attacks by a psychotic parent (Anthony, 1986), those who have been threatened and physically or sexually abused (George & Main, 1979; Terr, 1981), and those who have been abducted by a parent (Senior, Gladstone, & Nurcombe, 1982) and/or fought over in bitterly contested custody disputes (Johnston & Campbell, 1988) can develop an extreme identification with the perceived aggressor or with the victim of the aggression. The theory in this domain is not well developed. One explanation is that traumatic violation of the moral order, of what should and should not be, especially if it involves physical injury or threat of destruction to self or loved ones, appears to exacerbate the psychological defense of "splitting" in the child, so that one parent (the violator) is viewed as "all bad" and the other parent (the victim) is seen as "all good." The child then tries to become one with the good parent and to reject all contamination by the bad one. Alternately, the child, with an awareness of helplessness, may identify with the powerful parent (the aggressor) and reject the one who is perceived as weak and vulnerable. Gender-specific identifications may also influence the formation of such alignments. In extreme instances of trauma, dissociation or a profoundly confused amnesic state may prevail (Gil, 1988).

Some intensely aligned children from highly conflicted divorcing families in our studies had been exposed to considerable trauma, especially emotional and physical abuse between their parents. As a group, these children demonstrated the more extreme reactions and symptoms. Physical violence between parents had occurred in three-fourths of both samples of high-conflict litigating families. In about one-sixth of the first sample and one-fifth of the second sample, beatings or threats with or use of a weapon had occurred, which many of the children had either witnessed or heard about (Johnston, 1992). Some of these children had realistic fears about the dangerousness of a violent parent, particularly a battering father, and they resisted visitation because they did not feel safe with that parent. Alternatively, they did not feel it was safe to leave mother, home, or pets, perceiving these all to be vulnerable to attack by the violent parent. Other children became profoundly disturbed and entered into a state of *folie a deux* with an abused mother, with a narcissistically injured father, or with a paranoid parent, a state in which reality, fears, and fantasies about the excluded parent were inextricably entwined for the aligned parent and child.

Sometimes a child's alignment with one parent and refusal to visit the other appears to be partly rooted in early, barely remembered trauma of domestic violence. In the case of Christie, described above, it seems that she had never developed a secure attachment to her father during the first 3 years of her life in a home marred by his alcoholism and physical abuse. In fact, in counseling sessions she revealed she had "flashbacks" of traumatic scenes when she was an infant in her crib: She heard breaking glass, loud angry arguments, and her mother crying. Subsequently, although her father's drinking and violence had ceased, she never really trusted him, and her anxieties were confirmed by her mother's obvious fear of this man.

Counter-Rejection by the Rejected Parent and Others

The final factor that contributes to the intensity of the parent-child alignment and the child's refusal to visit after divorce is the part played by the rejected parent and his social network. To date, this has seldom been acknowledged as a problem. In the studies described here, both parents and clinicians perceived less warmth and more hostility, anger, and distance in the rejected parents' responses to their children. That is, the more likely the child was to align with one parent, refusing to visit and rejecting the other parent, the more counter-hostility was generated toward the child on the part of the derogated parent.

Most rejected parents are not only hurt but highly affronted, even outraged, by the child's challenge to their authority and the lack of respect accorded them. Some try to reassert their parental position forcibly and coercively, which not uncommonly ends in verbal abuse, physical struggles, and assaults between child and parent; as a result, the child may sometimes run away. Other parents pursue the child relentlessly with a barrage of phone calls, letters, unexpected appearances at the child's activities and functions, and through ongoing litigation. In these cases, the child's negative attitudes are denied and dismissed by the offended parent as simply "the other parent talking" or by declaring that the child has been "brainwashed." In response, the child is even more indignant at being so discounted. Preadolescents and adolescents, who cherish their emerging autonomy, are particularly angry when their own expressed opinions are ignored or invalidated.

The rejected parent's extended kin, friends, and community may become involved. Neighbors, the priest, or the father's therapist may be called upon to plead the father's cause. Grandparents may write guilt-inducing letters or may belittle and counter-reject the child as being "selfish," as having been "duped" by the other parent, or as being a "traitor" to the family. All of these shaming and guilt-inducing strategies invariably lead to more avoidance on the child's part. A child who is in the custody of the rejected parent is usually not able to tolerate this intense familial and social pressure.

At the same time the aligned child is stridently denouncing the rejected parent, he or she is usually hypersensitive to and hurt by the counter-rejection, and so the alliance is intensified. What becomes evident in these cases, from a clinical viewpoint, is that beneath all the overtly angry rejection and negativity, the aligned child is often confused and besieged by guilty feelings. The child longs pathetically for the rejected parent, wishes to be rescued from the intolerable dilemma, and seems to be continually testing, by more and more extreme, negative behavior, to prove how much the rejected parent does or does not care.

This is clearly illustrated in the case of 12-year-old Christie, who refused to visit her father. Christie was verbally abusive to her father and told him she would run away if the court compelled her to visit. Father retorted that if the court did not support his request, he would ask her stepfather to adopt her: He felt it was extremely unjust that he had to pay child support for a daughter whom he never saw! After this conversation, Christie became agitated and angry and punched a hole in the wall of her bedroom. Later, she expressed painful feelings of guilt, confusion, and hurt because of her father's rejection.

Implications for Research Policy and Practice

Parents of young children who resist visitation need help in soothing and making the child feel safe and competent in handling transitions between parental homes. Use of transitional objects, bedtime stories that explain the divorce and the child's living arrangement, decorated calendars that help explain the time schedule, liberal use of the telephone to keep in contact with each parent, and the use of photographs to keep alive the image of each parent, can all be encouraged. It is important to ensure that parents protect the child from their disputes with each other, and that they carry out the transitions at a place that feels neutral and safe for each parent and comfortable for the child. If these measures do not decrease the child's separation anxieties, schedule changes that reduce the number of transitions the child makes between parental homes may help.

Special care needs to be taken to monitor the adjustment of children under the age of 3 years. These children are often highly reactive to separations from and transitions between parents. It is proposed that they are vulnerable to having their attachments disrupted in a significant way by separations that are continually stressful. In general, parents need to be advised on how children of different ages react to separations, how they understand the nature of parental disputes, and how they are likely to react to conflict. Parents may need counseling on how to respond appropriately to their children's concerns, in order not to exacerbate developmentally expectable separation anxieties, shifting allegiances, loyalty conflicts, and alignments by their own anxious or punitive responses.

Children who have been traumatized by witnessing family violence may need to be treated for post-traumatic stress syndrome, which involves reexperiencing and working through the traumatic memories in a safe, supportive, therapeutic environment (Pynoos & Eth, 1986), before they can (re)engage in a secure relationship with both the perpetrator and the victim of abuse. When there is ongoing threat of violence by a parent, when children have been sexually molested by a nonresidential parent (or believe they have been molested despite the absence of definitive proof), they need therapeutic support and help to reevaluate their relationship with that parent, and they need the protection of supervised visits. In extreme cases of parental abuse and violence, parent-child contact may need to be suspended or terminated. (See proposed guidelines for custody and visitation for children of domestic violence, Johnston, 1992).

We have found that children who have incomplete psychological separation from an emotionally or mentally disturbed parent need longer-term therapy, which should include the therapist's supportive counseling relationship with both parents. It has been our experience that forcibly removing these children from the aligned parent and placing them in the custody of the rejected parent, as recommended by Gardner (1987), is a misguided resolution; it is likely to be not only ineffective but actually punitive and harmful because it usually intensifies the problem. Rather, the process needs to be one of effecting a gradual separation in a supportive, therapeutic environment. In general, the first step for the therapist is to advise the alienated parent how to empathically and patiently reach out without antagonizing or threatening the child. At the same time, a strong supportive relationship needs to be built up between the clinician and the aligned parent, thereby relieving the child of some of that burden. The therapist can then gradually decondition the child's phobic anxiety and manifest anger by acting as both a buffer against and a bridge to the alienated parent, while at the same time helping the child manage the fears and actual consequences of moving away from the aligned parent. The actual visitation time can be increased over several months, beginning with day visits that are short and protected by the presence of either the therapist, a relative, or an adult friend with whom the child feels comfortable. The duration of the visits can then be gradually lengthened to include overnights, first with, and later without, the presence of supportive others. When the child is caught in a *folie a deux* relationship with an extremely disturbed psychotic parent, the separation may need to be undertaken within the protective confines of an inpatient psychiatric unit or in a residential school for emotionally disturbed children.

There has been no systematic study of the vicissitudes of the visiting relationship between children of divorce and their nonresidential parents. The conditions under which it works well, to the gratification and benefit of the child, have not been distinguished from those in which it fails. Despite the fact that mental health professionals are recommending and courts are ordering visitation arrangements for thousands of children daily, there is yet a meager knowledge base to justify their decisions.

The findings reported in this chapter are tentative, based on simple correlations and clinical observations from relatively small samples of high-conflict divorcing families. The interpretations of these findings are also quite speculative, with theoretical ideas about separation-individuation, social-cognitive perspective taking, the effects of emotionally disturbed parents, and the effects of trauma on children largely drawn from bodies of theory and research not directly related to divorce. As such, they comprise no more than hypotheses, which, it is hoped, will guide more systematic inquiry into the origins of problematic visiting relationships. In the same vein, the mental health and legal interventions proposed should be regarded as preliminary suggestions, based on the author's clinical experience and understanding of methods that appear to help. These, too, need systematic evaluation. What is clear is that there is a great need for research based on a developmental framework that considers the child's perspective of changing relationships in the post-divorce family.

The overall thesis of this paper is that children's resistance and refusal to visit a noncustodial parent have their origins in diverse and multiple psychological, developmental, and family system factors that require careful differential assessment by experienced clinicians. Interventions and legal policy need to be fashioned from a clear understanding of the many threads that contribute to the problem.

References

Achenbach, T. M., & Edelbrock, C. S. (1983). *Manual for the child behavior checklist and revised behavior profile.* New York: Queen City Publishers.

Anthony, E. J. (1986). Terrorizing attacks on children by psychotic parents. *Journal of the Academy of Child Psychiatry, 25,* 299-305.

Bowlby, J. (1969). *Attachment & loss* (Vols. I & II). New York: Basic Books.

Buchanan, C. M., Maccoby, E. E., & Dornbusch, S. M. (1991). Caught between parents: Adolescents' experience in divorced homes. *Child Development, 62,* 1008-1029.

Derogatis, L. R., & Spencer, P. M. (1982). The brief symptom inventory (BSI), administration, scoring and procedures manual–I. *Clinical Psychometric Research.* Baltimore, MD: Johns Hopkins University School of Medicine.

Emery, R. E. (1982). Interparental conflict and the children of discord and divorce. *Psychological Bulletin, 92,* 310-330.

Flavell, J. H., Fry, C., Wright, J., & Jarvis, P. (1968). *The development of role-taking and communication skills in children.* New York: John Wiley.

Furstenberg, F. F., Jr., & Nord, C. W. (1985). Parenting apart: Patterns of childrearing after marital disruption. *Journal of Marriage and the Family, 47*(4), 893-904.

Furstenberg, F. F., Jr., Nord, C. W., Peterson, J. L., & Zill, N. (1983). The life course of children of divorce: Marital disruption and parental contact. *American Sociological Review, 48,* 656-668.

Gardner, R. (1987). *The parental alienation syndrome and the differentiation between fabricated and genuine child sex abuse.* Cresskill, NJ: Creative Therapeutics.

George, C., & Main, M. (1979). Sexual interaction of young abused children: Approach, avoidance and aggression. *Child Development, 50,* 306-318.

Gil, E. (1988). *Treatment of adult survivors of childhood abuse.* Walnut Creek, CA: Launch Press.

Glick, P. C. (1988). The role of divorce in the changing family structure: Trends and variations. In S. A. Wolchik & P. Karoly (Eds.), *Children of divorce: Empirical perspectives on adjustment* (pp. 3-34). New York: Gardner Press.

Hetherington, E. M., Cox, M., & Cox, R. (1982). Effects of divorce on parents and children. In M. Lamb (Ed.), *Nontraditional families* (pp. 233-288). Hillsdale, NJ: Laurence Erlbaum.

Hightower, A. D., Work, W. C., Cowan, E. L., Lotyczewski, B. S., Spinell, A. P., & Guare, J. C. (1986). The teacher-child rating scale: A brief objective measure of elementary children's school behavior problems and competencies. *School Psychology Review, 15,* 393-409.

Jaffe, P., Wolfe, D., & Wilson, S. (1990). *Children of battered women.* Newbury Park, CA: Sage.

Johnston, J. R. (1990). Role diffusion and role reversal: Structural variations in divorced families and children's functioning. *Family Relations, 39,* 405-413.

Johnston, J. R. (1992). *Guidelines for the resolution of disputed custody and visitation for children of domestic violence.* (Final report to the Judicial Council of California, Administrative Office of the Courts). San Francisco: Judicial Council of California.

Johnston, J. R., & Campbell, L.E.G. (1987). Instability in the networks of divorced and disputing families. In E. J. Lawler & B. Markovsky (Eds.), *Advances in group processes* (Vol. 4, pp. 243-269). New York: JAI Press.

Johnston, J. R., & Campbell, L.E.G. (1988). *Impasses of divorce: The dynamics & resolution of family conflict.* New York: Free Press.

Johnston, J. R., Kline, M., & Tschann, J. M. (1989). Ongoing postdivorce conflict: Effects on children of joint custody and frequent access. *American Journal of Orthopsychiatry, 59*(4), 576-592.

Kernberg, O. (1975). *Borderline conditions and pathological narcissism.* New York: Jason Aronson.

Kohut, H., & Wolf, E. S. (1978). The disorders of self and their treatment. *International Journal of Psychoanalysis, 59,* 413-424.

Maccoby, E., & Mnookin, R. (1992). *Dividing the child: The social and legal dilemmas of custody.* Cambridge, MA: Harvard University Press.

Mahler, M. S., Pine, F., & Bergman, A. (1975). *The psychological birth of the human infant: Symbiosis and individuation.* New York: Basic Books.

Main, M., Kaplan, N., & Cassidy, J. (1985). Security in infancy, childhood, & adulthood: A move to the level of representation. In I. Bretherton & E. Waters (Eds.), Growing points of attachment theory and research. *Monographs of the Society for Research in Child Development* (Serial No. 209, pp. 66-104).

Piaget, J. (1960). *The child's conception of the world.* New Jersey: Rowman & Allan Reid.

Piaget, J. (1965). *The moral judgement of the child.* New York: Free Press. (Original work published 1932)

Pynoos, R. S., & Eth, S. (1986). Witness to violence: The child interview. *Journal of the American Academy of Child Psychiatry, 25,* 306-319.

Selman, R. L. (1980). *The growth of interpersonal understanding*. New York: Academic Press.

Senior, N., Gladstone, T., & Nurcombe, B. (1982). Childsnatching: A case report. *Journal of the American Academy of Child Psychiatry, 21*, 579-583.

Straus, M. A. (1979). Measuring intrafamily conflict and violence: The conflict tactics (CT) scales. *Journal of Marriage and the Family, 41*, 75-86.

Terr, L. (1981). Psychic trauma in children. *American Journal of Psychiatry, 138*, 14-19.

Tschann, J. M., Johnston, J. R., Kline, J., & Wallerstein, J. S. (1989). Family process and children's functioning during divorce. *Journal of Marriage and the Family, 51*, 431-444.

Wallerstein, J. S., & Kelly, J. B. (1980). *Surviving the breakup: How children and parents cope with divorce*. New York: Basic Books.

Winnicott, D. W. (1971). *Playing and reality*. New York: Routledge.

Zaslow, M. J. (1989). Sex differences in children's response to parental divorce: II. Samples, variables, ages, and sources. *American Journal of Orthopsychiatry, 50*, 118-141.

7

Developing and Implementing
Post-Divorce Parenting Plans

Does the Forum Make a Difference?

JOAN B. KELLY

While there has been considerable focus in the past two decades on
parent-child relationships and visiting after divorce, little attention has
been paid to the process by which parents develop or arrive at custody
and parenting agreements when separation and divorce occur. Do parents candidly discuss their projected or desired parenting roles at the
point of separation and arrive at their own agreements? Do attorneys
and the adversarial divorce process influence the type of parenting plan
that results? To what extent do parents believe their custody and parenting agreements are in their children's best interests? Are parental
behaviors post-divorce influenced by the manner in which decisions are
reached during divorce? These questions take on importance in view of
accumulating research indicating that children's adjustment after divorce is in part dependent upon the nature of the coparental relationship
and the quality and extent of relationships that the child sustains with
each parent (Albiston, Maccoby, & Mnookin, 1990; Bisnaire, Firestone,
& Rynard, 1990; Buchanan, Maccoby, & Dornbusch, 1991, in press;
Camara & Resnick, 1989; Emery, 1988; Healy, Malley, & Stewart,
1990; Hetherington, Cox, & Cox, 1982; Tschann, Johnston, Kline, &
Wallerstein, 1989; Wallerstein & Kelly, 1980).

Until quite recently, culturally and legally embedded traditions of mother-custody of children after divorce preempted discussion or planning that considered a range of options for the post-divorce parenting roles of fathers or mothers. Except in unusual circumstances, fathers were, by default, expected to assume a nonresidential and limited part-time role in their children's lives after divorce. Many fathers were advised by attorneys and mental health professionals that their children's lives would be less confusing if they accepted limited access or ceased their contacts altogether. In this cultural context, when fathers strongly disagreed with the nonresidential role assignment, the options for settling the custody dispute were limited.

Most often, fathers reluctantly capitulated to the mothers' demand for full physical custody without any legal action. Others dropped pending legal action after attorneys advised them that litigation and judicial reliance on legal precedent would not result in greater involvement of the father (Kruk, 1992). When withdrawal from the legal conflict was not acceptable to the parent, and sufficient economic resources were available, the dispute was settled in the courts through a protracted process of litigation, evaluation, and judicial determination. Whether through capitulation or litigation, the intense dissatisfaction of interested nonresidential fathers with their limited parenting role has been well documented in many clinical and empirical studies (Ahrons, 1981; Jacobs, 1983; Kruk, 1992; Leupnitz, 1982; Maccoby, Depner, & Mnookin, 1988; Wallerstein & Kelly, 1980).

In the past decade, a new dispute settlement option, that of mediation, has become available in both the private and public sectors. Mediation is an alternative dispute resolution process in which the disputing parties meet with an impartial third party to reach mutually acceptable agreements. Decision making remains with the parties, not the mediator. In the public sector, most court-based mediation focuses exclusively on custody and access disputes (Depner, Cannata, & Simon, 1992; Pearson & Thoennes, 1989). Mandatory court mediation programs require at least one mediation session between disputing parents prior to proceeding with further legal action on custody matters. All support and property matters are handled concurrently by the parents' attorneys in the traditional adversarial process, and the advice given to parents in preparation for mediating custody and visiting disputes is framed within the context of winning or gaining advantage. In the private sector, parents more often use voluntary *comprehensive* divorce mediation, which enables them to resolve all aspects of the divorce, including property, child and spousal support, custody, and access, in an integrated manner. Given their greater complexity, comprehensive mediations generally require more sessions to reach final agreements (Kelly & Duryee, 1992).

Whether for custody mediation or comprehensive divorce mediation, proponents of mediation have advanced this alternative dispute resolution forum as superior to the adversarial process for multiple reasons. They have pointed to the collaborative problem-solving nature of the mediation process, the focus on children's interests and needs rather than the parents' adversarial positions, the potential for reducing conflict as a result of working together with a mediator in a process that contains anger and hostile communications, and considerable savings in time and expense. Opponents of mediation have argued that because women historically have had less access to wealth and positions of power, they are less capable of advancing their interests and therefore are disadvantaged in any negotiation process. Claiming that women fare better in the adversarial process, women's advocates fear that mediation both forces women to give up custodial entitlements that they would presumably achieve in the adversarial process and enables men to negotiate more residential time with their children than they deserve or really want.

It is important to note that an increasingly large group of divorcing men and women use neither the adversarial process nor a mediation intervention. These parents, acting *in pro per* without the advice of legal counsel, may represent up to 40% of the divorcing population (Duryee, 1992). As a group, this population, many of whom can not afford legal representation, is unstudied.

Research comparing custody mediation with adversarial approaches for settling custody and visiting disputes, while still limited, has demonstrated that mediation, when compared to adversarial divorce processes, is a more timely, cost-effective process (Emery & Wyer, 1987; Pearson & Thoennes, 1989), produces high levels of satisfaction among its participants (Depner et al., 1992; Duryee, 1992; Emery, Matthews & Wyer, 1991; Pearson & Thoennes, 1989), and results in small but significant increases in parental cooperation (Pearson & Thoennes, 1989). Mediation results in full or partial agreements between 60% and 80% of the time in both custody mediation and in comprehensive mediation services (Depner et al., 1992; Duryee, 1992; Emery & Jackson, 1989; Kelly & Gigy, 1989; Pearson & Thoennes, 1989).

Research comparing a comprehensive divorce mediation process inclusive of all issues with the traditional two-attorney adversarial divorce process has found similar and stronger effects with respect to cooperation, parent attitudes, client satisfaction, and cost savings (Kelly, 1989a, 1990a, 1991). Further, comprehensive mediation contained conflict during the divorce process more so than the adversarial process and led to more effective parental communication after divorce (Kelly, 1991). Mediation has not resulted in significantly more positive psychological functioning for either adults or children, compared to adversarial divorce, and the positive effects noted above are time-limited (Kelly, 1990b, 1991; Pearson & Thoennes, 1989).

One aspect of mediation that has received limited attention is whether the comprehensive mediation process, when compared to the traditional adversarial divorce process, affects the manner in which parents reach decisions about their children. When parents are given the opportunity to mutually address their children's emotional and financial needs, and articulate their own parenting interests, are the parenting and custody agreements they reach any different? When discussions are not framed by winning or losing, does the mediation setting produce positive changes in parental attitudes or behaviors, even in the presence of high levels of anger and conflict?

This chapter focuses on parental communication and decision making during divorce regarding custody issues, focuses on the custody and parenting plans that resulted, and reviews the interactions and behaviors of 284 parents using two different dispute resolution processes for reaching final divorce agreements. These parents were part of a larger longitudinal study comparing the effectiveness of a comprehensive divorce mediation to the more customary two-attorney adversarial process for reaching final property, child and spousal support, custody, and parenting agreements. The nature of the adversarial and mediative dispute resolution processes are discussed in relation to the findings, and suggestions for policy considerations offered.

The 284 parents described in this chapter included 113 men and women who had initiated divorce proceedings using two attorneys (adversarial sample), and 172 men and women who came to a nonprofit mediation center to resolve all their divorce issues (mediation sample). While characterized as adversarial and mediation groups for purposes of the larger study, the two groups were not totally pure. Mediation clients used outside attorneys for consultation and review, and 30% of the adversarial parents used court-based mandatory custody mediation to resolve custody and visiting disputes. Further, within the adversarial sample, final divorce agreements were reached through different pathways, including negotiated settlements, litigation, or both. Nevertheless, the two samples used a very different process overall to achieve full settlement of all their issues. Parent information was obtained through objective questionnaires mailed at five points in time, ranging from beginning of divorce to 2 years post-divorce. The data reported here were collected at Time 1 (6 weeks after filing a divorce petition, or at the beginning of mediation), Time 3 (final divorce), and Times 4 and 5 (1 and 2 years post-divorce). For those parents already separated, Time 1 was an average of 8 months since separation.

There were no significant baseline differences between parents in the two samples with respect to frequency of marital conflict, quality of marital communication, anger at spouse, overall cooperation, psychological adjustment scores, employment of women, and combined household income. Mediation respondents were better educated, and reported more depression and stress about the divorce than did adversarial parents. Women in both groups were significantly more angry than men, expressed more dissatisfaction with their marriages, and more often had made the decision to get the divorce. The adversarial parent group at Time 1 viewed their spouses as less competent parents, compared to the mediation parents, and anticipated less cooperation regarding their children by final divorce. Despite these more negative views, the adversarial parent group did not anticipate more conflict in settling child custody or visiting issues. Further, there were no group differences in the amount of child-specific conflict during the marriage, in the quality of child-related communications, or on a scale assessing the extent to which a parent assumed responsibility for a broad number of different parenting tasks and activities during the marriage (Kelly, 1991). While it is not possible to identify cause and effect, these findings raise the possibility that in meeting with their attorneys in preparation for filing a divorce petition (Time 1), adversarial parents may have adopted more polarized, negative views of each other. Where appropriate, all baseline group differences were controlled for through analyses of covariance. For a full discussion of the methodology, sample characteristics, measures, and major findings, see Kelly (1989a, 1990a, 1990b, 1991), Kelly & Gigy (1989), and Kelly, Gigy, & Hausman (1988).

Deciding Post-Divorce Custody and Parenting Roles

Parental Preferences and Their Correlates

When a parent communicates the intention to divorce to his or her spouse, each parent faces the crucial question of what parental role will be assumed in the children's lives after separation and divorce. Central to this question are the amount and pattern of time mothers and fathers will spend with their children after divorce (the parenting plan), and the extent to which each parent will be involved post-divorce in major decisions and responsibilities affecting the children's future. Many parents worry about whether a spouse will accept their proposal for custody and a parenting plan, or will litigate custody and access matters in the court. At Time 1, 75% of parents reported very high or moderate levels of anxiety about how they were going to work out the details of their parenting plan and roles.

Parental anxieties may stem from an awareness of gender-linked conflicting desires with respect to how much time each wanted to spend with their children after divorce. Indeed, the data lend support to this idea. In response to a forced choice question, asking parents to indicate how much time they wanted their children in residence with them after divorce, there were predictable and significant sex differences. Fifty-six percent of women wanted their children 80% or more of the time, compared to 16% of the men. Only 18% of the men indicated that visiting time of 20% with their children would be acceptable. Thirty-nine percent of the men wanted equal (50/50) shared residence; only 15% of the women wanted shared custody. It is not surprising, therefore, that at the beginning of divorce, 29% of the men and 25% of the women anticipated that they would have extreme or considerable conflict re-solving child custody, and 20% of parents anticipated similar high levels of conflict in settling visiting issues.

The anticipation of disputes about parent time with children may have been fueled as well by different psychological agendas for men and women. When levels of anger at their spouse about the divorce were very high, and when they either did not initiate or had less control over the decision to divorce, women in both groups wanted larger amounts of time with their children after divorce. Unemployed and part-time working mothers also wanted higher amounts of time with their children, as did mothers who perceived that the father was not a capable parent. In contrast, the extent of men's anger at their spouse was not significantly correlated with time desired with children, nor was control over the divorce decision. Fathers wanted larger amounts of time with their children when they had assumed more daily parenting tasks and responsibilities during the marriage. Desire for greater time was also associated with the perception that the mother was not a capable parent, or was perceived to be emotionally unstable and/or a substance abuser. These gender differences may have exacerbated anxiety about resolving post-divorce parenting roles.

Broaching Custody and Access Issues

As separation becomes imminent, to what extent do parents talk privately about their desires and attitudes regarding future custodial roles, parental responsibilities, and visitation plans? When do they settle these matters?

It was apparent that many parents with children under the age of 18 completely avoided discussions about child custody matters as they entered into the divorce process. Overall, 51% the parents reported that at the beginning of divorce they had not talked *at all* or only very little with their spouse about custody and parenting matters regarding their minor age children. Adversarial parents were significantly less likely to have talked to each other than mediation parents. Parents talked more with their children than they did with their spouses about visiting arrangements. Given the long-term psychological and economic consequences of the post-divorce parenting plan to the child, it is startling how little communication was devoted to a mutual consideration of children's psychological needs and parents' parental roles after divorce.

Sixty-three percent of the parents indicated at Time 1 that visiting and custody were essentially settled at separation, prior to Time 1. Given the widespread failure to communicate, it would appear that the majority of postdivorce parenting plans come about primarily by default. While one might assume that the parents' lack of communication about parenting arrangements at separation was related to a systemic problem with communication during the marriage, our findings do not support this. Communication about children in the marriage was reported by parents to be significantly better or more successful than communication measured in six other marital areas. Sixty-six percent of the women and 83% of the men reported that communication about their children was adequate or good during the marriage. This contradicts the common assumption that a failed marriage has failed in all respects, including parenting. Similarly, only 18% of parents reported very frequent conflict regarding their children during the marriage, although 50% reported very frequent conflict regarding other adult/marital issues. Parents' expectations regarding ability to cooperate about their children were surprisingly high at beginning of divorce, with 67% anticipating that their child-related cooperation would be reasonable or very good by final divorce.

Some understanding of why the majority of parents avoided discussing important parent-child relationship issues was gained from the comments of mediation parents, who told mediators in the first session that they were reluctant to initiate such discussions privately. They feared high conflict or premature closure. Anticipating a safer forum with an impartial mediator, parents deliberately deferred discussing what they really wanted for themselves and their children. Separated parents who had already established an interim parenting plan also viewed mediation as the place to refine or modify decisions through continued discussion.

The adversarial parents had no such setting. They were often advised by attorneys not to talk with their spouse about anything, including their children, and more often had formal court orders in place prohibiting contact. Attorneys for 55% of these parents had given specific advice to their clients about custody and parenting matters. When legal advice was given, the mothers' attorneys advocated strongly for sole physical custody for their clients and discouraged either shared residential arrangements or father custody. Attorneys for men, in comparison, were more likely to advise primary residence to mother or shared residential arrangements; few supported a desire for father custody, a finding reported elsewhere (Kruk, 1992). The adversarial context may have served to sharpen differences, heighten anger and suspicion, and reduce the potential for productive discussions between these parents.

Custody and Parenting Agreements

To determine whether final custody and parenting agreements varied according to the divorce process used by the parents, parent questionnaire data, mediation agreements, and court orders were combined and coded into two variables reflecting the amount of time children were spending with each of their parents. Where court orders lacked specificity, parent reports of monthly, holiday, and vacation time with children were used. Since the amount of time children were reported to spend with fathers was highly (negatively) correlated with mothers, the "dadtime" variable was used in subsequent analyses.

Legal Custody

The incidence of joint legal custody in the two groups was not significantly different. Ninety-four percent of the adversarial men, 86% of the adversarial women, and 100% of the mediation parents had joint legal custody. These findings confirm other reports that joint legal custody has become normative in California (Albiston, Maccoby, & Mnookin, 1990; Duryee, 1991), and is not dispute forum dependent.

There was a significant group difference with respect to whether joint legal custody was defined as to its intent. In the court orders of the adversarial group, there was no indication as to what decisions or responsibilities would be joint ones. This was true for the subsample of adversarial parents who used mandatory custody mediation, as well as those parents who did not have sufficient dispute regarding custody or access to warrant a referral to mandatory mediation. Since no opportunity was provided within the adversarial framework to work these parental responsibility issues out, and the majority of parents avoided talking about parenting and custody matters, the joint legal custody label was one of form rather than substance.

In contrast, all mediated agreements delineated those major child issues that would require discussion and joint consent. Mediation parents, and particularly nonresidential fathers, responded eagerly to the opportunity to discuss these matters. Parents typically agreed to future joint decision making on major educational issues, medical and dental care, religious training, and children's recreational activities that either interfered with a parent's access or were beyond the scope of child support (summer camp, lessons, recreational programs). It is not surprising that at 1 and 2 years post-divorce, mediation parents had more contact with each other than did adversarial parents, and were more likely to confer about their children on a variety of major issues, differences which remained significant after controlling for group baseline differences (Kelly, 1991).

Access

The average amount of dadtime in the entire sample was 30%. There were significant group differences in the amount of time that fathers spent with their children. The residential agreements in the adversarial sample reflected more extreme, either/or outcomes. Fathers in the adversarial group and spouses of adversarial women were significantly more likely to have limited time with their children (dadtime less than 20%) compared to the mediation group. Adversarial fathers were also more likely than mediation fathers to have sole physical custody (with dadtime of 80% or more).

Mediation parents significantly more often negotiated agreements that enabled the nonresidential father to have expanded access (dadtime = 20%-39%), compared to adversarial men and women. A typical pattern was for the father to have the children every other weekend from Friday after school until Monday morning, plus an additional overnight each midweek or during the week before mother's weekend.

Mediation parents were more likely to agree to the legal language of joint physical custody, compared to the adversarial parents, primarily as a result of the opportunity in mediation for nonresidential fathers to express their strong feelings about being formally designated a "visitor," if the mother had sole physical custody. However, the incidence of actual shared residential time, defined as between 40% and 60% of the time with children, was not significantly different for the two groups (overall, 27% of the sample). Where parents shared residential arrangements that were not equally divided, mothers always had the greater amount of time. Fathers never exceeded 50% time unless they had physical custody, in which case dadtime was 80% or more.

Parenting Plans

Inspection of final divorce decrees highlighted another difference in the two dispute resolution processes with respect to specificity of visiting or shared parenting plans. Nearly all mediation agreements described the specific plan of parent-child contacts for holidays, vacations, and specified days and times of transitions and responsibility for pick-ups or drop-offs for the weekly/monthly visiting or shared custody plan. In contrast, one-quarter of the final agreements of the adversarial parents failed to include any language at all about a parenting plan, and three-fifths of the custody agreements contained vague language, most often, "the father shall have reasonable visitation upon giving reasonable notice."

Other Provisions

Aside from differences in parenting plans and agreements, the mediation forum produced several different economic outcomes. In 32% of the mediated agreements between spouses with children, provisions for handling future college expenses of children were included, compared to 6% of the adversarial agreements, a difference reported by Pearson (1991) as well. Further, a significantly greater number of mediation agreements designated which parent was responsible for maintaining health insurance coverage, and addressed how unreimbursed medical and dental costs of children would be covered, compared to adversarial agreements.

Parental Behaviors and Attitudes During and After Divorce

When parents use a comprehensive divorce mediation intervention, does the process result in any different behaviors during the divorce, compared to the adversarial setting? Does the forum shape parental attitudes and influence communications after the divorce?

Adversarial respondents reported that the divorce proceedings had intensified their anger at their spouses. Strident declarations, depositions, and other legal procedures, as well as the desirability of taking extreme positions from which to negotiate or litigate final results, were often cited as creating outrage, frustration, and anger. Indeed, at final divorce, and again one year later, these parents had significantly higher co-parental anger scores and saw each other as more angry, compared to the mediation parents, despite the absence of differences in anger at spouse at the beginning of divorce (Kelly, 1991).

Mediation respondents at final divorce reported significantly fewer conflicts had occurred overall, and fewer conflicts occurred with respect to visiting, during the divorce process. At one year post-divorce, mediation respondents again reported significantly less conflict regarding visiting, and less conflict regarding medical and religious issues. During this same period, mediation parents communicated significantly more often, compared to the adversarial parents, and with respect to a larger number of child-specific topics. All differences remained significant after controlling for initial baseline differences (Kelly, 1991). Mediation seemed to diffuse or contain some of the hostility parents originally reported and was significantly more effective than the adversarial process in increasing the general level of cooperation between parents, from beginning of divorce to final divorce (Kelly, 1991; Kelly et al., 1988).

Mediation parents were also significantly more in compliance with their parenting plans and in making spousal support payments than were adversarial parents during the first year after divorce (Kelly, 1990b).

One year after divorce, the mediation intervention appeared to have enabled parents to have more favorable attitudes toward each other as parents, compared to the adversarial process. After partialling out baseline differences in attitudes toward each other as parents, the mediation group was significantly more likely to describe the other parent as more involved, as a more caring and competent parent, as more of a resource in child care, and as supportive of each other in their parenting roles, compared to the adversarial parents (Kelly, 1991).

Mediation parents were also significantly more satisfied overall with their divorce resolution process than were adversarial parents. Nonresidential adversarial fathers were the least satisfied, compared to nonresidential mediation fathers or women in both groups. While there was no significant difference in satisfaction with the custody and parenting agreements reached, mediation parents were significantly more likely to report that their custody and parenting plans would be better for everyone in their family. Adversarial parents perceived their attorneys as less helpful in identifying ways to arrange custody and visiting compared to parents' perceptions of mediators. Mediation parents were also significantly more likely to report that the mediation process increased their understanding of their children's psychological needs and reactions (Kelly, 1989a).

These differences favoring the mediation intervention remained through the first year after divorce, but were not significant 2 years post-divorce (Kelly, 1990b, 1991). By this time, the mediation parents diminished their communication somewhat, and the adversarial group had become slightly more cooperative over time.

How Do the Divorce Resolution Processes Differ?

These findings invite a comparison between mediated and adversarial divorce processes to understand what each offers to parents as they settle important child-related issues. Mediation provides joint sessions where parents can focus on their children's immediate and longer-range psychological and developmental needs in the presence of an impartial third party. When provided by trained, experienced mediators with good conflict management and negotiation skills, mediation enables angry and fearful parents the opportunity to voice their post-separation proposals and desires for how they will continue as parents with their children. With a strong problem-solving orientation that promotes collaboration, mediation encourages parents to shift from self-interest and polarized positions more familiar to the adversarial divorce to consider the separate and overlapping needs of all family members. Angry spouses are assisted in separating anger resulting from the failed marriage from their view of each other as parents (Kelly, 1983; Saposnek, 1983). Parents often effectively anticipate what issues may lead to future disputes and in mediation can design a process for settling disputes (Kelly, 1989b). By focusing on and clarifying future parental roles and the nature of the future co-parental relationship, mediation promotes the transformation of the marital relationship into a post-divorce partnership and may enhance the important process of family reorganization.

There is no comparable forum for parents in the customary adversarial divorce process. While settlement conferences with a judge may be required prior to a custody trial, they are often too late for productive negotiations, and are framed within the traditional adversarial perception that the parents have competing interests. The goal of each side is to gain a competitive edge or win at the expense of the other (Kressel, 1985; Kruk, 1992; Wolman & Taylor, 1991). Adversarial representation, by its nature, frequently creates or enhances distorted perceptions of the other spouse, which are hardened and memorialized in a spiraling series of legal pleadings that take on a reality of their own. The adversarial parents in this study confirmed that this process escalates preexisting parental hostilities.

When attorneys advise clients not to communicate with each other, they explicitly or implicitly convey messages that co-parental communication is undesirable, or dangerous, and may never be possible. Indeed, based on comments made to this author over two decades, the majority of attorneys believe that because parents are divorcing, they are incapable of productive communication and negotiation about their children. ("They wouldn't be getting a divorce if they could talk about their kids.") Such attitudes stem from a lack of understanding about why parents divorce (Gigy & Kelly, in press) and the strong belief, despite data to the contrary, that the majority of divorcing parents have pervasive and intense, frequent conflict (Bray, 1991).

The absence of a nonadversarial, structured forum for the mutual consideration of child and parent-child needs is a particular disadvantage for fathers who will become nonresidential parents. Short of full-scale custody litigation, nonresidential fathers who have been involved with their children during the marriage are not supported in their desire for meaningful time and continuity in their relationship with their children by their attorneys, legal presumptions and precedent, mothers angry about the divorce, and our culture. Fathers who want more time with their children, but not full physical custody, are often described as demanding, hostile, or unreasonable.

In jurisdictions such as California, which mandate custody mediation for parenting disputes, fathers who want to be involved meaningfully with their children after divorce have the opportunity to request expanded access in the presence of their spouses and an impartial mediator. While two studies found no forum differences in the number of days or type of parenting arrangement nonresidential fathers spend with their children (Emery & Wyer, 1987; Slater, Shaw, & Duquesnel, 1992), other data (this chapter; Duryee, 1992; Pearson & Thoennes, 1989) indicate custody mediation and comprehensive divorce mediation result in somewhat more expanded access to children for nonresidential fathers, compared to fathers using just an adversarial process. The differences may be related to the laws, societal and parenting norms that exist in each particular jurisdiction, the policies of the mediation services, and the manner in which the research samples were obtained. In jurisdictions where changes in law and cultural attitudes have led to greater acceptance of expanded access to children for nonresidential parents, fathers appear to be seeking, and getting, more time, regardless of type of dispute resolution forum (Duryee, 1992; Healy et al., 1990; Kelly, 1991). Even when nonresidential fathers participating in mediation do not get as much access to their children as desired, they are still highly satisfied with mediation (Emery & Jackson, 1989). The ability to be heard and to talk to one's spouse appears to be a key component of this client satisfaction.

The failure to develop and specify detailed parenting plans, delineating each parent's parenting responsibilities and rights, creates additional problems for nonresidential parents. Lack of specificity and language such as "reasonable access" in custody orders require that the nonresidential father make a *request* to the custodial mother each time he seeks time with the children. If the children have prior plans or if angry mothers deny visitation, the potential for a reciprocal spiral of decreasing contacts with children is very real. In contrast, when parenting plans specifying dates and times of transitions from one household to the other are recorded in final divorce orders, nonresidential fathers can exercise their parental roles in a predictable manner, without conflicts or power struggles. It is reasonable to postulate that the absence of specific post-divorce parenting orders is one major cause of diminished nonresidential parent-child contacts, as well as father dropout. The lack of specificity in custody and visiting agreements also leads to more post-divorce conflict, particularly before holidays and summer vacation, and is responsible for nearly one-third of the returns to custody mediation services (Duryee, unpublished data).

Implications for Policy, Research, and Practice

Research emerging from custody mediation settings (Depner et al., 1992; Duryee, 1991, 1992; Emery, Matthews, & Wyer, 1991; Kelly & Duryee, 1992; Pearson & Thoennes, 1989; Slater et al., 1992), and research comparing comprehensive divorce mediation with the two-attorney adversarial process for resolving all divorce issues (Kelly, 1989a, 1990a, 1990b, 1991), indicates that mediation is not only a viable but a preferable alternative for resolving divorce disputes for the majority of parents, compared to the traditional adversarial approach. When parents use custody mediation in the broader context of an adversarial divorce process, increased cooperation and higher levels of satisfaction are noted, compared to parents not using mediation for custody disputes. Mediation parents more often feel they both have "won" in reaching settlement, compared to litigating parents who clearly see the outcome as producing a winner and a loser (Emery & Jackson, 1989).

When parents using a comprehensive divorce mediation service to resolve all divorce issues are compared to parents using the more traditional adversarial divorce proceeding, the effect of the mediated divorce appears to be more powerful and pervasive. Mediation contains rather than escalates conflict, facilitates more positive post-divorce parental communication, and enhances compliance with agreements. When the mediation is comprehensive of economic issues, mediation parents reach financial agreements that are more beneficial for their children, compared to those reached in the traditional adversarial process.

Given the difficulty parents have in discussing their children's post-divorce needs at the time of separation, and the culturally embedded presumption of mother custody and limited father visitation, mediation may provide nonresidential fathers their only opportunity to discuss their strongly felt desires for post-divorce involvement with their children.

In those few jurisdictions mandating mediation for custody and visiting disputes, from 18% to 33% of divorcing parents are using court-connected custody mediation services to reach agreements (Duryee, 1991; Kelly, unpublished data; Mnookin, Maccoby, Albiston, & Depner, 1990). Therefore, it is assumed that two-thirds of the divorcing parent population is not in sufficient dispute to warrant a referral to mediation. This group is most likely to arrive at parenting plans through default rather than thoughtful consideration of their children's immediate and longer-term needs. As a policy matter, the widespread availability of mediation services seems important, not just for those parents in high conflict, but also as a planning process for parents who simply need some assistance. These parents with lesser disputes, or who lack knowledge about what post-divorce arrangements would be beneficial for their children, do not currently have any collaborative forum for resolving parenting matters unless private mediation services are available and affordable. Our data indicate that such parents, and particularly nonresidential fathers, actively welcome the opportunity to develop specific parenting agreements so that they are workable for both parents and children and will be complied with after divorce. Most often, with lower-conflict parents, 1 to 2 hours is sufficient time to mediate a comprehensive custody and parenting agreement and redefine parental responsibilities.

Mediation not only works on a personal level for the majority of its participants, but the process also succeeds from a legal systems perspective. Among disputed custody cases coming to the court, 77% of those cases randomly assigned to custody mediation settled their dispute, compared to 31% of those randomly assigned to the adversary settlement process, a significant difference (Emery & Wyer, 1987). Of those not reaching agreement in mediation, one-half settled later, prior to appearing for a court hearing. Settlements are reached more quickly in mediation, and the cost savings to the individuals and society are considerable.

From a policy standpoint, it is important that mediators have specialized, intensive training and experience in custody and divorce mediation. This is particularly critical in jurisdictions mandating the use of custody mediation as an entry-level intervention for all custody and access disputes. Indeed, the quality of court-connected mediation services has improved considerably in California since policymakers recognized this need and provided funding for training and continuing-education programs for court-based mediators.

Policymakers must understand that mediation will not be an effective or appropriate intervention for as many as 30% of parents who have custody or access disputes (Depner et al., 1992; Kelly & Duryee, 1992; Slater et al., 1992). Serious concerns regarding domestic violence, parental substance abuse, child neglect and abuse, and mental illness must often be addressed, following the first (unsuccessful) session, through a combination of more adversarial proceedings, including investigations, settlement conferences, court hearings, and custody trials. Mediation should not supplant these more costly options; they should be used when mediation fails or is inappropriate (Kelly & Gigy, 1989). It is important in assessing the success of court-based mediation services that agreement rates not be used as a sole criterion for measuring effectiveness. Agreement rates in excess of 80% would suggest that coerciveness or arbitration has replaced the central underlying principle of mediation, which is that decision making remains with the clients.

While much has been learned about custody and divorce mediation in the past decade, further research is necessary to advance our knowledge and refine mediation practices. Further studies utilizing random assignment to mediated and litigated samples will address lingering questions about the possible effects of self-selection of mediation in several studies, including that described in this chapter. Research investigating the limitations and uses of specialized mediation services in cases where domestic violence is alleged or has occurred is critical, particularly since the number of such cases is large (Depner et al., 1992). Sophisticated conceptual and research approaches to assessing power issues in custody and divorce mediation are essential for answering the critical voices of those believing that women lack sufficient power to present and address their own interests. Thus far, however, a number of major findings cited in this chapter have been replicated in studies utilizing different samples, methodologies, and measures, which have been conducted in jurisdictions with wide variations in laws and presumptions.

The weight of research and practice indicates that it is important for all jurisdictions to embrace a dispute resolution service that collaboratively addresses the interests of all family members, that focuses not on the competing interests of the parents, as represented by their attorneys, but instead on the developmental and psychological needs of children whose parents are divorcing.

References

Ahrons, C. (1981). Continuing co-parental relationship between divorced spouses. *American Journal of Orthopsychiatry, 51,* 415-428.

Albiston, C., Maccoby, E., & Mnookin, R. (1990). Does joint legal custody matter? *Stanford Law & Policy Review, 2,* 167-179.

Bisnaire, L., Firestone, P., & Rynard, D. (1990). Factors associated with academic achievement in children following parental separation. *American Journal of Orthopsychiatry, 60,* 67-76.

Bray, J. (1991). Psychosocial factors affecting custodial and visitation arrangements. *Behavioral Sciences and the Law, 9,* 419-437.

Buchanan, C., Maccoby, E., & Dornbusch, S. (1991). Caught between parents: Adolescents' experience in divorced homes. *Child Development, 62,* 1008-1029.

Buchanan, C., Maccoby, E., & Dornbusch, S. (in press). Adolescents and their families after divorce: Three residential arrangements compared. *Journal of Research on Adolescence.*

Camara, K., & Resnick, G. (1989). Styles of conflict resolution and cooperation between divorced parents: Effects on child behavior and adjustment. *American Journal of Orthopsychiatry, 59,* 560-574.

Depner, C., Cannata, K., & Simon, M. (1992). Building a uniform statistical reporting system: A snapshot of California Family Court Services. *Family and Conciliation Courts Review, 30,* 169-184.

Duryee, M. (1991). *Demographic and outcome data of a court mediation program* (Report to the Judicial Council of California). San Francisco: The Judicial Council of California.

Duryee, M. (1992). Mandatory court mediation: Demographic summary and consumer evaluation of one court service—executive summary. *Family and Conciliation Courts Review, 30,* 260-267.

Emery, R. (1988). *Marriage, divorce, and children's adjustment.* Newbury Park, CA: Sage.

Emery, R., & Jackson, J. (1989). The Charlottesville Mediation Project: Mediated and litigated child custody disputes. *Mediation Quarterly, 24,* 3-18.

Emery, R., Matthews, S., & Wyer, M. (1991). Child custody mediation and litigation: Further evidence on the differing views of mothers and fathers. *Journal of Consulting and Clinical Psychology, 59,* 410-418.

Emery, R., & Wyer, M. (1987). Child custody mediation and litigation: An experimental evaluation of the experience of parents. *Journal of Consulting and Clinical Psychology, 55,* 179-186.

Gigy, L., & Kelly, J. (in press). Reasons for divorce: Perspectives of divorcing men and women. *Journal of Divorce.*

Healy, J., Malley, J., & Stewart, A. (1990). Children and their fathers after parental separation. *American Journal of Orthopsychiatry, 60,* 531-543.

Hetherington, E., Cox, M., & Cox, R. (1982). Effects of divorce on parents and children. In M. Lamb (Ed.), *Nontraditional families* (pp. 233-288). Hillsdale, NJ: Lawrence Erlbaum.

Jacobs, J. (1983). Treatment of divorcing fathers: Social and psychotherapeutic considerations. *American Journal of Psychiatry, 140,* 1294-1299.

Kelly, J. (1983). Mediation and psychotherapy: Distinguishing the differences. *Mediation Quarterly, 1,* 33-44.

Kelly, J. (1989a). Mediated and adversarial divorce: Respondents' perceptions of their processes and outcomes. *Mediation Quarterly, 24,* 71-88.

Kelly, J. (1989b). Dispute systems design: A family case study. *Negotiation Journal, 5,* 373-380.

Kelly, J. (1990a). Is mediation less expensive? Comparison of mediated and adversarial divorce costs. *Mediation Quarterly, 8,* 15-26.

Kelly, J. (1990b). Mediated and adversarial divorce resolution processes: An analysis of post-divorce outcomes. *Final report.* Washington, DC: Fund for Research in Dispute Resolution.

Kelly, J. (1991). Parent interaction after divorce: Comparison of mediated and adversarial divorce processes. *Behavioral Sciences and the Law, 9,* 387-398.

Kelly, J., & Duryee, M. (1992). Women & men's views of mediation in voluntary and mandatory mediation settings. *Family and Conciliation Courts Review, 30,* 34-49.

Kelly, J. & Gigy, L. (1989). Divorce mediation: Characteristics of clients and outcomes. In K. Kressel, D. Pruitt & Associates (Eds.), *Mediation research: The process and effectiveness of third-party intervention* (pp. 263-283). San Francisco: Jossey-Bass.

Kelly, J., Gigy, L., & Hausman, S. (1988). Mediated and adversarial divorce: Initial findings from a longitudinal study. In J. Folberg & A. Milne (Eds.), *Divorce mediation: Theory and practice* (pp. 453-473). New York: Guilford Press.

Kressel, K. (1985). *The process of divorce.* New York: Basic Books.

Kruk, E. (1992). Psychological and structural factors contributing to the disengagement of noncustodial fathers after divorce. *Family and Conciliation Courts Review, 30,* 81-101.

Leupnitz, D. A. (1982). *Child custody: A study of families after divorce.* Lexington, MA: Lexington Books.

Maccoby, E., Depner, C., & Mnookin, R. (1988). Custody of children following divorce. In E. M. Hetherington and J. Arasteh (Eds.), *The impact of divorce, single-parenting and step-parenting on children* (pp. 91-114). Hillsdale, NJ: Laurence Erlbaum.

Mnookin, R., Maccoby, E., Albiston, C., & Depner, C. (1990). Private ordering: What custodial arrangements are parents negotiating? In S. Sugarman & H. Kay (Eds.), *Divorce reform at the crossroads* (pp. 37-74). New Haven, CT: Yale University Press.

Pearson, J. (1991). The equity of mediated divorce agreements. *Mediation Quarterly, 9,* 179-197.

Pearson, J., & Thoennes, N. (1989). Reflections on a decade of research. In K. Kressel, D. Pruitt & Associates (Eds.), *Mediation research: The process and effectiveness of third-party intervention* (pp. 9-30). San Francisco: Jossey-Bass.

Saposnek, D. (1983). *Mediating child custody disputes: A systematic guide.* San Francisco: Jossey-Bass.

Slater, A., Shaw, J., & Duquesnel, J. (1992). Client satisfaction survey: A consumer evaluation of mediation and investigative services. *Family and Conciliation Courts Review, 30,* 252-259.

Tschann, J., Johnston, J., Kline, M., & Wallerstein, J. (1989). Family process and children's functioning during divorce. *Journal of Marriage and the Family, 51,* 431-444.

Wallerstein, J., & Kelly, J. (1980). *Surviving the breakup: How parents and children cope with divorce.* New York: Basic Books.

Wolman, R., & Taylor, K. (1991). Psychological effects of custody disputes on children. *Behavioral Sciences and the Law, 9,* 399-417.

8

Nonresidential Parent-Child Relationships Following Divorce and Remarriage

A Longitudinal Perspective

JAMES H. BRAY
SANDRA H. BERGER

Divorce and remarriage have a profound impact on children's relationships with their residential and nonresidential parents and their kinship systems. Despite the increased participation of fathers in childrearing, fathers are named nonresidential parents in 85% to 90% of the cases following divorce (Glick, 1988). Demographic projections reveal that more than 50% of American children will spend some time in a single-parent home and more than 33% will live some part of their childhood in a stepfamily following the remarriage of a parent (Glick, 1989; Hofferth, 1985). Millions of children and adolescents are indirectly affected by the dissolution and reorganization process as their families change from nuclear families to post-divorce single-parent families to stepfamilies (Glick, 1988, 1989). There is a dearth of information on the relationship between nonresidential parents and their children beyond

AUTHORS' NOTE: This chapter is partially based on Bray, J. H., & Berger, S. H. (1990). Noncustodial parent and grandparent relationships in stepfamilies. *Family Relations, 39,* 414-419. Copyright 1990 by the National Council on Family Relations, 3989 Central Ave. NE, Suite 550, Minneapolis, MN 55421. Used with permission. This research was supported by NIH grants RO1 HD18025 and RO1 HD22642 from the National Institute of Child Health and Human Development to James H. Bray.

the years immediately following divorce (Depner & Bray, 1990; Spanier & Furstenberg, 1987). In addition, even less research has examined the nonresidential parent's relationship with children subsequent to the remarriage of the custodial parent.

This chapter will discuss the changes in the nonresidential parent-child relationship following the remarriage of the custodial parent and the long-term effects of this relationship on children's adjustment. We will draw from our research in the *Developmental Issues in StepFamilies (DIS) Research Project* and present findings and case examples that address this area. The *DIS Research Project* is studying stepfather families and first-marriage nuclear families to evaluate children's development, the unique transitional issues, and family relationship patterns in stepfamilies over the first 10 years after parental remarriage (Bray, 1988; Bray & Berger, 1990, 1992; Bray, Berger, & Boethel, 1993; Bray, Berger, Silverblatt, & Hollier, 1987). The *DIS Research Project* also investigates how stepfamily relationships in the broader kinship network are distinct from nuclear families and how they relate to children's adjustment.

Developmental Family Systems Model of Divorce and Remarriage

Divorce and remarriage involve a series of marital and family transitions that interact with individual and family development. Initially we used family systems theory as a basis for examining the divorce and remarriage process. Family members are viewed as parts of an interdependent emotional and relational system that mutually influences other aspects of the family system. Change within one component of the system is believed to induce change in other parts of the system. We found that examining only the interactional and relational aspects of stepfamilies was not sufficient to understand the divorce and remarriage process. The stepfamily is an evolving system that is continually influenced by the individual developmental paths of each family member. Therefore, the developmental aspects of the stepfamily and individual members were integrated with a family systems approach, which we refer to as a developmental family systems model (Bray & Berger, 1990; Bray et al., 1987). Insufficient research has focused on the normative stages and transitions of the remarried family and wider kinship system. Forging successful interventions and social policy supportive of stepfamilies is limited by our lack of knowledge (Depner & Bray, 1990; Giles-Sims

& Crosbie-Burnett, 1989; Spanier & Furstenberg, 1987). A primary goal of the *DIS Research Project* is to document the developmental processes and issues of divorce and remarriage.

Understanding the remarriage process and stepfamilies includes knowledge about the marital transitions and family history from the first marriage through the remarriage. Many factors that affect stepfamily relations, and particularly nonresidential parents and children, have their origins in the first marriage and in the separation and divorce processes. A prime example is interparental conflict. Conflict between biological parents often starts before the divorce, may continue for many years after, and has serious effects on family members. In this chapter, the focus is on the developmental issues for stepfamilies that may influence nonresidential parent-child relationships. A more comprehensive discussion of the model is beyond the scope of this chapter. Table 8.1 presents salient issues identified at each point in the divorce and remarriage life cycle that are part of a model based on work from the *DIS Research Project*, McGoldrick and Carter (1980), Ransom, Schlesinger, and Derdeyn (1979), and Whiteside (1982). At each transition, factors that may affect the nonresidential parent-child relationship are identified. These factors and processes also may continue to have an impact during subsequent family transitions.

First Marriage

First marriages vary in length from a few days to many years, with the average length of marriages in the United States between 7 and 10 years. The probability of divorce decreases with the length of the marriage (London, 1991). Length of the first marriage is salient as it often reflects the level of commitment to the spouse and perhaps children. The length of the marriage interacts with the developmental stages of individual family members and the life cycle of the family. As an illustration, consider the marriages of individuals in early adulthood (in their twenties). These marriages may be impacted by the differentiation process within each spouse's family of origin and the realignment of family relationships when joining two families through marriage (Carter & McGoldrick, 1980). In addition, the individual developmental issues of forming an intimate peer network outside the family, identity development, and career choice will also influence the marriage. The birth

Table 8.1 Developmental Family Systems Model of Divorce and Remarriage

Factors Affecting Nonresidential Parent-Child Relations

First Marriage
    Length of First Marriage
    Developmental Stage of Marriage:
      Family Life Cycle Stage
      Individual Life Cycle Stages
    Parent-Child Relations
    Parenting Involvement During Marriage

Separation and Divorce
    Developmental Stage at Separation:
      Family Life Cycle Stage
      Individual Life Cycle Stages
    Process of Divorce: When and How
    Legal and Emotional Divorce
    Parent-Child Relations and Parenting Involvement

The Divorced Family
    Parent-Child Relations and Parenting Involvement
    Relationship Between Former Spouses
    Psychological Adjustment of the Nonresidential Parent
    Binuclear Households and Extended Family Relationships

Planning for Remarriage
    Remarriage of Nonresidential Parent
    Remarriage of Custodial Parent
    Planning for Parenting
    Evaluating Complexity and Multiple Roles in the Stepfamily
    Planning for Family Environment Changes

Early Years of Remarriage
    Parenting and Family Changes
    Integrating Nonresidential Parent Family System
    Developing Realistic Expectations
    Resolution of Previous Marriage: Completing the Psychological Divorce

Later Years of Remarriage
    Changes in Visitation and Custody
    Children From Remarriages
    Remarriage or Divorce of Nonresidential Parent
    Separation and Divorce of Stepfamily

of children further influences the marriage, as the couple has to make psychological "space" for the children in their relationship. Disruptions in the maturation process can interfere with a young adult's assuming a parental role and may contribute to the breakup of the family. The attachment and quality of involvement between each parent and child often influences their later relationship and the child's psychological adjustment and also may affect the type of custodial arrangement following the divorce (Lowery, 1986).

Separation and Divorce

About 50% of marriages are expected to end in divorce, and approximately 60% of divorcing couples have children (Glick, 1988, 1989). Approximately 40% of couples that separate will reconcile and may not eventually divorce (Bumpass, Castro Martin, & Sweet, 1991). Because of parental separation, divorce, or death, it is estimated that more than 50% of children will spend some time in a single-parent home before reaching age 18 (Bumpass, 1984; Hofferth, 1985). The age and developmental status of the children impact their reactions to marital conflict and separation, their understanding of the process, and their bonding and attachment to each parent (Bray, 1990; Hetherington & Camara, 1984; Wallerstein & Kelly, 1980). For example, preschool children often experience temporary developmental regressions and do not have the cognitive capacity to understand both separation from a parent and the divorce process. School age children frequently develop behavioral problems and may blame themselves for their parents' divorce, while adolescents typically respond with increased behavior problems, but are able to establish more emotional distance from their parents' divorce.

Individual and family life cycle stages are frequently important indicators of factors that contribute to the marital breakup. For example, marriages with teenage parents and very young children may represent a failed attempt at leaving the parental home, a problem with differentiation within the family, or some other type of family dysfunction (Carter & McGoldrick, 1980). Further, a family with middle-aged parents and adolescents represents the termination of a long-term relationship (12 to 20 years) and may indicate some problems in resolving midlife issues for one or both adults. Longer marriages have a greater impact on the partners' self-concept.

The process of divorce can have long-lasting effects on the post-divorce adjustment and relationships among family members. Not all divorces occur because of high conflict and poor relationships; some couples report just growing apart (Kelly, 1988). However, those that have high conflict involving children are detrimental to children's adjustment, particularly if the conflict continues after the divorce (Johnston, Kline, & Tschann, 1989). If the divorce results in termination of the conflict, then the divorce may be beneficial for the children (Hetherington & Camara, 1984; Peterson & Zill, 1986). The legal process may also affect the level of family and interparental conflict. Contested and prolonged litigation serves to continue or exacerbate interparental conflict with negative results for children (Kelly, 1991). The legal divorce is only one aspect of the process, as adults must also emotionally divorce their spouses. The emotional divorce may take longer and, if not resolved, will also contribute to ongoing interparental conflict.

The pattern of relationships between nonresidential parent and child established during the separation period often sets the stage for later development; however, the relationship may be quite different from what it was prior to the separation. Hetherington, Cox, and Cox (1978) found virtually no correlation between the father-child relationship during the marriage and after the divorce. Some men who had good relationships and significant involvement with their children dropped out of their children's lives after the divorce, while some men who had limited involvement before the divorce developed close, more involved relationships with their children after the divorce. Nonresidential mothers are more likely than nonresidential fathers to remain in contact with their children (Furstenberg, Nord, Peterson, & Zill, 1983). This is probably due to the socialization process of women as caretakers of children.

The Divorced Family

Families of divorce are rapidly becoming a normative family form (Glick, 1988, 1989). Divorce can occur at most points during the family life cycle and thus interacts with and alters the traditional course of family life. Divorce is best conceptualized as a series of transitions, rather than a static event (Hetherington & Camara, 1984). As with other aspects of the family life cycle, family relationships, particularly within the wider kinship system, are altered by divorce (Anspach, 1976; Hetherington & Hagan, 1986; Spicer & Hampe, 1975). Contact between the custodial parent and the kinship system of the ex-spouse frequently diminishes following divorce (Hetherington et al., 1978). The decrease in contact with the nonresidential parent may indirectly restrict access between paternal grandparents and grandchildren and decrease payment of child support by the nonresidential parent (Gladstone, 1989; Peterson & Nord, 1990).

The impact of the nonresidential father-child relationship is complex, variably associated with children's adjustment, and may differ according to the age and sex of the child and the time since marital separation (Bray, 1991; Hetherington & Hagan, 1986). Nonresidential parents usually form a pattern of involvement and visitation early during the divorce process and subsequently continue this pattern for several years after the divorce (Furstenberg, 1987; Maccoby & Mnookin, 1982). Studies on the influence of the nonresidential father-child relationship on child adjustment in the post-divorce family also demonstrate the importance of the family context, particularly the degree of conflict and cooperation between ex-spouses. For example, Healy, Malley, and Stewart (1990) conducted a 2-year longitudinal study of the effect of the quality of the nonresidential parent-child relationship on adjustment of children, aged 6 to 12 years, following parental separation. Frequency of contact with nonresidential fathers during early separation was consistently associated with higher self-esteem but *more* behavior problems for boys. For girls, however, early visitation frequency was persistently related to *lower* self-esteem and fewer behavior problems. Both boys and girls had more behavior problems if parents were in conflict and visitations were neither frequent nor regular at the initial separation. These gender variations may reflect the differential impact on children's adjustment and self-concept of same-sex parent-child relationships (Santrock & Warshak, 1979).

Nonresidential fathers are more likely to maintain contact with sons than daughters (Hess & Camara, 1979) and to have sons later shift residence to the fathers' homes (Hetherington, Cox, & Cox, 1982; Tepp, 1983). Research using large national samples, however, shows contradictory results. Furstenberg and colleagues (Furstenberg et al., 1983; Furstenberg, Morgan, & Allison, 1987), using data collected in 1981, found that the child's gender had no effect on involvement of the nonresidential father, while a more recent survey by Seltzer (1991) found that nonresidential fathers are more likely to visit and pay support for daughters than sons. Adolescent boys and girls and adult children of divorce have poorer ego functioning when rejected by one or both parents following divorce (Lewis & Wallerstein, 1987). Daughters, however, demonstrate a greater vulnerability to rejection of the parental role by one parent, most frequently nonresidential fathers, regardless of either parent's current marital status. Lewis and Wallerstein's findings suggest that the father-child relationship is of particular importance to daughters confronting adolescent identity issues. It is unclear, however, if the saliency of this relationship remains in longer remarried stepfamilies, where the stepfather may be a more important role model for the children.

However, studies focusing on the post-divorce patterns of continuing contact between nonresidential fathers and children reflect disturbing findings. While some authors have reported a gradual decline in contact over time (Hetherington & Hagan, 1986; Hetherington et al., 1982; Seltzer, 1991; Weiss, 1975), others found that divorce resulted in an abrupt cessation of contact or a rapid decline in visitation 12 months post-divorce (Furstenberg et al., 1983, 1987). Changes in these relationships following remarriage and the impact on children's adjustment are not well understood.

The interparental relationship is a key factor in children's adjustment. Ongoing high levels of conflict between divorced adults involving children is associated with poor adjustment and increased behavioral problems (Hetherington et al., 1978, 1982; Johnston et al., 1989). The relationship between interparental conflict and children's problems continues several years after the divorce (Kurdek & Sinclair, 1988). Frequent contact with the nonresidential father, low levels of interparental conflict, co-parental agreement, and ex-spouses who support each other's approaches to childrearing and discipline are characteristics of the post-divorce family that are associated with better adjustment for children, and particularly for boys (Camara & Resnick, 1987, 1988; Guidubaldi, Cleminshaw, Perry, & McLoughlin, 1983; Hess & Camara, 1979; Hetherington & Hagan, 1986; Wallerstein & Kelly, 1980).

When nonresidential parents continue their relationship with their children, the children are part of two households, called a binuclear family, with their own sets of roles and rules (Ahrons & Rodgers, 1987). Even with joint custody, most parents do not have shared and joint parenting (Maccoby & Mnookin, 1992). The pattern tends to be *parallel* parenting in which each parent conducts parenting independently and separately from the other parent (Furstenberg, 1987). If custodial and nonresidential parents have disparate parenting styles and home environments, children may have a more difficult time adjusting to transitions between households (Bray, 1991). When children reach adolescence, they may respond to these differences by playing one parent against the other or refusing to visit the parent with more structured or authoritarian parenting.

While there is often an increase in contact between custodial mothers and maternal grandparents following divorce (Hetherington et al., 1978), the divorce process may negatively impact continuation of relationships between children and paternal grandparents (Gladstone, 1989; Spanier & Furstenberg, 1987). This may be due to the reliance of the paternal grandparents on the nonresidential father to facilitate visits with grandchildren, and the lack of a continuing relationship between the custodial mother and the paternal grandparents (Gladstone, 1989). Similarly, Spanier and Furstenberg allude to the enabling role of the nonresidential parent in maintaining the relationship between children and paternal grandparents, noting that frequency of contact between children and the paternal kinship system follows the pattern of contact with the nonresidential father.

The psychological adjustment of the nonresidential parent may be an important factor in the post-divorce adjustment of children. Parents suffering from emotional problems or personality disorders may adversely influence their children's adjustment through projection of parental problems onto the child, diminished parenting abilities, and inadequate attention to the child's needs (Hetherington, 1981; Johnston & Campbell, 1988; Kelly, 1988). Adults with psychopathology are often rigid or unstable. Therefore, they are less likely to provide a stable or nurturing environment for the child. With two parents in the home, the negative impact of a disturbed parent can be buffered by a psychologically healthy parent who has a good relationship with a child (Baumrind, 1991; Bray, 1991; Hetherington, 1981). However, following the divorce, buffering by the healthy parent is not possible because of the separate home environments. Thus, a child's psychological adjustment may suffer with frequent visitation with a disturbed or emotionally unstable parent (Johnston & Campbell, 1988; Wallerstein & Kelly, 1980).

Planning for Remarriage

Most men, up to 85%, remarry and they do so more quickly than women following a divorce (London, 1991; Norton & Moorman, 1987). Thus, the children usually first become nonresidential members of a stepfamily. The remarriage of the nonresidential parent often results in changes in visitation, access, and routines between nonresidential parent and child. There are likely to be changes in living arrangements, and children are often concerned about how the remarriage will affect visits with their fathers. The changes frequently include a decrease in child support payments and visitations by the nonresidential father

(Furstenberg, 1987; Peterson & Nord, 1990). When the emotional divorce has not been completed, remarriage of the ex-spouse elicits unresolved feelings of anger, hurt, and disappointment, contributing to an increase in conflict between family members.

Demographic projections indicate that up to 75% of women remarry, usually within 3 to 5 years of their divorce (London, 1991; National Center for Health Statistics, 1990; Norton & Moorman, 1987). Thus, most children who experience a parental divorce will spend some time in a residential stepfamily before they reach adulthood (Glick, 1989). When adults plan to remarry, many evaluate these changes and develop plans for life after remarriage; unfortunately, many others do not. It is important to consider the changes that will occur in the parent-child relationships for both the residential and the nonresidential parents. Many adults cohabitate before marriage (Bumpass et al., 1991), but only 52% eventually marry following cohabitation (London, 1991). Thus, children are often exposed to multiple adults through parental dating or other relationships before the remarriage. Little is known about the impact of cohabitation on the nonresidential parent or children's adjustment following divorce or remarriage.

Early Years of Remarriage

Remarriage involves the joining of multiple family systems whose family life cycles have been disrupted by death, desertion, or divorce (McGoldrick & Carter, 1980). The new family context includes the developmental tasks of the residential family and adds further issues created by the remarriage. In addition, there may be disparities between individual and family life cycle stages in the new stepfamily. For example, in a new stepfamily with adolescents, the stepfamily is moving to develop a cohesive unit, while the adolescents are moving to disengage from the family and thus want to be *less* cohesive and more separate from the family unit. Further, some stepparents may have been married previously and may have children from that marriage, while other stepparents are marrying for the first time. The presence of children from each adult's previous marriage creates an even more complicated family system.

Remarriage of the custodial parent initiates a series of changes that impact most aspects of family members' lives. Many families move after the remarriage, which involves new schools and friends for the children. New relationships are formed and old relationships may be terminated. The introduction of the stepparent into the family usually results in changes in parenting by all adults, and there may be disparities, conflict, or competition among the adults over parenting issues and parent-child relationships. These changes prompt an increase in both positive and negative stress for family members (Bray, 1988).

As the stepfamily is attempting to develop a cohesive family unit, the role of the nonresidential parent and kinship system may vary considerably (Bray, 1990). If the nonresidential parent and kinship system were active with the children before the remarriage, then more integration is required. However, even in cases where there is limited or no contact between nonresidential parents and children, the remarriage may result in reinvolvement of this parent. This issue is discussed more fully later.

It is important that residential parents, stepparents, and nonresidential parents develop realistic expectations for the new stepfamily. Stepfamilies frequently attempt to consciously or unconsciously model themselves after a first-marriage nuclear family. This is likely due to the prevailing image of the family as a two-parent intact family with children. However, if the adults in the stepfamily attempt to recreate a nuclear family, additional stress and conflict may occur within the residential family and between the residential and nonresidential family members because of the complexity and differences between stepfamilies and nuclear families (Bray, 1988; Bray, Berger, & Boethel, 1993). The stress and conflict are often over attempts to exclude the nonresidential parent and kinship system and replace that family system with the stepparent's family. These attempts may promote loyalty conflict for the children, even when there is little contact with the nonresidential parent.

The remarriage of the custodial parent often signals the end to dreams and fantasies of reconciliation held by various family members. Thus, unresolved emotional attachments or a lack of emotional divorce finally may be settled with the remarriage of the custodial parent. Increased conflict or grief reactions may resurface during this period as family members come to terms with their feelings. Paternal grandparents may also feel threatened in their connection with their grandchildren, particularly if their usual contact is disrupted following the remarriage.

Later Years of Remarriage

Remarriage involves ongoing and unexpected changes in family living. The complex web of family relationships often results in multiple entrances and exits to the family and changes in visitation and custodial arrangements (Jacobson, 1987; Tepp, 1983; Tropf, 1984). These changes may result from positive developmental issues for children or may be due to problems between children and their custodial parents (Bray, 1991; White & Booth, 1985). Children may seek to have more contact with their nonresidential parent during adolescence when they are struggling with the normal developmental issues of identity formation. On the other hand, adolescents may attempt to live with the nonresidential parent to avoid conflict or parental control by the stepparent and custodial parent, or may be moved to the nonresidential parent's home by the custodial parent due to problems in the stepfamily (White & Booth, 1985).

Many couples in stepfamilies have children in this marriage. There is no unique name for stepfamilies that procreate. We refer to these children as "our babies." There is no indication that these children "cement" the relationships between stepfamily members, as had been hypothesized (Ganong & Coleman, 1988). However, when the new half-siblings are treated differently or favored over the stepchildren, the nonresidential parents may become reinvolved in interparental conflict out of loyalty to the children.

Since the divorce rate for remarriages is higher than for first marriages, up to 60%, and the average length of remarriages is only 5 years, many children will experience the breakup of their nonresidential parent's and residential parent's second marriages (Brody, Neubaum, & Forehand, 1988; Glick, 1988, 1989; Spanier & Furstenberg, 1987). This creates another stressful transition for family members. In addition, many of these children will experience the second remarriage of one of their parents and must cope with the stresses of forming another new stepfamily. It is not clear what role, either to enhance or to buffer stress for the children, the nonresidential parent plays in these transitions.

There is only limited research on the role of the nonresidential parent following remarriage. A central question concerns changes in the nonresidential parent's and kinship system's roles and relationships following remarriage. Is it important or useful for the nonresidential father and paternal grandparents to continue to have contact with their children after the remarriage, or does continued contact negatively impact the children? The remainder of this chapter will examine the effects of contact and relationship quality with the nonresidential father and the paternal grandparents on children's psychological adjustment following the mother's remarriage. In addition, common patterns identified in the *DIS Research Project* of involvement between children and their nonresidential fathers will be described.

The Developmental Issues in StepFamilies Research Project

The *DIS Research Project* is investigating the relationship of family structure, family process, family organization, and adult/child psychosocial variables in stepfather families and first-marriage nuclear families across the first 10 years of remarriage. To determine developmental differences in family organization and process during this period, stepfather families at 6 months, 2.5 years, and 5 to 7 years after remarriage were studied. We conducted longitudinal assessments of these families 3 to 4 years after the initial assessments to determine changes in family and individual functioning during the first 10 years after parental remarriage.

The *DIS Research Project* uses a multimethod, multisource design to study families. Ninety-nine stepfather families and 100 first-marriage nuclear families were studied. The nuclear families were selected to match the ages of the children in the stepfamilies and were similar in demographic background to the stepfamilies. Boys were studied in about one-half of the families, and girls were studied in the remainder. These families were reinterviewed 3 to 4 years after the initial assessment to determine longitudinal changes. The data at both interviews include self-reports of family and individual relationships, family process, adult/child outcomes, standardized assessments of parent and child behavior, observations and ratings of videotaped family interactions, and structured and unstructured interviews of family members. These data provide a rich source of information about family life after divorce and remarriage. In addition, the comparisons to families and children in nuclear families enable us to evaluate the normative and non-normative changes following remarriage. See Bray (1988), Bray and Berger (1990, 1992), and Bray et al. (1987) for further details on the methodology of the project.

Summary of DIS Research Findings on Nonresidential Parent-Child Relations

Cross-Sectional Finding. Using the cross-sectional data from the original *DIS Research Project*, Bray and Berger (1990) examined correlations between the amount of contact and relationship quality of nonresidential parents and children and children's behavioral adjustment. There was no difference in contact and relationship quality for children and their fathers at 6 months post-remarriage, 2.5 years post-remarriage, or 5 to 7 years post-remarriage. The study also found that more contact and a better relationship were related to better behavioral adjustment, but lower self-esteem, for boys after living 6 months in a stepfather family. After 2.5 years of remarriage there was no correlation between contact and relationship quality with the nonresidential parent and the boys' adjustment or self-esteem. For girls, more contact and a better relationship were related to better behavioral adjustment, but not self-esteem, after 6 months and 2.5 years of remarriage life. However, after 5 years in a stepfamily there was no relationship between contact and relationship quality with the nonresidential parent and girls' adjustment or self-esteem.

Bray and Berger (1990) also examined the correlations between children's adjustment and relationships with paternal grandparents after remarriage. Better relationships between paternal grandparents and boys in 6-month and 5- to 7-year stepfamilies were related to poorer self-esteem. In addition, better relationships with grandparents were related to more externalizing behavior problems (i.e., conduct problems, aggression) for boys in 5- to 7-year stepfamilies, according to stepfathers. More contact and better relationships between paternal grandparents and girls in the 6-month and 2.5-year stepfamily groups correlated with fewer behavior problems. At 2.5 years and 5 to 7 years post-remarriage, girls' self-esteem was associated with better grandparent relationships.

Longitudinal Findings. A preliminary analysis was conducted on a subset of the families to examine the longitudinal changes in nonresidential parent-child contact and relationships. We evaluated 78 stepfamilies in which the custodial mother was remarried in the original interview at Time 1 and continued to be married to the same person at Time 2. Families in which the mother had divorced between Time 1 and Time 2, or in which the target child had moved to the nonresidential father's residence, were not included in this analysis.

The results indicate that children's contact with their nonresidential fathers decreased over time, but the quality of the relationship improved during the same time frame. Girls tended to have less contact with their nonresidential fathers, but the father-daughter relationship quality tended to remain constant. Boys and their fathers tended to continue the same amount of contact; however, boys reported an improvement in relationship quality with their nonresidential fathers over time.

The median number of contacts with nonresidential fathers at Time 1 was 6 to 12 times per year for boys and girls, and the range of contacts was from twice a month (10.6%) to less than once a year (10%). At Time 2 the median number of contacts with nonresidential fathers was 3 to 6 times a year for boys and girls, and the range of contacts was from twice a month (11.7%) to less than once a year (25%). Thus, there was an increase in the number of children who had no contact with their nonresidential fathers in the past 12 months.

More contact and a better relationship between fathers and sons at Time 1 was predictive of mothers' ratings of *more* internalizing problems (i.e., anxiety, depression, worry) for boys at Time 2. At Time 2, higher self-esteem ratings by boys were related to poorer nonresidential father-son relationships. An increase in the quality of the nonresidential father-son relationship from Time 1 to Time 2 was predictive of stepfathers' ratings of more internalizing and externalizing behavior problems and boys' ratings of lower self-esteem at Time 2. There were no longitudinal or Time 2 predictors of girls' adjustment. There were also no correlations between changes in contact or the quality of the nonresidential father-daughter relationship from Time 1 to Time 2 and outcomes for daughters at Time 2.

These findings, in contrast to those of earlier studies (Hess & Camara, 1979; Tepp, 1983), suggest fewer differences between the father-daughter relationship and the father-son relationship. Maintenance of relationship between father and child through the early and later stages of stepfamily formation may have mitigated younger girls' fear of loss of the father's love as a result of acceptance of the stepfather and may have also alleviated the anxiety accompanying loosening of the mother-child bond with the mother's remarriage (Knaub & Hanna, 1984; Visher & Visher, 1988). These findings indicate that girls' relationships with nonresidential fathers are less important to their longer-range behavioral adjustment following the remarriage of the mother.

The amount of contact and quality of the relationship between children and their nonresidential fathers changes over time after maternal remarriage. In contrast to the *DIS Research Project* cross-sectional findings (Bray & Berger, 1990), the longitudinal study indicated that nonresidential fathers significantly decreased the amount of contact with their children, but increased their quality of relationships over a 3- to 4-year period. These findings are consistent with previous longitudinal studies that found a decline in contact between nonresidential fathers and children over time (Furstenberg, 1987; Hetherington et al., 1982). While there are long-range effects of the previous nonresidential parent-child relations, after several years of remarriage there are few concurrent effects of contact with the nonresidential father on children's behavioral adjustment (Clingempeel & Segal, 1986; Furstenberg et al., 1987; Jacobson, 1987). Given the ages of the children at the time of the follow-up interviews and the limited amount of time that children spend with their nonresidential fathers, it is not surprising that the amount of contact and quality of relationship have little impact on children's behavioral adjustment. During adolescence, children are often influenced more by their peer relationships than family relationships (Baumrind, 1991), and family relationships might have even less effect on adolescents' adjustment in divorced and remarried homes.

The unexpected finding that boys in early stepfather families who have a better relationship with the nonresidential father report lower self-esteem is similar to results from Clingempeel and Segal (1986). Examining the adjustment of boys and girls in stepmother and stepfather families, these authors reported a trend that the frequency of visitation with the nonresidential mother was associated with lower self-esteem for girls in stepmother families. In the Bray and Berger (1990) study the negative correlation between the quality of the relationship with nonresidential fathers and self-esteem for boys continued as a trend during later remarriage. These results reflect the sensitive relationship between children and the nonresidential parent of the same sex and indicate the importance of this relationship to the psychological adjustment of the child in the divorce and remarriage process (Hetherington & Hagan, 1986; Santrock & Warshak, 1979).

The causal relationship among these variables remains uncertain. Following the remarriage of the custodial mother, boys' lower self-esteem may be the result of a close relationship with the father, or fathers may form a closer attachment to sons who are having problems. Other unexamined considerations, however, may explain this finding. Time spent on visitations may inhibit boys' participation in out-of-school activities important to the development of a sense of mastery and self-esteem. Also, unremitting hostility toward and negative criticism of the nonresidential parent by the mother and stepfather could contribute to the son's feeling bad about himself because of his identification with the father. This may also negatively impact the quality of the relationship between custodial mother and child. These processes may reflect an incomplete emotional divorce or the unacknowledged attempts of the mother and stepfather to replicate the structure of the first-marriage nuclear family. Furthermore, more frequent visits with a nonresidential father may add stress to a child's life through moves between households, changes in routines and schedules, or additional negative family process.

Regular but infrequent contact with paternal grandparents was related to better behavioral adjustment, especially for girls, during the early years of remarriage. Surprisingly, this relationship reversed itself for boys but remained as a trend for girls after 5 years of remarriage. Additionally, boys tended to have poorer self-esteem with better relationships with grandparents, while girls had the opposite relationship. Nonresidential fathers and their parents are reinvolved with an adolescent with problems and utilized as a solution to handling an acting-out child by the mother and stepfather (Bray & Berger, 1990). More behavior problems for boys after 5 years may also be due to some moderating variable, such as the relationship between the mother and grandparents or mother and nonresidential father. In general, these findings support a developmental family systems conceptualization of the divorce and remarriage process in which multiple family systems are important correlates of children's adjustment.

Patterns of Nonresidential Parent-Child Relationships Following Remarriage

One of the limitations of the quantitative data on these families is that they provide snapshots of the family at only one point in time. During the longitudinal assessments we conducted semistructured interviews with the families in order to create a context in which the families could "tell us their family story." The interviews were designed to allow each family member to describe how family relations remained stable or changed over time. It is apparent from the interviews that relationships between nonresidential parents and children shift over time, and often in dramatic ways. There are a variety of relationship patterns that emerge from these interviews. In the following sections we describe common patterns of nonresidential parent-child relationships based on our clinical impressions of these families. These patterns were not derived from empirical examination of the data. Thus, the groups should be viewed with some caution until empirical verification can take place.

Cooperative Co-Parenting. Although all of the divorced mothers in the *DIS Research Project* were sole custodial parents, a small group of former spouses were interdependent in decision making and providing support and nurturance for their children. Frequently these couples lived in proximity, which facilitated more frequent visitations and interactions than were legally prescribed. This arrangement allowed fathers to actively participate in school and extracurricular activities with their children. In addition, visitations were less disruptive to the children's social activities. Visitation schedules appeared flexible and easily renegotiated in these families. In one case the nonresidential father took the half-sibling from the remarriage on weekend visits with the other children. His explanation was that this gave his former spouse and the stepfather some time without children, and also because his children wanted their new sibling to be with them during visits.

Standard Visitation and Access. The majority of families had a standard visitation arrangement in which the children were supposed to visit with their nonresidential fathers on alternate weekends and holidays. In these cases, the fathers appeared to be involved with their children in limited ways, although most of the children reported that the visits were beneficial and desirable. There was considerable variability within this group, with many children wanting more access to their nonresidential fathers, while others wanted less access. For many of these children it appeared that the stepfather played an important paternal role, although he did not replace the biological father for the children. With the paucity of contact, the fathers' lack of influence on the children's adjustment is not surprising.

Ongoing Interparental Conflict. Despite the numerous changes and many years following the initial divorce, a number of couples sustained high levels of animosity and conflict (Dudley, 1991). Ahrons and Rodgers (1987) labeled these couples "fiery foes" because of their intense and antagonistic relationships. The range of interparental conflict in these families was from mild tension between ex-spouses to protracted, high levels of discord. Several of these families also "fought it out" in the courts and continued to have problems over child support payments, visitation, and custody. As with interparental conflict following divorce, children's adjustment is adversely affected by their involvement in interparental conflict following remarriage.

The Suddenly Appearing Parent. For some stepfamilies, remarriage occasions the sudden reappearance of an absent nonresidential parent who wants to resume a relationship with the child. The impetus for this change may be due to a number of factors, including competition with the stepparent, legal actions taken by the custodial parent that reinvolve the absent parent, or developmental needs of the child. Custodial mothers are more likely to file a lawsuit to recover unpaid child support following their remarriage (Peterson, 1986). The lawsuit reinvolves the nonresidential father in the family and he may demand to exercise his visitation rights with the children. This can be disruptive for the stepfamily, particularly in cases where there has not been contact between the non-residential parent and the child for some time. Alternatively, after being brought back into the family through litigation, some men sever their ties with the children at this point and attempt to disappear (Peterson & Nord, 1990).

The Suddenly Vanishing Parent. The reverse of the above situation occurs when the nonresidential parent has had contact and a relationship with the children and suddenly stops or significantly decreases the amount of contact. This may occur because of the father's remarriage, instability in the father, and/or a sudden relocation. When a nonresidential father remarries, there may be pressures on him to reduce his level of involvement with his children. The most extreme reaction is to terminate all contact, but more often there is a gradual or immediate decrease in visitation and access. The nonresidential father may suddenly announce that he is not going to have the children over for visitations. An alternative cause of this type of change is when the nonresidential parent moves because of a job change or career opportunities (Dudley, 1991). In these cases the visitation may go from alternate weekends to visits only a few times a year during holidays and vacations. Another version of this pattern occurs when the nonresidential father exercises his visitation sporadically, cancels visits at the last minute, or simply does not show up when expected.

Changes in Access and Custody. There are many formal and informal changes in living and visitation arrangements between children and their parents (Maccoby & Mnookin, 1992). As previously discussed, these changes often occur during adolescence and are influenced by developmental needs of the children. However, the changes are also stimulated by problems between the custodial parent and the child.

As children enter adolescence and their social interactions outside of the family increase, many do not want to continue with a rigid visitation schedule. In some cases they may refuse visitation completely or demand that the visits be on their terms (see Chapter 6, by Johnston, on children who refuse visitations). However, some adolescents who had limited contact with their nonresidential parents may seek more access during this period. The increase in contact may be due to the developmental issues of identity formation; adolescents may want to interact with the nonresidential parent during this process (Bray, 1991). However, residential parents may view this as a critique of their parenting, causing old wounds to be reopened, which generates an increase in interparental conflict. As a result, the adolescent may be caught in a loyalty conflict between parents.

Adolescents also request to live with their nonresidential parents as a way of avoiding conflict with their residential parents, or because the nonresidential parent is perceived as more lenient. Such a change may place additional stress on the family of the nonresidential parent, and the outcome may not be as the child idealistically projects. In some cases the adolescent may "bounce" back and forth between households, and may not receive sufficient supervision and parenting. In addition, if the adolescent is having trouble with the stepparent, then a change in custody may occur (White & Booth, 1985). This move can serve to stabilize the remarried family.

Fathers With no Contact. A substantial number of fathers have no contact with their children following divorce and remarriage. Reasons for no contact vary from hostility and conflict between ex-spouses, to fathers having personal problems that prevent visitation, to long-distance parenting (Dudley, 1991). Results from the *DIS Research Project* indicate that up to 25% of fathers have no contact with their children, which is less than that found by other studies from the early 1980s (Furstenberg et al., 1983, 1987). The absence of the parent, however, does not mean that he or she has no impact on the family. Many children continue to feel close to their absent fathers and may idealize them in their absence (Furstenberg et al., 1987). Thus, these parents are present psychologically for the children and may influence the family and parent-child relationships. Custodial parents also keep the absent parent alive in the family through projective identification of the nonresidential parent onto a particular child. Statements such as, "You act just like your father," or "Your father used to do that to me," keep the nonresidential parent part of the family, even when there is no contact with that parent. Alternatively, some mothers help the child develop a more empathic understanding of the father's absence and do not necessarily denigrate the absent parent.

Termination of Parental Rights. In a small number of cases, the nonresidential parent's parental rights are legally terminated. This usually occurs in two cases. First, the nonresidential parent voluntarily gives up parental rights due to lack of involvement with the children. Second, the nonresidential parent's rights may be terminated in absentia or because it is judged to be in the children's best interests because of major problems with the nonresidential parent (e.g., psychiatric problems, sexual or physical abuse). In these cases the children usually have no relationship with this parent and consent to the termination.

Adoption by the Stepparent. Termination of the nonresidential parent's rights may be stimulated by the desire of the custodial parent and stepparent to have the stepparent adopt the stepchildren. Adoption of children by the stepparent is an infrequent arrangement. After adoption, the family is no longer a stepfamily because the stepparent has full legal rights and responsibilities with respect to the children.

It should be noted that these patterns may change over time and interact with the developmental changes and needs of children and changes in family relationships throughout the complex stepfamily system. During the longitudinal assessments many families related how nonresidential parent-child relationships were often in flux and the patterns of relationships changed as the children matured, as unresolved feelings reemerged or faded away, or as other changes, such as moves, remarriages, or changes in child support, emerged within the family system.

Clinical and Social Policy Implications

Problems in access to and affiliations with nonresidential parents and their kinship system are areas that educators and clinicians can impact to enhance positive outcomes for children and better relationships with family members. Parents can be educated that denigration or "bad-mouthing" the ex-spouse may cause boys to develop lower self-esteem because of their identification with their fathers. Most parents do not understand that speaking negatively about an ex-spouse in front of the child is implicitly criticizing their child because of the biological connection, which further places the child in a loyalty conflict. In addition, nonresidential fathers may need to be more mindful that visitation can disrupt peer and social activities that are important to their children's development. Stepfamilies face difficult choices in weighing the relative benefits of ongoing contact with the nonresidential parents and the needs and desires of the children and stepfamily. Further investigation is needed to develop interventions that bolster the positive influences and minimize the negative impact of these relationships.

The relationship between children and their paternal grandparents is also related to children's adjustment, their developmental path, and the evolving stepfamily. The pattern of contact generally follows the arrangement found for fathers. Educating parents and grandparents in stepfamilies about the importance of ongoing contact between children, especially girls, and paternal grandparents is supported by this research. Anecdotal evidence from paternal grandparents suggests that they feel abandoned, forgotten, or left out of their grandchildren's lives after the divorce, and particularly after the remarriage. Many grandparents experience distress and sorrow over the loss of their grandchildren. These results support the importance of ongoing grandparent visitation following divorce. However, it is important to identify the other factors that mediate these relationships, such as ex-spousal conflict, rather than to assume that regular contact between paternal grandparents and children is always in the children's best interests. Further longitudinal research is necessary to understand the complex nature of extended family relationships after remarriage and how these relationships change over time and impact children's adjustment.

The evolving relationships between nonresidential parents and children have many implications for our society as a whole. It is clear that the changing nature of American families will require modifications in social policy. Recent research on the positive effects of mediated rather than adversarial divorces suggests that alternative dispute resolution strategies need to be developed and practiced (Kelly, 1991). Continued financial support of children by the nonresidential parent following divorce is an important factor that contributes to children's well-being. Changes in the laws to facilitate child support payments are necessary (see Teachman & Paasch, this volume).

Separation, divorce, and remarriage are events that create ongoing family transitions and processes that affect all aspects of family members' lives. During the heat of the marital disruption many adults feel that by divorcing their spouse they will eliminate that person from their lives. Nothing could be further from the truth. In most cases, however, the long-term changes and consequences of divorce are not reflected in the crafting of divorce settlements. This seems to ignore the reality of family life following marital separation and may contribute to the ongoing difficulties experienced by some divorcing families. It appears that divorce and remarriage will continue to occur in our society as common family transitions for many years to come. It is important that a long-term perspective on family transitions be fostered to help people through these trying times and facilitate their positive adjustment. A long-term perspective would include consideration of changes that may occur in the family due to parental remarriage, developmental needs of children and adolescents, career and economic changes in the family, and long-term financial needs of children. Many of these factors occur with such frequency that they can be anticipated at the time of the separation and divorce. It is clear that more research is necessary to document and understand the progression of these relationships and the impact they have on adults and children. As we understand the common developmental paths and issues that impact nonresidential parents and their children, we can foresee and develop constructive solutions and modify social policies that support adults and children through the transitions in modern American families.

References

Ahrons, C. R., & Rodgers, R. H. (1987). *Divorced families: A multidisciplinary developmental view*. New York: Norton.

Anspach, D. F. (1976). Kinship and divorce. *Journal of Marriage and the Family, 38*, 323-330.

Baumrind, D. (1991). Effective parenting during the early adolescent transition. In P. A. Cowan & E. M. Hetherington (Eds.), *Family transitions* (pp. 111-164). Hillsdale, NJ: Lawrence Erlbaum.

Bray, J. H. (1988). Children's development in early remarriage. In E. M. Hetherington & J. Arasteh (Eds.), *The impact of divorce, single-parenting and step-parenting on children* (pp. 279-298). Hillsdale, NJ: Lawrence Erlbaum.

Bray, J. H. (1990). Impact of divorce on the family. In R. E. Rakel (Ed.), *Textbook of family practice* (4th ed, pp. 111-122). Philadelphia: W. B. Saunders.

Bray, J. H. (1991). Psychosocial factors affecting custodial and visitation arrangements. *Behavioral Science and the Law, 9*, 419-437.

Bray, J. H., & Berger, S. H. (1990). Nonresidential parent and grandparent relationships in stepfamilies. *Family Relations, 39*, 414-419.

Bray, J. H., & Berger, S. H., (1992). Stress, conflict, and children's adjustment in stepfather families and nuclear families. Manuscript submitted for publication.

Bray, J. H., Berger, S. H., & Boethel, C. L. (1993). Role integration and marital adjustment in stepfather families. In K. Pasley & M. Ihinger-Tallman (Eds.), *Stepfamilies: Issues in research, theory, and practice.* New York: Greenwood Press.

Bray, J. H., Berger, S. H., Silverblatt, A. H., & Hollier, A. (1987). Family process and organization during early remarriage: A preliminary analysis. In J. P. Vincent (Ed.), *Advances in family intervention, assessment, and theory* (Vol. 4, pp. 253-279). Greenwich, CT: JAI Press.

Brody, G. H., Neubaum, E., & Forehand, R. (1988). Serial marriage: A heuristic analysis of an emerging family form. *Psychological Bulletin, 103*, 211-222.

Bumpass, L. L. (1984). Children and marital disruption: A replication and update. *Demography, 21*, 71-82.

Bumpass, L. L., Castro Martin, T., & Sweet, J. A. (1991). The impact of family background and early marital factors on marital disruption. *Journal of Family Issues, 12*, 22-42.

Camara, K. A., & Resnick, G. (1987). The interaction between marital and parental subsystems in mother-custody, father-custody, and two-parent households: Effects on children's social development. In J. P. Vincent (Ed.), *Advances in family intervention, assessment, and theory* (Vol. 4, pp. 165-196). Greenwich, CT: JAI Press.

Camara, K. A., & Resnick, G. (1988). Interparental conflict and cooperation: Factors moderating children's post-divorce adjustment. In E. M. Hetherington & J. Arasteh (Eds.), *The impact of divorce, single-parenting and step-parenting on children* (pp. 169-196). Hillsdale, NJ: Lawrence Erlbaum.

Carter, E. A., & McGoldrick, M. (Eds.). (1980). *The family life cycle.* New York: Gardner Press.

Clingempeel, W. G., & Segal, S. (1986). Stepparent-stepchild relationships and the psychological adjustment of children in stepmother and stepfather families. *Child Development, 57,* 474-484.

Depner, C. E., & Bray, J. H. (1990). Modes of participation for nonresidential parents: The challenge for research, policy, education and practice. *Family Relations, 39,* 378-381.

Dudley, J. R. (1991). Increasing our understanding of divorced fathers who have infrequent contact with their children. *Family Relations, 40,* 279-285.

Furstenberg, F. F., Jr. (1987). The new extended family: The experience of parents and children after remarriage. In K. Pasley & M. Ihinger-Tallman (Eds.), *Remarriage and stepparenting: Current research and theory* (pp. 42-61). New York: Guilford.

Furstenberg, F. F., Jr., Morgan, S. P., & Allison, P. D. (1987). Paternal participation and children's well-being after marital dissolution. *American Sociological Review, 52,* 595-601.

Furstenberg, F. F., Jr., Nord, C. W., Peterson, J. L., & Zill, N. (1983). The life course of children of divorce: Marital disruption and parental contact. *American Sociological Review, 48,* 656-668.

Ganong, L. H., & Coleman, M. (1988). Do mutual children cement bonds in stepfamilies? *Journal of Marriage and the Family, 50,* 687-698.

Giles-Sims, J., & Crosbie-Burnett, M. (1989). Stepfamily research: Implications for policy, clinical interventions, and further research. *Family Relations, 38,* 19-23.

Gladstone, J. W. (1989). Grandmother-grandchild contact: The mediating influence of the middle generation following marriage breakdown and remarriage. *Canadian Journal on Aging, 8,* 355-365.

Glick, P. C. (1988). The role of divorce in the changing family structure: Trends and variations. In S. A. Wolchik & P. Karoly (Eds.), *Children of divorce: Empirical perspectives on adjustment* (pp. 3-34). New York: Gardner Press.

Glick, P. C. (1989). Remarried families, stepfamilies, and stepchildren: A brief demographic profile. *Family Relations, 38,* 24-27.

Guidubaldi, J., Cleminshaw, H. K., Perry, J. D., & McLoughlin, C. S. (1983). The impact of parental divorce on children: Report of the nationwide NASP study. *School Psychology Review, 12,* 300-323.

Healy, J. M., Malley, J. E., & Stewart, A. J. (1990). Children and their fathers after parental separation. *American Journal of Orthopsychiatry, 60,* 531-543.

Hess, R. D., & Camara, K. A. (1979). Post-divorce family relationships as mediating factors in the consequences of divorce on children. *Journal of Social Issues, 35,* 79-96.

Hetherington, E. M. (1981). Children and divorce. In R. Henderson (Ed.), *Parent-child interaction: Theory, research, and prospects.* New York: Academic Press.

Hetherington, E. M., & Camara, K. A. (1984). Families in transition: The processes of dissolution and reconstitution. In R. D. Parke (Ed.), *Review of child development research: Vol. 7. The family* (pp. 398-439). Chicago: University of Chicago Press.

Hetherington, E. M. Cox, M., & Cox, R. 1978). The aftermath of divorce. In J. H. Stevens & M. Mathews (Eds.), *Mother/child, father/child relationships* (pp. 110-155). Washington, DC: National Association for the Education of Young Children.

Hetherington, E. M. Cox, M., & Cox, R. (1982). The effects of divorce on parents and children. In M. Lamb (Ed.), *Nontraditional families* (pp. 233-288). Hillsdale, NJ: Lawrence Erlbaum.

Hetherington, E. M., & Hagan, M. S. (1986). Divorced fathers: Stress, coping, and adjustment. In M. E. Lamb (Ed.), *The father's role: Applied perspectives* (pp. 103-134). New York: John Wiley.

Hofferth, S. L. (1985). Updating children's life course. *Journal of Marriage and the Family, 47,* 93-115.

Jacobson, D. S. (1987). Family type, visiting patterns, and children's behavior in the stepfamily: A linked family system. In K. Pasley & M. Ihinger-Tallman (Eds.), *Remarriage and stepparenting: Current research and theory* (pp. 257-272). New York: Guilford.

Johnston, J. R., & Campbell, L.E.G. (1988). *Impasses of divorce: The dynamics and resolution of family conflict.* New York: Free Press.

Johnston, J. R., Kline, M., & Tschann, J. M. (1989). Ongoing postdivorce conflict: Effects on children of joint custody and frequent access. *American Journal of Orthopsychiatry, 59,* 1-17.

Kelly, J. B. (1988). Longer-term adjustment in children of divorce: Converging findings and implications for practice. *Journal of Family Psychology, 2,* 119-140.

Kelly, J. B. (1991). Parent interaction after divorce: Comparison of mediated and adversarial divorce processes. *Behavioral Sciences and the Law, 9,* 387-398.

Knaub, P. K., & Hanna, S. L. (1984). Children of remarriage: Perceptions of family strengths. *Journal of Divorce, 7,* 73-90.

Kurdek, L. A., & Sinclair, R. J. (1988). Adjustment of young adolescents in two-parent nuclear, stepfather, and mother-custody families. *Journal of Consulting and Clinical Psychology, 56,* 91-96.

Lewis, J. M., & Wallerstein, J. S. (1987). Family profile variables and long-term outcome in divorce research: Issues at a ten-year follow-up. In J. P. Vincent (Ed.), *Advances in family intervention, assessment, and theory: Vol. 4* (pp. 121-142). Greenwich, CT: JAI Press.

London, K. A. (1991). Cohabitation, marriage, marital dissolution, and remarriage: United States, 1988. *Advance data from vital and health statistics; No. 194.* Hyattsville, MD: National Center for Health Statistics.

Lowery, C. R. (1986). Maternal and joint custody: Differences in the decision process. *Law and Human Behavior, 10,* 303-315.

Maccoby, E. E., & Mnookin, R. H. (1992). *Dividing the child: The social and legal dilemmas of custody.* Cambridge, MA: Harvard University Press.

McGoldrick, M., & Carter, E. A. (1980). Forming a remarried family. In E. A. Carter & M. McGoldrick (Eds.), *The family life cycle* (pp. 265-294). New York: Gardner Press.

National Center for Health Statistics. (1990). Advance report of final marriage statistics, 1987. *Monthly vital statistics report* (Vol. 38, No. 12, Supp.). Hyattsville, MD: Public Health Service.

Norton, A. J., & Moorman, J. E. (1987). Marriage and divorce patterns of U.S. women. *Journal of Marriage and the Family, 49*, 3-14.

Peterson, J. L. (1986). Post-divorce events and the provision of child support payments. *Proceedings of the Research and Evaluation Track, 35th Annual Conference, National Child Support Enforcement Association.*

Peterson, J. L., & Nord, C. W. (1990). The regular receipt of child support: A multistep process. *Journal of Marriage and the Family, 52*, 539-551.

Peterson, J. L., & Zill, N. (1986). Marital disruption, parent-child relationships, and behavior problems in children. *Journal of Marriage and the Family, 48*, 295-307.

Ransom, J. W., Schlesinger, S., & Derdeyn, A. P. (1979). A stepfamily in formation. *American Journal of Orthopsychiatry, 49*, 36-43.

Santrock, J. W., & Warshak, R. A. (1979). Father custody and social development in boys and girls. *Journal of Social Issues, 35*, 112-125.

Seltzer, J. A. (1991). Relationships between fathers and children who live apart: The father's role after separation. *Journal of Marriage and the Family, 53*, 79-101.

Spanier, G. B., & Furstenberg, F. F., Jr. (1987). Remarriage and reconstituted families. In M. B. Sussman & S. K. Steinmetz (Eds.), *Handbook of marriage and the family* (pp. 419-434). New York: Plenum.

Spicer, J., & Hampe, G. (1975). Kinship interaction after divorce. *Journal of Marriage and the Family, 37*, 113-119.

Tepp, A. V. (1983). Divorced fathers: Predictors of continued paternal involvement. *American Journal of Psychiatry, 140*, 1465-1469.

Tropf, W. D. (1984). An exploratory examination of the effect of remarriage on child support and personal contacts. *Journal of Divorce, 7*, 57-73.

Visher, E. B., & Visher, J. S. (1988). *Old loyalties, new ties: Therapeutic strategies with stepfamilies.* New York: Brunner/Mazel.

Wallerstein, J. S., & Kelly, J. B. (1980). *Surviving the breakup: How children cope with divorce.* New York: Basic Books.

Weiss, R. S. (1975). *Marital separation.* New York: Basic Books.

White, L. K., & Booth, A. (1985). The quality and stability of remarriages: The role of stepchildren. *American Sociological Review, 50*, 689-698.

Whiteside, M. F. (1982). Remarriage: A family developmental process. *Journal of Marital and Family Therapy, 4*, 59-68.

9

Nonresidential Parenting

Multidimensional Approaches in Research, Policy, and Practice

CHARLENE E. DEPNER
JAMES H. BRAY

The focus of this volume is on nonresidential parents—the nature and amount of their family participation as well as the implications of their involvement for the family system. Despite the call for a comprehensive national family policy that recognizes the diversity of family patterns (Moynihan, 1986), we are only beginning to build frameworks that can handle variations across families and over time. Nonresidential parents can play viable and consequential roles in the lives of their children (Ahrons & Rodgers, 1987; Depner & Bray, 1990; Nock, 1988); but an understanding of the dynamics of nonresidential parenting is fragmented when the full spectrum of relevant variables is not integrated into a multidimensional model. The chapters in this book illustrate the value of a multidimensional approach that considers the perspectives of different family members, recognizes family pluralism and the sig-

AUTHORS' NOTE: This chapter is partially based on Depner, C. E., & Bray, J. H. (1990). Modes of participation for nonresidential parents: The challenge for research, policy, education and practice. *Family Relations, 39,* 378-381. Copyright 1990 by the National Council on Family Relations, 3989 Central Ave. NE, Suite 550, Minneapolis, MN 55421. Used with permission. Dr. Bray's contribution was partially supported by NIH grant RO1 HD22642 from the National Institute of Child Health and Human Development.

nificance of cultural heritage, and extends the temporal dimension of the inquiry.

A multidimensional analysis lends support to the position that a monolithic vision of nonresidential parenting is a poor basis for policy. A single image excludes the experiences of many families. Distinctions based on ethnicity, marital history, non-normative gender roles, and changes in family roles should be factored into policy formulation. Together, our authors send a compelling message that, although nonresidential fathers and mothers collectively constitute a large sector of all parents, social policy should not treat this group as homogeneous, but must make provisions that respect and support diversity.

This final chapter reviews multidimensional approaches that are being adopted in research, practice, and policy. There is increased recognition that research, practice, and policy should operate together in a reticular process to understand and facilitate contemporary family relationships (Brownstein, 1991). Research interweaves with policy and practice in various ways. One stream of scholarship uses demographic data to lend historical perspective to rapid changes in family patterns and to make projections that equip social institutions to anticipate the needs of American families (Cherlin, 1983; Moroney, 1986; Noble & Sussman, 1987; Thornton & Freedman, 1983). Research is sometimes explicitly designed to explore particular public concerns (Brownstein, 1991; Mayer & Greenwood, 1980; Merton, 1945) or to evaluate specific policy initiatives (Aldous & Dumon, 1990; Grych & Fincham, 1992). On other occasions it inadvertently redirects policy as evidence mustered to support or refute proposed programs (Depner, 1991). The need for information about the operations of alternative family structures is also an impetus for further development of family research. For example, policy questions posed by nonresidential parenting reveal lacunae in an empirical knowledge base that has relied extensively on the study of nuclear families. Perhaps most important, recognition of family multiplicity introduces new ways of conceptualizing family issues that, in turn, inspire unprecedented policy strategies.

An integrated agenda for research, policy, and practice would adopt a multidimensional perspective in seven key areas: (1) defining parental roles; (2) evaluating the effects of the law on parental behavior; (3) facilitating parental involvement; (4) determining the impact of legislation on the family system; (5) understanding the role of cultural and kinship systems; (6) considering life course issues in the relationship between nonresidential parents and their children; and (7) increasing the responsiveness of social systems to the reality of family pluralism.

Defining Parental Roles

This is a period of experimentation with and reappraisal of parental role definitions. There is increased recognition of diversity in the expression of parent-child relationships, and at the same time, specific policies are being initiated to forge stronger financial and emotional bonds between nonresidential parents and their children.

Social science is beginning to identify modes of nonresidential parenting by describing the plethora of parental and quasi-parental connections and their significance in the lives of children. Several chapters in this volume touch on the changing social expectations for divorced mothers and fathers. Others question whether models of post-divorce parenting extend to situations in which a child has never lived with both parents, as is the case with millions of children born outside of marriage. Remarriage introduces new adults who may assume some parenting activities (Bray & Berger, this volume; Braver, Wolchik, Sandler, & Sheets, this volume). Advances in reproductive technology are posing complex dilemmas about the rights and responsibilities of adults who play functional and biological roles in the life of a child (Polikoff, 1990). Del Carmen and Virgo (this volume) introduce the provocative notion that a multicultural perspective may detect successful models of parent-child interaction that have been overlooked in a heretofore exclusionary research tradition.

Despite the multiplicity of roles that parents may play in the lives of their children, stereotypes are prevalent. A simplistic "single parent" caricature accords preeminence to policy initiatives consistent with that image, but may be ill-advised in light of a multicultural perspective (del Carmen & Virgo, this volume). Much needs to be done to eradicate the stigma of the "broken home" and the self-fulfilling prophecy that certain family structures inevitably lead to developmental deficit. For example, children from divorced homes are often expected to behave distinctively and are treated differently from children from intact homes, even when there are no observable behavioral problems or dissimilarities (Hetherington, Cox, & Cox, 1982; Santrock & Tracey, 1978).

Biases about nonresidential parents and their children have far-reaching implications. At least half of all school children will spend some time in a single-parent household (Bumpass, 1984; Castro Martin & Bumpass, 1989). Positive and empowering images of their experience need to find their way into textbooks and the popular media. Public education and the media play a crucial role in their portrayal of the nonresidential parent and the possibilities for relationships between parents and children who do not live together.

In a similar vein, practitioners raise concern about the vocabulary used to refer to nonresidential parents and their families. Such terms as *only parent, absent parent*, and *custodial parent* send powerful messages about social expectations for family relationships. The paucity of affirmative labels and the tenacity of "stinkweed terms" (Ricci, 1980) reflect narrow and exclusionary criteria for relationships in the Anglo-American tradition (Kydd, 1992). Other cultural legacies in our society may prove to be a reservoir of untapped possibilities—alternative models of interpersonal connection and more inspirational terminology.

Recent legislation has sought modifications in language, eliminating the monolithic term *custody*, which implies possession by one party, to introduce a more fully articulated vocabulary of *parenting plans*, which inspires a wider spectrum of participation by both parents (Ricci, 1989).

Evaluating the Impact of Law on Parental Behavior

Legislation enacted in the past decade was explicitly designed to increase the participation of nonresidential parents in the lives of their children. As custody reform sought to augment parent-child interaction, child support reform insisted that nonresidential parents assume greater financial responsibility for their children. Some formulas for child support determination explicitly link time allocation with the amount of the child support award. It is too early to tell how the simultaneous policy thrusts for financial and social connection will solely or jointly shape parent-child relationships. This should be the subject of intensive empirical investigation.

Changes in child custody standards have been rapid and pervasive, and innovative strategies for sharing parental responsibilities have captured public attention (Folberg, 1991). Architects of the new legislation were hopeful that legal provisions for joint custody would bolster continued involvement of nonresidential parents (Clingempeel & Reppucci, 1982). Available evidence suggests that a sizable number of parents are electing joint legal custody and that generalized rates of nonresidential parent participation appear to be increasing (Bray & Berger, this volume; Braver et al., this volume; Johnston, this volume; Mnookin, Maccoby, Albiston, & Depner, 1990).

Recent evaluations of the impact of custody labels on parent behavior raise doubts that custody reform, in and of itself, can guarantee sustained parental involvement and child adjustment (Albiston, Maccoby, & Mnookin, 1990; Kline, Tschann, Johnston, & Wallerstein, 1989). If it is not enough to simply legislate the opportunities to participate, what causal agents determine whether nonresidential parents will exercise their legal rights and responsibilities? We will turn to this question shortly.

In a similar vein, child support reform under the Child Support Enforcement Program of 1975, the 1984 Child Support Enforcement Amendments, and the Family Support Act of 1988 was directed toward increasing the economic role of nonresidential parents (Stipek & McCroskey, 1989). Early child support research identified the need to modify economic policies to ensure adequate financial support for children who do not live with both parents (Nichols-Casebolt, 1986). The economic plight of single parents and their children is poignantly described in the chapter by Teachman and Paasch. Public awareness of and censure for nonpayment of child support elevated with the initiation of rigorous federal enforcement policies; but research must play a pivotal role in the evaluation of the new programs (Aldous & Dumon, 1990).

Effective economic policies must be informed by a better understanding of the determinants of nonsupport (Besharov & Tramontozzi, 1988) and its causal links to visitation (Seltzer, Schaefer, & Charng, 1989). Teachman and Paasch report that surprisingly little is known about the situation of the nonresidential parent. Initial assessments suggest that most fathers are financially able to comply with support awards (Garfinkel & Oellerich, 1989). Characteristics of fathers, particularly motivation to pay, appear to be the most powerful predictors of sustained financial involvement. Wage withholdings have been advocated by some scholars to enhance the likelihood of financial transfers by reducing the discretionary element of payment (Teachman and Paasch, this volume) or as means of standardizing the payment process and simplifying enforcement (Garfinkel & McLanahan, 1986). Conversely, motivation to pay might be elevated by enhancing the relationship between nonresidential parents and their children (Teachman & Paasch, this volume).

Facilitating Parental Involvement

Although nonresidential parents express the desire to assume an active role in the lives of their children (Depner, this volume; Kelly, this volume), this aspiration is not always realized. What are the obstacles? How can involvement best be facilitated? This section focuses on interventions directed toward the co-parental relationship as well as the parent-child relationship.

Interventions Focused on the Co-Parental Relationship

Several policy initiatives emphasize the co-parental relationship, attempting to foster an emotional climate and problem-solving orientation that permits parents to work collaboratively in rearing their children.

An early point of intervention is the juncture when provisions for custody, visitation, and child support are established. There is substantial concern that litigation can erode the last vestiges of parental accord (Kruk, 1992). Enthusiasm for nonadversarial methods, such as mediation, is echoed in high rates of client satisfaction (Depner, Cannata, & Simon, 1991). More important, a shift in objectives from "winning" custody to creating viable parental roles for both parents may set the stage for sustained participation of nonresidential parents. Indeed, at least in the short term, it appears that mediation helps parents contain conflict, improve communication, and maintain agreements (Kelly, this volume). More research is needed to evaluate the long-range implications of alternative processes (Kelly, 1990; Pearson, 1990) and to sustain their effects on family interaction and functioning.

The range of dispute resolution strategies can be extended beyond the global categories of litigation and mediation. Innovation and experimentation should be encouraged in the realms of practitioners, processes, and strategies employed. The development of new models could be enhanced by approaches that are multidisciplinary and multicultural in orientation. Comparative research can play a crucial role in identifying dispute resolution techniques best suited for particular families and disputes (Ricci, 1989).

Regardless of whether custody terms are disputed, a sound collaborative planning process has the potential to allow parents to forge viable parenting roles (Kelly, this volume). Obviating continual renegotiations and circumventing potential misunderstanding, a planning forum can spell out common understandings, establish realistic expectations, clarify future roles, and make provisions for family transitions over the life course (see also Bray & Berger, this volume).

Interventions have also been created to sustain visitation through ongoing support and follow-up. Pearson & Anhalt (1992) compared five programs across the country that were designed explicitly to resolve ongoing problems with visitation. Program components could include providing information, specifying visitation rights and responsibilities, holding telephone or personal conferences with parents to resolve disputes about access, giving referrals to counseling or community services, monitoring visitation, documenting deviations from visitation agreements, supervising visitation, or formally enforcing visitation rights. Analysis of the programs and their users indicate that when visitation goes awry, a complex set of factors may be operating. Pearson and Anhalt found that cases seen in enforcement programs also involved child support arrearages, protracted litigation over visitation and support matters, and concerns of the residential parent about safety, substance abuse, or violence. There is increased recognition that comprehensive service integration will be needed to coordinate the efforts of various public and private agencies engaged in maintaining different facets of the nonresidential parent's family involvement (Depner, 1992b).

Other interventions focus specifically on the effects of conflict on parenting behavior. Acrimony associated with the parental breakup has potentially corrosive effects for all family members. It is unrealistic to assume that the termination of a relationship will have no emotional repercussions, but it is also inaccurate to assume that all parents are locked in unremitting conflict (Kelly, this volume). Left to their own devices, high-conflict parents are unlikely to transform hostile relationships into cooperative co-parenting (Maccoby & Mnookin, 1992); but follow-up intervention has proven successful in helping parents work through the aftermath of custody conflict (Solomon, 1991). The goal of practitioners and policymakers is to assist parents so that their children can witness and benefit from successful resolution of family disputes.

Short of resolving parental hostilities, it is crucial to identify factors that shield children from the pernicious effects of interparental disputes. Despite the established finding that children exposed to protracted conflict do less well than their peers on various indicators of adjustment, few studies have measured the underlying mechanisms that account for this association (Depner, Leino, & Chun, 1992; Emery,

1982). Some notable exceptions offer promising directions for the design of future research and interventions (Bray, 1991). For example, Hetherington, Cox, and Cox (1982) have examined the implications of conflict for decrements in parenting behaviors. Dodge (1980) and other social learning theorists have discussed the role of modeling and vicarious learning, and behaviorists point to the role of reinforcement of behavior. Differentiation of conflict themes (Kelly, this volume) and strategies (Camara & Resnick, 1988) may further isolate particular expressions of conflict that are most harmful to children. Reciprocal effects over time need to be explored. For example, children's behavior problems, such as coercion and aggression, are often followed by more coercive and hostile behaviors by parents (Hetherington, 1987, 1991; Patterson, 1982).

New strategies for evaluating parental competence and potential risks for children are another crucial direction for the further development of family services. In the current legal climate, there is substantial concern about responsibly adjudicating allegations and counter-allegations of abuse, neglect, or deficits in parenting ability. In addition to diagnostic skills, there is a need for a wider range of remedies to address these problems. Provisions for continued contact with nonresidential parents must adequately safeguard the child. Innovative procedures, such as supervised visitation, need to be evaluated for their feasibility and effectiveness.

Interventions Focused on the Parent-Child Relationship

Braver and his colleagues illustrate the heuristic value of existing theory for the examination of parent-child dynamics. Their chapter identifies several potential areas for educational and therapeutic interventions. For example, parent education could reinforce symbolic and social rewards for sustaining a relationship with one's child and validate the nonresidential parent's sense of the importance of continued contact. Education can also offer models for arranging visitation to minimize awkwardness, painfulness, and other disincentives.

Johnston's analysis of visitation problems suggests further ways in which educators and mental health practitioners can intervene. Her work points out that parents need to have adequate information in order to identify children's developmental needs and to recognize signals of poor adaptation to visitation. Parent education programs or work with individual practitioners could impart such knowledge. Parent education could also alert parents to the effects of conflict and undermining on the well-being of the child (Bray & Berger, this volume). Signs of deeper problems, according to Johnston, may require more intensive therapeutic intervention.

Determining the Effects of Legislation on the Family System

Families operate within a larger legal context that has introduced widespread reform affecting options and obligations of the nonresidential parent. Research will figure prominently in analysis of the ramifications of legal transformation for the separate and sometimes conflicting interests of different members of the family system (Depner, 1987; Entmacher, 1990; Scanzoni, 1983).

New strategies for child custody decision making are being mandated by courts and elected by parents. Some theoretical articles raise the disquieting possibility that nonadversarial forums systematically compromise the interests of mothers, particularly victims of violence (Bruch, 1988; Gagnon, 1992; Germane, Johnson, & Lemon, 1985; Grillo, 1991). Empirical work does not support the position that this is the experience of most women who use mediation, but it remains a lingering concern in a minority of cases (Depner & Cannata, 1992). More research is in order to determine the best fit of dispute and intervention in light of implications for mothers, fathers, and their children (Depner, Cannata, & Simon, 1991; Ricci, 1989; Rosenberg, 1991).

Disenchantment with gender-neutral child custody standards reflects a broader sociolegal debate about social rights and gender (Mezey, 1992; Scott, 1988). Chapters by Depner and by Teachman and Paasch (this volume) track the legacy of gender-based differentiation of responsibility for the emotional and financial needs of children. Current debate focuses on how a family's history of role assignments should influence provisions for the economic and caregiving options of the nonresidential parent. Feminists contend that inequity is perpetuated by the failure of the law to acknowledge the persistence of female responsibility for the care of children and by policies blind to intractable gender-based disparities, such as the wage gap, that render women ill-equipped for the financial burdens of single parenting (MacKinnon, 1989; Villmoare, 1991).

Challenges to the philosophical underpinnings of child support policy also call for consideration of the implications for all family members. The polarities of the debate are represented on one hand by those who advocate "cost sharing" (basing support awards on some estimate of the cost of raising children) and on the other by those who endorse "income sharing" (efforts to equalize financial circumstances in the two parental households) (Bruch, 1986; Hunter, 1983). One important function of research has been to point out the vast state-to-state discrepancies in practices and their implications (Williams & Price, 1990). Comparative research can speak to the ramifications of alternative formulations for different family members. Research could also contribute to a better understanding of the resource pool available from all family members (Teachman & Paasch, this volume).

Understanding the Role of Cultural and Kinship Systems

Extending the analysis still further, to consider the kinship and cultural contexts of the nonresidential parent, will help policymakers craft effective strategies for facilitating nonresidential parenting. For example, Bray and Berger draw attention to the implications of the nonresidential parent's role for the paternal kinship system. Ties to grandparents may atrophy if the nonresidential parent cannot sustain contact with the child.

A culturally competent system must recognize and collaborate with existing structures in the extended family and community. Del Carmen and Virgo suggest that the extended network of kinship and culture may offer important mechanisms for defining and supporting modes of nonresidential involvement and for resolving disputes about parental rights and responsibilities. Attention to cultural heritage invokes ignored factors that may figure prominently in the dynamics of nonresidential parent involvement, such as religion, patriarchal gender roles, familism, acculturation, and migration. Moreover, because cultural dynamics often are confounded with the vicissitudes of poverty, migration, and urbanization, a multicultural perspective offers models of resilience and accommodation to transitions and disruptions (del Carmen & Virgo, this volume).

A multicultural perspective also challenges conventional policy objectives of the dominant culture. Variations in the normative ordering of responsibility for children should be examined. For example, the policy emphasis on economic transfers obscures a wider range of indicators of family adaptation to nonresidential parenting. A culturally based expression of involvement might emphasize contact, access to kin, or lineage rather than financial transfers. In some social systems, other family members might be expected to assume financial or care-giving responsibilities that are assigned to the nonresidential parent in the dominant culture. The family system would then evolve to a configuration quite different from one in which the mother provides care and the father contributes financial support.

Considering Life Course Issues

Policy analysis should also be expanded to incorporate a clear understanding of the temporal dynamics of nonresidential parenting (Depner, 1992a). Theory and research have been grounded in the episode of family breakup; yet recent research illustrates the wisdom of extending the analysis retrospectively to evaluate precursing and historical events in the family (Braver et al., this volume; Cherlin et al., 1991). Family dynamics and individual differences may precede rather than flow from the circumstances of the rupture of the parental relationship. Likewise, extended longitudinal observation following the dissolution of the parental relationship makes it possible to determine whether effects observed in short-term observations are transient reactions to family change or enduring effects that set a trajectory for child adjustment (Bray & Berger, this volume).

Bray and Berger's Developmental Systems model illustrates the complex intersections of individual and family life cycles. For example, plans to integrate nonresidential parents into their children's lives must foresee family transitions, such as remarriage, as well as the social development of the child over time. Still other stochastic processes may influence the family relationships of nonresidential parents, such as the rate of acculturation or the pace of custodial innovation in a particular community.

Information about the sequence of family processes and outcomes is crucial in the design and timing of successful interventions. Adopting a temporal perspective permits comparison of alternative causal explanations, each with different policy implications. For example, an observed relationship between a form of custody and child adjustment might be attributed to arrangement duration (e.g., children might initially have difficulty adapting to the logistics of joint custody), coordination of family and individual timetables (e.g., the alternation schedule might be poorly coordinated with developmental needs of the child), or cumulative effects over time (the number of ecological changes in the child's environment).

New considerations emerge as nonresidential parenting is analyzed within a temporal framework that anticipates likely changes in family structure over the course of a child's minority. For example, remarriage is a common transition that poses a new set of adaptation tasks and subsequent family issues (Bray & Berger, this volume). The nonresidential parent assumes new responsibilities for stepchildren and/or children of the remarriage. In addition, there is no policy consensus about whether new resources or obligations of remarried households, particularly the wages of a new spouse, are salient factors in the reevaluation of the nonresidential parent's financial obligations (Williams & Price, 1990). Economic policymakers need to make provisions for changes in family economics that are triggered by life course transitions, such as remarriage, the birth of new children, or financial responsibilities for aging parents.

Contemporary policy specifications of nonresidential parents' obligations may have dramatic long-term ramifications for children's ability and willingness to provide care and also create unprecedented demands on government assistance. Although legal obligations often cease when a child reaches the age of majority, social ties and transactions continue (Depner & Bray, 1990). Insufficient attention is devoted to transfers between nonresidential parents and adult children; for example, whether nonresidential parents feel obligated to share in the costs of their children's college education, contribute to establishing their first home, or facilitate entry into the work world. Children from divorced homes are less likely to attend college because many custodial parents often cannot sustain the costs of higher education, and noncustodial parents fail to provide financial assistance (Wallerstein & Corbin, 1986). This is an alarming phenomenon, since it is unlikely that alternative resources, such as government funds, will be adequate to meet the educational expenses of the increasing numbers of children with nonresidential parents.

A reciprocal concern is the care of aging nonresidential parents. Will adult children's sense of obligation for elder care mirror the level of investment that their nonresidential parents made in them? That is, if contact and support were intermittent in childhood, will adult children be unwilling to provide support and care to an aging nonresidential parent? Since the majority of care for elderly persons is provided by marital partners and other family members (Walsh, 1988), it is unclear who will assume this burden. Men seem to have a more difficult time coping with the death or loss of a spouse (Stroebe & Stroebe, 1983). Given the more limited contact between fathers and children, nonresidential fathers may be at greater risk than residential mothers for morbidity and mortality during old age. Again, people are likely to look to the government for assistance, but the government may not be equipped to handle this level of demand.

Making Social Systems Responsive to Family Pluralism

Virtually every social system that interacts with families must confront the realities that family structure is not stable over time and that many boys and girls will not live with both of their parents throughout the course of childhood. The adaptation of social policies and institutions to profound changes in family demographics remains unexamined. Indeed, some policy analysts bemoan the tendency of social institutions to operate as if our nation is populated exclusively by nuclear families. New models need to be developed for working with family change and diversity.

Health Care. Decision makers and individual parents must sort out the role of the nonresidential parent in health care for the child. Explicit provisions for health insurance should not be overlooked in legal parenting obligations. Kelly's chapter underscores the importance of specifying parental responsibilities, such as those for health care. Rights of the nonresidential parent in the determination of elective treatment or in acute medical crises are another facet of parental decision making that could be specified in custody plans. Preventive care (e.g., periodic checkups and inoculations), long-term treatment, and medication must be coordinated with access arrangements. Medical systems should anticipate special issues in the logistics of delivering care to the increasing numbers of children who spend time in nonresidential households.

Education. Strober and Dornbush (1988) entreat schools to act as child advocates, educating both parents and policymakers about the importance of a coordinated effort between the schools and all adults involved with children. New models for enhancing nonresidential parent involvement incorporate participation in educational decision making, parent-teacher conferences and receipt of reports, and communication about assignments that may span visitation periods.

Schools play a pivotal role in the adaptation of children during family transitions (Hetherington, Cox, & Cox, 1982). Working with both parents to monitor and bolster the child's progress is an important step in promoting the child's adjustment. Parent-child communication is particularly crucial as arrangements for visitation or parental time-sharing are developed and evaluated. School-based programs for children experiencing family change also have yielded promising results (Kalter, Pickar, Lesowitz,

1984; Pedro-Carroll & Cowen, 1985; Roseby & Deutsch, 1985). Grych and Fincham (1992) credit the success of such programs to the fact that they are situated in a familiar location, accessible to most children, and draw on a natural support network of schoolmates and teachers. Damon (1979) recommends annual in-service workshops for educators to assist them in working with nontraditional families.

We have also noted several junctures where public education may equip the nonresidential parent to assume parental responsibilities and overcome barriers to sustained involvement. Many states are formalizing parent education programs (Lehner, 1991). Curricula differ, but often assist nonresidential parents in building basic child-rearing skills and address the special challenges of co-parenting from separate households. Parent education also may act as a countervailing force to general education deficits of the nonresidential parent that have been linked to disengagement (Furstenberg, Nord, Peterson, & Zill, 1983), offering basic training on topics ranging from the developmental needs of children to the fundamentals of household management.

Housing and Urban Design. The physical structure of homes and communities can reinforce peripheral involvement of nonresidential parents. For example, the conspicuous Saturday morning presence of fathers and children at shopping malls and fast-food restaurants reflects a need to transform residences of nonresidential parents into homes conducive to the needs and interests of children. Availability of parks, play areas, and space for children to interact with others could send the message that children can have a home with a nonresidential parent, rather than a makeshift place to visit. Availability of supplemental or convertible space that could be used to accommodate overnight stays might enable nonresidential parents to provide home-like environments for their children.

Strober and Dornbusch (1988) call for architects and planners to consider the needs of families in the design of new structures, zoning, and housing codes. Substantial advantages could be realized with the creation of communal spaces that permit sharing tasks such as cooking and facilitate social interaction among families. The objective would be to create welcome environments in the residence of each parent.

Future Directions

The foregoing analysis points out many ways in which knowledge of nonresidential parenting is fragmented by exclusive attention to particular relationships, outcomes, or time frames. This book illustrates the value of a multidimensional perspective. Future initiatives must attend to the wider social system in which the parent-child dyad operates—immediate and extended family members, culture, community, and social institutions that interact with families. A new generation of scholarship will need to synthesize information from multiple systems and flesh out the connections most crucial to viable family roles for nonresidential parents. The effectiveness of practice and policy initiatives will hinge on how well they incorporate the complex systems in which the nonresidential parent operates. Without a systems perspective, problems are less likely to be resolved than merely shifted to other family members or social institutions (Capra, 1988). For example, efforts to assign and enforce child support obligations may create custody disputes, or custody standards focused on the nonresidential parent's relationship with the child may have unforeseen consequences for custodial parents, stepparents, or kinship systems. Policy must be evaluated at several levels of analysis, considering implications for children, parents, kin, community, and the wider society.

A multidimensional perspective on nonresidential parenting will incorporate a broader range of salient variables. Research has now revealed a host of factors that may influence the dynamics of nonresidential parent participation. Further work must consider the simultaneous operation of multiple determinants of involvement as well as disentangle the complex causal etiology of successful adaptation to nonresidential parenting. A multivariate perspective also introduces alternative indicators of adaptation (e.g., linked to cultural heritage or individual and family life cycle considerations) and reveals that different factors optimize alternative outcomes (Bray & Berger, this volume). Further, recognition of family pluralism suggests that salient outcomes and processes will vary across family configurations.

Future professional training and development must also be guided by a multidimensional perspective. Work with nonresidential parents and their families demands a broad range of expertise. Practice requires specific knowledge of legal requirements and awareness of ethical concerns for these families. For example, the rights of nonresidential parents to seek treatment for their children are defined by state law and vary across the United States. Issues of confidentiality among divorced family members are also complex and challenge professionals to maintain neutral therapeutic alliances. A multicultural perspective points out the need to insure the training of minority practitioners and to develop training curricula, programs, instruments, and treatment models that are culturally competent (Markman, 1992). Finally, the function of bridging research, policy, and practice will be personified in the scientist-practitioner, a professional role that seeks to integrate work within the various facets of family scholarship and practice (Hoshmand & Polkinghorne, 1992; Peterson, 1991). In a similar vein, better utilization of research by policymakers will require liaison professionals with expertise in both areas (Liddle, 1992).

These complex dynamics may be played out in regional and community-based programs. In an era of decreased spending, family policy strategies are being implemented at the local level, even though principles are debated in a nationwide forum. Some policy dictates, most particularly those governing child support, are initiated at the federal level. Most other provisions for parental obligations, such as custody decision making, are regulated by state or local jurisdiction. One serendipitous effect of localized policies and programs is that they forge stronger collaborations among policymakers, practitioners, and community interests. They may more closely reflect the observations of professionals who work with nonresidential parents and also ratify quotidian values and objectives of a particular community. However, in order to maximize the cumulative power of such decentralized efforts, new channels of communication must be established so that effective programs are visible and can be replicated in new settings.

Throughout this chapter, we have argued for an alliance of research, policy, and practice to develop a multidimensional approach to nonresidential parenting. Such a strategy could have far-reaching implications for the development of policies and service models that are grounded in an accurate understanding of the constraints on and possibilities for nonresidential parenting.

References

Ahrons, C. R., & Rodgers, R. H. (1987) *Divorced families: A multidisciplinary developmental view.* New York: Norton.

Albiston, C. R., Maccoby, E. E., Mnookin, R. H. (1990). Does joint legal custody matter? *Stanford Law and Policy Review,* 167-179.

Aldous, J., & Dumon, W. (1990). Family policy in the 1980s: Controversy and consensus. *Journal of Marriage and the Family, 52*(4), 1136-1151.

Besharov, D. J., & Tramontozzi, P. N. (1988, December). *Seven key issues for child support research.* Symposium sponsored by the American Enterprise Institute and the

Office of the Assistant Secretary for Planning and Evaluation, U.S. Dept. of Health and Human Services, Washington, DC.

Bray, J. H. (1991). Psychosocial factors affecting custodial and visitation arrangements. *Behavioral Science and the Law, 9*, 419-437.

Brownstein, H. H. (1991). The social construction of public policy: A case for participation by researchers. *Sociological Practice Review, 2*(2), 132-140.

Bruch, C. S. (1986). And how are the children? The effects of ideology and mediation on child custody law and children's well-being in the United States. *International Journal of Law and the Family, 2*, 106-126.

Bruch, C. S. (1988). Problems inherent in designing child support guidelines. In *Essentials of child support guidelines development: Economic issues and policy considerations* (pp. 41-64). Proceedings of the Women's Legal Defense Fund's National Conference on the Development of Child Support Guidelines, Queenstown, MD. Washington, DC: Women's Legal Defense Fund.

Bumpass, L. L. (1984). Children and marital disruption: A replication and update. *Demography, 21*, 71-82.

Camara, K., & Resnick, G. (1988). Interparental conflict and cooperation: Factors mediating children's post-divorce adjustment. In E. M. Hetherington & J. Arasteh (Eds.), *The impact of divorce, single-parenting and step-parenting on children* (pp. 169-195). Hillsdale, NJ: Lawrence Erlbaum.

Capra, F. (1988) *The turning point*. New York: Bantam.

Castro Martin, T., & Bumpass, L. (1989). Recent trends and differentials in marital disruption. *Demography, 26*, 37-51.

Cherlin, A. J. (1983). Changing family and household: Contemporary lessons from historical research. *Annual Review of Sociology, 9*, 51-66.

Cherlin, A. J., Furstenberg, F. F., Chase-Lansdale, P. L., Kiernan, K. E., Robins, P. K., Morrison, D. R., & Teller, J. O. (1991). Longitudinal studies of effects of divorce on children in Great Britain and the United States. *Science, 252*, 1386-1389.

Clingempeel, W. G., & Reppucci, N. D. (1982). Joint custody after divorce: Major issues and goals for research. *Psychological Bulletin, 91*(1), 102-127.

Damon, P. (1979). When the family comes apart: What schools can do. *The National Elementary Principal, 59*(1), 66-75.

Depner, C. E. (1987, August). *The evaluation of differential fates: A value/policy interaction*. Paper presented at the annual meeting of the American Psychological Association, New York City.

Depner, C. E. (1991, October). *Bridging the gap between social science and legal policy*. Presented at the annual meeting of the California Sociological Association, Oakland, CA.

Depner, C. E. (1992a, May). *Social science research on joint custody: A critical review*. Paper presented at the annual meeting of the Law and Society Association, Philadelphia.

Depner, C. E. (1992b, June). Trends in characteristics of users of juvenile and family courts: Child custody, visitation, and family court service In G. Melton (Chair), *Children, families, and the justice system in the 21st century*. Symposium sponsored by the Family and Juvenile Court Committee Commission on 2020 Vision: A plan for the future of the California courts, San Francisco.

Depner, C. E., & Bray, J. H. (1990). Modes of participation for noncustodial parents: The challenge for research, policy, practice and education. *Family Relations, 39*(4), 378-381.

Depner, C. E., & Cannata, K. (1992, May). *A state court study of 1700 family court clients.* Paper presented at the annual meeting of the Association of Family and Conciliation Courts, San Diego, CA.

Depner, C. E., Cannata, K. V., & Simon, M. B. (1991). Building a uniform statistical reporting system: A snapshot of California Family Court Services. *Family and Conciliation Courts Review, 30*(3), 185-206.

Depner, C. E., Leino, V., & Chun, A. (1992). Interparental conflict and child development: A decade review and meta-analysis. *Family and Conciliation Courts Review, 30*(3), 323-342.

Dodge, K. A. (1980). Social cognition and children's aggressive behavior. *Child Development, 51*, 162-172.

Emery, R. E. (1982). Interpersonal conflict and the children of discord and divorce. *Psychological Bulletin, 92*(2), 310-330.

Entmacher, J. (1990, May). *Dissonant discourses: Legal ideology and feminist theory in the work of task forces on gender bias in the courts.* Paper presented at the annual meeting of the Law and Society Association, Berkeley, CA.

Folberg, J. (1991). Custody overview. In J. Folberg (Ed.) *Joint custody and shared parenting* (2nd ed., pp. 3-15). New York: Guilford Press.

Furstenberg, F. F., Jr., Nord, C. W., Peterson, J. L., & Zill, N. (1983). The life course of children of divorce: Marital disruption and parental contact. *American Sociological Review, 48*(3), 656-668.

Gagnon, A. G. (1992). Ending mandatory divorce mediation for battered women. *Harvard Women's Law Journal, 15*, 272-294.

Garfinkel, I., & McLanahan, S. (1986). *Single mothers and their children: A new American dilemma.* Baltimore, MD: Urban Institute Press.

Garfinkel, I., & Oellerich, D. (1989). Non-custodial fathers' ability to pay child support. *Demography, 26*, 219-233.

Germane, C., Johnson, M., & Lemon, N. (1985). Mandatory custody mediation and joint custody orders in California: The dangers for victims of domestic violence. *Berkeley Women's Law Journal*, 175-200.

Grillo, T. (1991). The mediation alternative: Process dangers for women. *Yale Law Journal, 100*(6), 1545-1610.

Grych, J. H., & Fincham, F. D. (1992). Interventions for children of divorce: Toward greater integration of research and action. *Psychological Bulletin, 111*(3), 434-454.

Hetherington, E. M. (1987). Family relations six years after divorce. In K. Pasley & M. Ihinger-Tallman (Eds.), *Remarriage and stepparenting today: Research and theory.* New York: Guilford.

Hetherington, E. M. (1991). The role of individual differences and family relationships in children's coping with divorce and remarriage. In P. A. Cowan & E. M. Hetherington (Eds.), *Family transitions* (pp. 165-194). Hillsdale, NJ: Lawrence Erlbaum.

Hetherington, E. M., Cox, M., & Cox, R. (1982). Effects of divorce on parents and children. In M. E. Lamb (Ed.), *Nontraditional families: Parenting and child development* (pp. 233-288). Hillsdale, NJ: Lawrence Erlbaum.

Hoshmand, L. T., & Polkinghorne, D. E. (1992). Redefining the science-practice relationship and professional training. *American Psychologist, 47*(1), 55-66.

Hunter, N. D. (1983). Women and child support. In I. Diamond (Ed.), *Families, politics and public policy* (pp. 209-221). New York: Longman.

Kalter, N., Pickar, J., & Lesowitz, M. (1984). School-based developmental facilitation groups for children of divorce: A preventive intervention. *American Journal of Orthopsychiatry, 54*, 613-623.

Kelly, J. (1990, May). *Does the process make a difference? Comparing adversarial and mediated divorces.* Paper presented at the annual meeting of the Law and Society Association, Berkeley, CA.

Kline, M., Tschann, J. M., Johnston, J. R., & Wallerstein, J. S. (1989). Children's adjustment in joint and sole physical custody families. *Developmental Psychology, 25*(3), 430-438.

Kruk, E. (1992). Psychological and structural factors contributing to the disengagement of noncustodial fathers after divorce. *Family and Conciliation Courts Review, 30*(1), 81-101.

Kydd, J. (1992, February). *Language and the family: The poverty of English.* Paper presented at the annual Child Custody Colloquium of Los Angeles Superior Courts, Los Angeles.

Lehner, L. (1991). Mediation parent education programs in the California Family Courts. *Family and Conciliation Courts Review, 30*(2), 207-216.

Liddle, H. A. (1992). Family psychology: Progress and prospects of a maturing discipline. *Family Psychology, 5*(3/4), 249-263.

Maccoby, E. M., & Mnookin, R. H. (1992). *Dividing the child: The social and legal dilemmas of custody.* Cambridge, MA: Harvard University Press.

MacKinnon, C. A. (1989). *Toward a feminist theory of the state.* Cambridge, MA: Harvard University Press.

Markman, H. J. (1992). Marital and family psychology: Burning issues. *Journal of Family Psychology, 5*(3/4), 264-275.

Mayer, R. R., & Greenwood, E. (1980). *The design of social policy research.* Englewood Cliffs, NJ: Prentice-Hall.

Merton, R. K. (1945). Role of the intellectual in public bureaucracy. *Social Forces, 23*, 405-415.

Mezey, S. G. (1992). *In pursuit of equality.* New York: St. Martin's Press.

Mnookin, R. H., Maccoby, E. E., Albiston, C. R., & Depner, C. E. (1990). Private ordering revisited: What custodial arrangements are parents negotiating? In S. Sugarman & F. Zimring (Eds.), *Perspectives on the no fault revolution* (pp. 37-74). New Haven: Yale University Press.

Moroney, R. (1986). *Shared responsibility: Families and social policy.* New York: Aldine.

Moynihan, D. P. (1986). *Family and nation.* San Diego, CA: Harcourt Brace Jovanovich.

Nichols-Casebolt, A. (1986). The economic impact of child support reform on the poverty status of custodial and noncustodial families. *Journal of Marriage and the Family, 48*, 875-880.

Noble, J., & Sussman, M. (1987). *Government and family.* New York: Haworth.

Nock, S. L. (1988). The family and hierarchy. *Journal of Marriage and the Family, 50*(4), 957-966.

Patterson, G. R. (1982). *Coercive family processes: A social learning approach* (Vol. 3). Eugene, OR: Castalia.

Pearson, J. (1990, May). *The equity of mediated divorce agreements.* Paper presented at the annual meeting of the Law and Society Association, Berkeley, CA.

Pearson, J., & Anhalt, J. (1992, May). *The enforcement of visitation rights: A preliminary assessment of five exemplary programs.* Paper presented at the annual meeting of the Law and Society Association, Philadelphia.

Pedro-Carroll, J. L., & Cowen, E. L. (1985). The children of divorce intervention program: An investigation of the efficacy of a school-based prevention program. *Journal of Consulting and Clinical Psychology, 53,* 603-611.

Peterson, D. R. (1991). Connection and disconnection of research and practice in the education of professional psychologists. *American Psychologist, 46*(4), 422-429.

Polikoff, N. (1990). This child does have two mothers: Redefining parenthood to meet the needs of lesbian-mother and other nontraditional families. *Georgetown Law Journal, 78,* 459-575.

Ricci, I. (1980). *Mom's house, dad's house.* New York: Macmillan.

Ricci, I. (1989). Mediation, joint custody and legal agreements: A time to review, revise and refine. *Family and Conciliation Courts Review, 27*(1), 47-55.

Roseby, V., & Deutsch, R. (1985). Children of separation and divorce: Effects of a social role-taking group intervention on fourth and fifth graders. *Journal of Clinical Child Psychology, 14*(1), 55-60.

Rosenberg, J. (1991). In defense of mediation. *Arizona Law Review, 33*(3), 467-507.

Santrock, J. W., & Tracey, R. L. (1978). Effect of children's family structure status on the development of stereotypes by children. *Journal of Educational Psychology, 70,* 754-757.

Scanzoni, J. (1983). *Shaping tomorrow's family.* Beverly Hills, CA: Sage.

Scott, J. W. (1988). Deconstructing equality-versus-difference: Or, the uses of poststructuralist theory for feminism. *Feminist Studies, 14,* 33-56.

Seltzer, J. A., Schaeffer, N. C., & Charng, H. (1989). Family ties after divorce: The relationship between visiting and paying child support. *Journal of Marriage and the Family, 51*(4), 1013-1031.

Solomon, C. R. (1991). A critical moment for intervention: After the smoke of the battle clears and custody has been won. In C. A. Everett (Ed.), *The consequences of divorce* (pp. 325-335). New York: Haworth.

Stipek, D., & McCroskey, J. (1989). Investing in children: Government and workplace policies for parents. *American Psychologist, 44*(2), 416-423.

Strober, M. H., & Dornbusch, S. M. (1988). Public policy alternatives. In S. M. Dornbusch & M. H. Strober (Eds.), *Feminism, children and the new families* (pp. 327-357). New York: Guilford.

Stroebe, M. S., & Stroebe, W. (1983). Who suffers more? Sex differences in health risks of the widowed. *Psychological Bulletin, 93,* 279-301.

Thornton, A. D., & Freedman, D. (1983) The changing American family. *Population Bulletin, 38*(4), 1-44.

Villmoore, A. (1991). Women, differences, and rights as practices: An interpretive essay and a proposal. *Law and Society Review, 25*(2), 385-410.

Wallerstein, J. S., & Corbin, S. B. (1988). Father-child relationships after divorce: Child support and educational opportunities. *Family Law Quarterly, 20,* 109-128.

Walsh, F. (1988). The family in later life. In B. Carter & M. McGoldrick (Eds.), *The changing family life cycle* (pp. 311-334). New York: Gardner Press.

Williams, R. G., & Price, D. A. (1990). *Analysis of California's child support guidelines.* Final report of a grant from the Judicial Council of California.

Author Index

Subject Index

About the Authors

Sandra H. Berger, M.S.W., is a research associate in the Department of Family Medicine at Baylor College of Medicine. Ms. Berger has been an investigator on the *Developmental Issues in StepFamilies Research Project.* She has published and presented papers in the areas of divorce and remarriage.

Sanford L. Braver, Ph.D., has been at Arizona State University since 1970. He is now Professor of Psychology and on the faculty of the Program for Prevention Research. He received his Ph.D. in Social Psychology from the University of Michigan in 1971. He is principal investigator in the NICHD grant "Non-Custodial Parents: Parents Without Children," and co-principal investigator on the NIMH grant "Center for the Prevention of Child and Family Stress." He has written extensively on the social psychology of divorce. His research interests also include conflict resolution and methodology and statistics.

James H. Bray, Ph.D., is an Associate Professor in the Department of Family Medicine at Baylor College of Medicine. For the past 8 years, Dr. Bray has been the principal investigator of the longitudinal study, *Developmental Issues in StepFamilies Research Project.* This study has been investigating the impact of divorce and remarriage on children's development and adjustment, the unique transitional issues in remarriage, and family relationship patterns in stepfamilies. The *DIS Research Project* also investigates how stepfamily relationships in the broader kinship network are distinct from nuclear families and how these relationships influence children's adjustment. Dr. Bray has published and presented numerous works in the areas of noncustodial parents, divorce, and remarriage and also has extensive experience as an editorial reviewer for professional journals and book publishers.

Rebecca del Carmen, Ph.D., is a clinical child psychologist and is currently a Senior Staff Fellow in the Child and Adolescent Research Branch of the National Institute of Mental Health. She received her Ph.D. from The Ohio State University. Her research interests include ethnic and cultural issues, developmental psychopathology, and attachment theory.

Charlene E. Depner, Ph.D., has published extensively on family transitions and social policy. She holds a Ph.D. in social psychology from the University of Michigan. Dr. Depner has worked as a primary researcher at Michigan's Institute for Social Research and Stanford University's Center for the Study of Children, Youth and Families. She is the founding coordinator for Research, Evaluation and Statistics at California's Statewide Office of Family Court Services, which is responsible for evaluation research and statistical reporting on child custody and other family law matters. Dr. Depner is active in several professional organizations devoted to bridging research and social policy, including the Society for the Psychological Study of Social Issues, the Law and Society Association, and the American Psychological Association's Divisions on Psychology of Women and Family Psychology.

Janet R. Johnston, Ph.D., is the Director of Research at the Center for the Family in Transition, Corte Madera, California, and Consulting Associate Professor in Sociology at Stanford University. As a researcher and an experienced clinical social worker, she has focused her efforts during the past decade on research, intervention, and social policy with high-conflict and violent families who are litigating about the custody and care of their children. She is co-author with Linda Campbell, Ph.D., of the book *Impasses of Divorce: The Dynamics and Resolution of Family Conflict* (1988).

Joan B. Kelly, Ph.D., is Executive Director of the Northern California Mediation Center. She received her Ph.D. in clinical Psychology from Yale University. An experienced mediator in divorce, family, and interpersonal disputes, Dr. Kelly also provides training seminars and workshops in conflict resolution and mediation, and psychological aspects of family law. She recently completed a major study of the effectiveness of divorce mediation as compared to the traditional adversarial divorce proceedings, and has published widely concerning both mediation and the impact of divorce on family members. Co-author of *Surviving the Breakup: How Children and Parents Cope with Divorce,* Dr. Kelly has written often of nonresidential parenting dilemmas and the child's need for continuity in relationships with fathers and mothers after divorce. Dr. Kelly is a past president and founding board member of the Academy of Family Mediators, a Fellow of the Division of Family Psychology of the American Psychological Association, and on the board of directors of the Northern California Council for Mediation and the California Chapter of the Association for Family and Conciliation Courts.

Kathleen Paasch is a graduate student in the Department of Sociology at the University of Maryland. She has published work in the area of family demography which has appeared in the *Journal of Family Issues* and *Demography.* She is currently finishing her dissertation dealing with the effects of military service on divorce among veterans of the Vietnam era.

Irwin N. Sandler, Ph.D., is a Professor of Psychology and the Director of the Program for Prevention Research at Arizona State University. He received his Ph.D. in Clinical/Community Psychology from the University of Rochester in 1971. His professional career has focused on the development and evaluation of preventive mental health programs for children. In 1975 he joined Arizona State University, where he has pursued research on a wide range of topics, including the assessment of stress and social support in children, mediators of the effects of bereavement and divorce on children's mental health, the development and evaluation of preventive interventions for children of divorce, bereaved children, and children of alcoholic parents. He is currently Director of an NIMH-funded Preventive Intervention Research Center, which focuses on the development and evaluation of prevention programs for children in stressful situations.

Virgil L. Sheets is a doctoral candidate in the Social/Environmental Psychology Program at Arizona State University. His research interests include gender differences, social problems, environmental preferences, and issues of methodology and statistics in psychological research.

Jay D. Teachman, Ph.D., is Professor of Sociology and a member of the Center on Population, Gender and Social Inequality at the University of Maryland. His research focuses on processes of family formation and dissolution and the consequences of change in family structure. He recently completed a National Science Foundation-supported project examining the determinants of child support award and receipt. Some of this work has been published in the *Journal of Marriage and the Family* and *Social Problems*. He is beginning a new project that will investigate the short- and long-term implications of economic distress for families. Of particular interest is the impact of downsizing on the economic situation of families and how related changes in economic well-being affect family processes and outcomes.

Gabrielle N. Virgo, M.D., is a pediatrician and is currently completing a National Research Service Award for postdoctoral research training in the Laboratory of Comparative Ethology at the National Institutes of Health. She received her M.D. from the University of Michigan Medical School in Ann Arbor. Her research interests include normal child development, both physical and emotional, and pediatric preventive health.

Sharlene A. Wolchik, Ph.D., is a Professor of Psychology at Arizona State University in the Clinical Psychology Program, where she has taught since 1980. She received her B.A. at Vassar and her Ph.D. from Rutgers University. She is currently co-principal investigator on two federal grants relating to divorce research. She is editor of *The Community Psychologist* and has co-edited (with Paul Karoly) the book *Children of Divorce: Empirical Perspectives on Adjustment*. Her research interests involve the impact of divorce on children and adults, and interventions to facilitate their adjustment. She has authored or co-authored more than 65 published articles or presentations on these topics.